SIMPSON

IMPRINT IN HUMANITIES

The humanities endowment
by Sharon Hanley Simpson and
Barclay Simpson honors

MURIEL CARTER HANLEY

whose intellect and sensitivity
have enriched the many lives
that she has touched.

The publisher and the University of California Press Foundation gratefully acknowledge the generous support of the Simpson Imprint in Humanities.

The Lure of the Image

The Lure of the Image

Epistemic Fantasies of the Moving Camera

Daniel Morgan

UNIVERSITY OF CALIFORNIA PRESS

University of California Press
Oakland, California

© 2021 by Daniel Morgan

Library of Congress Cataloging-in-Publication Data

Names: Morgan, Daniel, 1977– author.
Title: The lure of the image : epistemic fantasies of the moving
    camera / Daniel Morgan.
Description: Oakland, California : University of California Press,
    [2021] | Includes bibliographical references and index.
Identifiers: LCCN 2021005040 (print) | LCCN 2021005041 (ebook) |
    ISBN 9780520344259 (cloth) | ISBN 9780520344273 (paperback) |
    ISBN 9780520975446 (epub)
Subjects: LCSH: Motion pictures—Production and direction. | Motion
    pictures—Aesthetics. | Cinematography.
Classification: LCC PN1995.9.P7 M57 2021 (print) |
    LCC PN1995.9.P7 (ebook) | DDC 791.4301—dc23
LC record available at https://lccn.loc.gov/2021005040
LC ebook record available at https://lccn.loc.gov/2021005041

Manufactured in the United States of America

30 29 28 27 26 25 24 23 22 21
10 9 8 7 6 5 4 3 2 1

The film image . . . is what? *A lure.*

—Roland Barthes

Contents

Acknowledgments

Although I have been interested in the moving camera for about as long as I have been seriously interested in cinema, I began work on this book a decade ago when I was teaching at the University of Pittsburgh. A graduate seminar I taught there on the intersection of camera movement and philosophical aesthetics proved incredibly generative, not least because of the range of students and colleagues who were present: Katie Bird, Veronica Fitzpatrick, Kevin Flanagan, Joseph Franke, Beach Gray, Jedd Hakimi, Jeff Heinzl, Matt Lambert, Ryan Pierson, John Rhym, Jordan Schonig, Kieran Setiya, Kyle Stevens, Gordon Sullivan, and Jen Waldron. A later class at the University of Chicago helped take these ideas further, and I am grateful to the graduate students who were there: Blake Beaver, Hannah Frank, Trevor McCulloch, Xin Peng, Kate Schlachter, Jordan Schonig, Pao-chen Tang, Tyler Tennant, and Panpan Yang. Over these two classes, it became clear that while I was aiming to write a more general account of the history and aesthetics of the moving camera, I was in fact stuck on the topic of point of view and why it seemed to be an inextricable problem for thinking about camera movement. It wasn't until a conversation with Jim Chandler in Chicago during the summer of 2018 that I realized that point of view and camera movement could be a book of its own.

Over the past dozen years, I have been fortunate to teach at two wonderful programs for thinking about film and other moving image media. I have learned from and been shaped by my colleagues at each institution. At the University of Pittsburgh: Mark Lynn Anderson, Mark Best, Nancy Condee, Josh Ellenbogen, Charles Exley, Jane Feuer, Lucy Fischer, Randall Halle, Marcia Landy, Adam Lowenstein, Colin Mac-Cabe, Neepa Majumdar, Vladimir Padunov, David Pettersen, and Kun Qian. At the University of Chicago: Robert Bird, Dominique Bluher, Jim Chandler, Marc Downie, Xinyu Dong, Allyson Nadia Field, Tom Gunning, Judy Hoffman, Patrick Jagoda, Kara Keeling, Jim Lastra, David Levin, Rochona Majumdar, Richard Neer, David Rodowick, Salomé Skvirsky, Noa Steimatsky, Jacqueline Stewart, Yuri Tsivian, and Jennifer Wild.

I have given talks and presentations of the material in this book at a range of places: Columbia University, Indiana University Bloomington, Jawaharlal Nehru University, Johns Hopkins University, Pomona College, Triangle Film Salon (the University of North Carolina at Chapel Hill, Duke University, and North Carolina State University), the University of California Los Angeles, the University of Chicago, the University of Pittsburgh, Vanderbilt University, and the Society for Cinema and Media Studies. I am grateful for the invitations, and for the conversations that took place there. In October 2016, I organized a conference with Jordan Schonig on camera movement, "Seeing Movement, Being Moved: An Exploration of the Moving Camera," which was an intellectually exhilarating experience; I am deeply grateful to the presenters and audience who produced a conversation that seemed to cover most of the possible areas for thinking about camera movement.

Many people have read part or all of this book and offered suggestions along the way: Dudley Andrew, Brooke Belisle, Lauren Berlant, Kristin Boyce, Matthew Boyle, Warren Buckland, Jim Chandler, Marc Downie, Noam Elcott, Jen Fay, Frances Ferguson, Gregg Flaxman, Kata Gellen, Marah Gubar, Adam Hart, Steffen Hven, Paola Iovene, Usha Iyer, Patrick Jagoda, Sarah Keller, Jim Lastra, Tamar Lando, Rochona Majumdar, Josh Malitsky, Joe McElhaney, Michelle Menzies, Andrew Miller, Davide Panagia, Vladimir Padunov, Gilberto Perez, Robert Pippin, Inga Pollman, John Rhym, Ariel Rogers, Kieran Setiya, Noa Steimatsky, Kyle Stevens, Julie Turnock, Rick Warner, and Mark Wilson. Tom Gunning provided deep insight and advice about camera movement (and much else) over multiple decades. I have been in conversation with Ryan Pierson since I began this project, and I have learned much from his work on animation and camera movement. Shane Denson graciously shared a copy of his book before its publication. I also bear a deep debt of gratitude to the reviewers of the manuscript for the University of

California Press; both Patrick Keating and Kristen Whissel understood what I was trying to do and gave me criticism and support that helped me along the way. It is a privilege to have one's work read in the way they did.

At the University of California Press, Madison Wetzell oversaw the production of the book, guiding it through the various stages; Sharon Langworthy provided copyediting that improved the manuscript; and Alexander Trotter expertly created the index. I am especially indebted to Raina Polivka, who not only helped bring this book into being but gave invaluable advice as I was developing its core organizational ideas. I am lucky to have her as an editor.

I wrote this book in regular dialogue with three people in particular. Jordan Schonig started as a student but has taught me more about how to think about camera movement than anyone else I know. Richard Neer has been a constant interlocutor for the ideas that underpin this project and gave me tools for thinking about problems that I hadn't yet noticed. And over a number of years, I had few ideas that I did not discuss with Jen Waldron, whose intelligence and insight shaped the way I think about media, theory, and style.

At various stages, I benefited from sustained conversation with three friends whose deaths have haunted my writing. Miriam Hansen provided the initial impetus to write about camera movement, urging me to work on Ophuls. Hannah Frank showed me all the tricks that animation did with camera movement and pushed me not to be complacent in my formulations. Edward Branigan served as a sounding board for ideas about point of view, philosophy, and film style (as well as baseball). I miss them all.

Last, I want to thank my family. Barbara Herman has continued to teach me how to think hard and carefully without sacrificing the ambition of ideas, and to allow me to learn from her; Mickey Morgan first showed me how to be excited by thinking about the moving camera, so many years ago, and this book bears the mark of those conversations throughout its pages. Ally Field is the love that has guided this book, not only in the many ways I have learned from her how to think about films in and out of history—but also in the life that we have built together. It is a perpetual joy, a sense of morning, to be with her. When I began working on this book a decade ago, it felt as though I had indefinite amounts of time to think and write. I finished writing this book in the midst of a global pandemic, when time is largely oriented around my children, Theo and Zoe. For a project that is centrally about considerations of fantasy and imagination and about the importance of complexity, they have been reminders of the value and pleasures of each of those things. They are, and have been, happiness.

A version of chapter 3 was originally published by Taylor & Frances as "Where Are We? Camera Movements and the Problem of Point of View," *New Review of Film and Television Studies* 14, no. 2 (2016): 222–48.

A version of part of chapter 4 was originally published by Wiley Blackwell as "Beyond Destiny and Design: Camera Movement in Fritz Lang's German Films," in *A Companion to Fritz Lang*, ed. Joe McElhaney (Malden, MA, 2015): 259–78.

A version of chapter 5 was originally published by the University of Chicago Press as "Max Ophuls and the Limits of Virtuosity: On the Aesthetics and Ethics of Camera Movement," *Critical Inquiry* 38 (Autumn 2011): 127–63.

CHAPTER I

Talking about the Moving Camera

I.

Perhaps something new begins with Agnès Varda's *Les glaneurs et la glaneuse* (*The Gleaners and I*, 2000), her poetic meditation about the practice of gleaning as both a means for survival and an artistic practice. At one moment, filming a field of potatoes, Varda forgets to turn off her small digital camera as she returns to her car. What results is a shot she calls the "dance of the lens cap": the dangling cap jangles around in front of the camera, swinging wildly as she walks. A shot reclaimed, or gleaned, by Varda, and expressive of the mood of many of her late films, the "dance of the lens cap" is a unique product of the then-emerging terrain of digital cinema. Varda would not have forgotten to turn off a 16mm camera, and its bulkiness—like that of early video cameras—would have precluded the shot's casual feel. If the pleasures of the shot come in part from the confirmation of the way that a small digital camera can pick up new kinds of images, they also come from the camera's movement, the way it is both within and outside Varda's control: how its bouncing both responds to her own movements and suggests a kind of autonomy of its own.

Cinema has had, almost since its beginning, a fascination with the moving camera. Less than two years after the screening of the first films in December 1895, the moving camera had become a prominent feature. Cameras were placed on moving sidewalks and elevators, on the front of trams, boats, and (especially) trains; such shots constituted one of the main attractions in early cinema. The moving camera has also of course been central to the history of narrative cinema, with everything from extended tracking shots to subtle reframings that convey narrative information. And there is also something else. For many cinephiles, part of the treasured informal knowledge of the history of cinema was a celebration of famous tracking shots, such as the ride down the hotel elevator and out the revolving door in F. W. Murnau's *Der letzte Mann* (*The Last Laugh*, 1924)—or, staying with Murnau, the magic flight in *Faust* (1926) and the glorious movement through the swamp in *Sunrise: A Song of Two Humans* (1927). The shot that reveals the effects of Anna May Wong's kitchen dance in E. A. Dupont's *Piccadilly* (1929); the ballroom sequence in Orson Welles's *The Magnificent Ambersons* (1942), chopped into multiple shots by the studio executives; the exploration of the crowd in the *danse macabre* sequence from Jean Renoir's *La Règle du jeu* (*The Rules of the Game*, 1939); the tracking shots that enact Genjuro's infatuation with the spirit in Kenji Mizoguchi's *Ugetsu monogatari* (1953); the repeated movements through the trenches in Stanley Kubrick's *Paths of Glory* (1957); the extended shot following Antoine as he runs to the sea in François Truffaut's *Les quatres cents coups* (*The 400 Blows*, 1959); the spectacular virtuosity of Mikhail Kalatozov's *The Cranes Are Flying* (1957) and *Soy Cuba* (*I Am Cuba*, 1964); the triple 360-degree tracking shot of the courtyard in which a pianist plays Mozart in Jean-Luc Godard's *Week-end* (1967), or the horizontal tracking shots that litter his films of that period, from *La Chinoise* (1967) to *British Sounds* (1969) to *Tout va bien* (1972); the seemingly impossible movement of the camera in the final shot of Michelangelo Antonioni's *The Passenger* (1975); the first use of a Steadicam in Hal Ashby's *Bound for Glory* (1976), showing Woody Guthrie walking through camp; the Copacabana scene in Martin Scorsese's *Goodfellas* (1990); the opening shot of Robert Altman's *The Player* (1992), echoing the extraordinary opening from Welles's *Touch of Evil* (1958); the haunting circling of the camera in the train station in Chantal Akerman's *D'Est* (*From the East*, 1993): all these are cinematic currency. And there are the directors broadly renowned for their use of the moving camera: Jean Epstein, Frank Borzage, Alfred Hitchcock, Max Ophuls, Maya Deren, Otto Preminger, Marie Menken, Vincente Minnelli, Bruce Baillie, Kira Muratova, Miklós Jancsó, Andrei Tarkovsky, Béla Tarr, and so on.

Despite the length and depth of this history, it is no exaggeration to say that we are now living in the age of the moving camera. It's everywhere we look. Some of these new camera movements are spectacular, as in the single-shot films *Timecode* (Mike Figgis, 2000), *Russian Ark* (Alexsandr Sokurov, 2002), *Birdman* (Alejandro Iñárritu, 2014), and *1917* (Sam Mendes, 2019). The last of these even occasioned an article in the *New York Times* on Christmas Day 2019 that listed the great camera movements to which it ought to be compared, encompassing not only the history of single-shot films—such as Hitchcock's *Rope* (1948)—but also extended sequences of virtuosic camera movement, like the fight sequence in Park Chan-wook's *Oldboy* (2003).[1] Everywhere we turn we find extraordinary mobile shots: the opening seventeen-minute shot of Alfonso Cuarón's *Gravity* (2013), which moves in and around a spacewalk and the ensuing chaos after a collision with a field of debris, or the opening shot of *Wolf Warrior 2* (Wu Jing, 2017), in which the hero defeats a group of Somali pirates while the camera follows the fight across two boats and even underwater. Any moviegoer in recent years can fill in their own favorites.

Such virtuosic and thematized use of the moving camera has also taken place outside the cinema. It's not just in the "walk and talk" sequences made famous by *The West Wing*, in which the movement of the camera is guided by the movement of the characters. We see it celebrated in sequences like the six-minute tracking shot of the "Who Goes There" episode of *True Detective* (2014). Camera movement also occupies a central role in moving image work in gallery spaces, such as Sharon Lockhart's *Lunch Break* (2008), comprised of a shot that moves slowly through a corridor where workers eat their lunch, and Philippe Parreno's *The Crowd* (2015), in which the camera swirls through people inhabiting gallery spaces. Or there is Amie Siegel's *Provenance* (2013), in which a series of horizontal tracking shots traces the history of mid-century modernist design back to the Indian city of Chandigarh.

It is not too much to say that the moving camera is now present as a steady undercurrent to the contemporary grammar of film style. Shots that would have been taken on a tripod in classical Hollywood cinema are now done with a handheld camera. Beyond the unsteadiness that expresses the tension radiating through the characters in Kathryn Bigelow's *The Hurt Locker* (2008), even a standard shot/reverse-shot sequence in *Men in Black: International* (F. Gary Gray, 2019), during which Molly is being interviewed by Agent O, uses a handheld camera for its over-the-shoulder shots, creating a subtle instability that refuses to settle down. It's a kind of framing that would never have been used twenty-five years ago; now, the moving camera is narrative cinema's default option.

This is a book about camera movement. It is not an account of the current state of camera movement, though it does aim to contribute to that. Nor is it a history of the moving camera and its different uses, though it does address that. Rather, it is about one of the most persistent and intuitive ways of thinking about the moving camera: that spectators identify with the position and movement of the camera within the world of the film, that it serves as a surrogate for the spectator. Already in accounts of "phantom rides," early films in which the camera was placed on the front of a moving train—such as *Conway Castle* (William Dickson, 1898)—audiences reported that "suddenly we're right in the midst of it all," or that they were "swept along in the rush" of the camera through the world.[2] Much later, at the turn of the twenty-first century, a cinematography manual described how the Steadicam can "almost be an additional character in the scene," one with whom the spectator identifies.[3] A century apart, these accounts rely on the same premise: as the camera moves within the world of the film, we move—or take ourselves to move—within that world as well.

Such accounts are not confined to spectators, critics, and theorists but appear in the ambitions of filmmakers themselves. They surface most clearly in the attempts to create a "subjective cinema," one in which the viewpoint of the camera—hence, the spectator—is identified with the viewpoint of a character. Especially prominent from the 1920s through the 1940s, and ranging from experiments by Joris Ivens to films such as *Dr. Jekyll and Mr. Hyde* (Rouben Mamoulian, 1932), *Dark Passage* (Delmer Daves, 1947), and, most (in)famously, *Lady in the Lake* (Robert Montgomery, 1947), the subjective camera has returned in works such as Gaspar Noé's *Enter the Void* (2009), Ilya Naishuller's *Hardcore Henry* (2015), and, as many have noted, the first-person video game. The subjective camera is often criticized when it is used to structure an entire film, where it is described as at best a gimmick, but its recurrence across the history of cinema is due in no small part to the way it literalizes the intuitive assumption about our relation to the moving camera.

"A history of camera movement," Patrick Keating writes toward the beginning of his study of the moving camera in classical Hollywood cinema, "must also be a history of ideas about camera movement."[4] What Keating neglects to mention, however, is that not all the ideas are good ones. The logic of the camera-eye, the sense that the way we look at the world of a film proceeds through the look of the camera, that we are with the camera when it moves through the world, is the most dominant and important account of the moving camera, one that returns each time the moving camera is in need of reinvention. Yet the logic behind this fundamental idea is deeply flawed. To put it bluntly, we are not within the world of the film, seeing it from the perspective of the camera; that is an illusion, and showing this to be the case is a central aim of this book. At the same time, however, and importantly, even though we recognize this, even though we *know* that we cannot be in the world of the film with the camera, we still *feel* it to be the case.[5]

The Lure of the Image is about the relation between these two features of camera movements and our experience of them. It makes a theoretical argument that shows the implications—the dangers, the traps—of thinking about camera movement as a surrogate for the look and movement of the spectator. Rather than treating this mode of experience as an uncontested given, or as false to fact, I describe it instead as a *fantasy*: a fantasy that camera movements place us within the world of the film itself, actually or virtually. More precisely, I argue that it is an *epistemic fantasy*, one of being granted access to the film world in a way that is in fact impossible to achieve. The book shows how this fantasy recurs across the history of cinema, and that it is more than just a trap for critics and theorists. I show that filmmakers have often used this fantasy to lure audiences into a certain way of seeing and a belief in how they relate to the world of the film. Yet I also argue that this intuitive model has fundamentally prevented us from recognizing how the moving camera functions.

This book is an attempt to undo that blind spot, that guiding assumption, and so to clear conceptual space in which to develop a different model—not only for thinking about camera movement but also for addressing a range of problems in film theory. I argue that camera movements do not carry with them point of view, a position from which the spectator perceives the world of the film. While we *can* be at the position of the moving camera, we need not be—and indeed often are not. By attending to a range of examples of camera movements, both virtuosic and mundane, I show that how we relate to the image is not a given, fixed by the way the moving camera lures us into the image. Rather, I argue that our point of view is *an effect* of this movement, a secondary production. This way of grasping the relation of the spectators to the moving camera allows for a more flexible account of point of view as well as a more expansive understanding of the stakes—political, ethical, even ontological—of this key component of cinematic style.

2.

Camera movement remains a topic in search of a debate. Despite their prominence across the history of cinema, camera movements have been surprisingly marginal and elusive in theoretical accounts. Indeed, only recently has a range of positions and topics emerged as part of a sustained engagement with the moving camera. Part of the lack of discourse is due to the way the two dominant topics throughout the twentieth century, ontology and montage, had little to do with camera movements. In critical writing on both topics, the model for thinking about the cinema is predicated on the assumption that the basic unit to be analyzed is a static shot, a fixed frame, a still image. The result is that these theoretical traditions were not only ill-equipped to deal with the problems that camera movements pose; they were, to a large extent, indifferent to them. As a result, while essays and fragments of theoretical treatises have been devoted to camera movement, they are nothing compared to the volumes spent discussing film's photographic basis or its reliance on montage as a language-like form of communication.[6] The study of camera movement has no Bazin or Eisenstein, no Kracauer or Metz. In this section, I tell a brief story about the history of thinking about the moving camera. My aim is not to be exhaustive, or even synoptic, but in the absence of sustained theoretical work on camera movement I hope to give a sense of the critical tradition out of which work can be done. Against the background of this fragmented history, we can see some of the missteps of more recent theoretical work and what a better path might involve.

Like the cinephile's history of camera movement, the history of the critical literature has proceeded by largely informal means. Some of this involves classic accounts, such as André Bazin's description of the end of Renoir's *Le crime de monsieur Lange* (1936), when Lange descends the staircase to confront Batala. The camera executes a counterclockwise sweep of almost 360 degrees, taking in the entire courtyard and only returning to Lange as he comes up to Batala and shoots him. Bazin writes that, while the shot "has perhaps psychological or dramatic justification (it gives an impression of dizziness, of madness, of suspense) . . . its real *raison d'être* is more germane to the conception of the film: it is the pure spatial expression of the *mise en scène*."[7] Another familiar example is Annette Michelson's discussion of the extended zoom that comprises Michael Snow's *Wavelength* (1967), which she argues is at once a drama of consciousness itself and a revelation of cinema as a temporal narrative form. Michelson writes: "The film is the projection of a grand reduction; its 'plot' is the tracing of spatio-temporal *données*, its 'action' the movement of the camera as the movement of consciousness."[8] A third is Brian Henderson's argument that the horizontal tracking shots in Godard's films of the late 1960s and early 1970s emphasized the flatness of the image, which he reads—in their refusal of depth—as a rejection of "the principal mode of bourgeois self-presentment in cinema."[9]

Most often, discussions of camera movement tend to follow one of two directions. The first involves the idea of motivation. This is often connected to narrative, such as when Hitchcock remarked about *Rope*, "I believe in using camera movement when it helps tell the story more efficiently"—an exceedingly odd claim for a film that so ostentatiously displays its camera movements.[10] But it need not be. "The most important thing," writes Jean Mitry, "is that camera movement should be justified—physically, dramatically, or psychologically." Proper justification is, he says, the "law" that governs the proper use of camera movement, which allows us to distinguish between proper artistic uses of the moving camera and less organized ones.[11] Nick Hall describes this form of judgment as a "use and abuse" model for determining "appropriateness," a way of thinking that is central to criticism but that can be limited—and limiting.[12] The criteria, after all, aren't hard and fast: excessive camera movements can seem to be without motivation at the time of their appearance, yet later be revealed as part of a larger pattern. The hyper, swirling camera movements at the beginning of *Lola Rennt* (*Run Lola Run*, Tom Tykwer, 1998) are one example. Or there is the beginning of *Festen* (*The Celebration*, Thomas Vinterberg, 1998), in which the ringing of a mobile phone sends the camera scurrying into Michael's pocket to find it, a gesture that feels wildly disproportionate to the mundane event but suggests the intensity of the disclosures to come.

A second way of talking about camera movement sees the moving camera as part of the expressive arsenal of filmmakers, a way to convey an experience, impression, or mood to the spectator. This is often treated as an authorial flourish, as in Éric Rohmer and Claude Chabrol's description of a camera movement in Hitchcock's *Notorious* (1946): "When Devlin, come to save Alicia from death, steps from the shadows—in the same way he had appeared after the Miami drinking bout—and the camera, in a movement of extreme tenderness and sensuality, circles around the two lovers, the screen sparkles with an indescribable beauty, the secret of which Hitchcock learned from Murnau."[13] Or there is Gilberto Perez's discussion of the different "cameras" employed by filmmakers:

> The epic camera of Mizoguchi, the devil's camera Hitchcock employs, not only knows what to show us but makes palpable to us its stance of knowledge. The explorer's camera Flaherty employs has scouted the territory for us, has discovered what to show us. Renoir's camera is another kind of explorer, one who hasn't gone ahead of us into the territory and can't presume to know exactly what to show us. Antonioni's camera is like Renoir's in this respect, an inquiring rather than a knowing camera, though Renoir's camera takes the point of view of a friend rather than a stranger. Always in Antonioni we are made to sense what the photographer in *Blow-Up* (1966) is brought up against: the incompleteness of any view of appearances, the inconclusiveness of any perspective.[14]

This way of approaching the moving camera does not aim to get at a general account of what camera movement is or does, but it contains a vital point about flexibility. Unlike debates over the linguistic structure of montage or the ontological foundations of photographic realism, these writings insist that there is no a priori logic that determines the contours of how camera movements operate. David Bordwell articulates this principle when he writes that "camera movement has usually been considered too elusive to be analyzable."[15]

In recent years, however, thinking about the moving camera has begun to shift as new writings have generated compelling and important accounts of the different issues that camera movements can raise. Much of the attention has been on particular problems. Sometimes this involves debates about technology, from the history of the zoom lens to the dynamics of the Steadicam.[16] At other points it involves specific kinds of shots, from types of movement—like the "cosmic zoom" that opens some recent films, in which the camera moves through the sky (or across space) to focus on specific characters—to animation practices, to handheld cinematography.[17]

These new writings, various as they are, have had several important consequences. First, and perhaps most significantly, they have created genuine debates, and hence also terms of disagreement—the conditions for a dialogue over forms and types that has long been a part of the way that montage has been discussed. That is, these writings enable the kind of critical activity that J. L. Austin describes as the "field work" of a topic, so that "we should be able to unfreeze, to loosen up and get going on agreeing about discoveries."[18] Second, they have introduced historical analysis into discussions of the moving camera, whether that history is institutional, intellectual, or technological. Many of these studies also draw on interviews and/or oral histories to provide accounts of how operators understood the possibilities of the cameras they moved. And third, they have drawn broad conclusions without losing the insight that there is no one thing that camera movements do or can do, and that how camera movements work is not fixed by any essence but instead predicated on the range of norms, ideas, and uses that attend them.

The most representative work of this new trend is Keating's study of camera movement in classical Hollywood cinema. Keating gives a production history, one that includes not only technology and labor but also the work of writers and cinematographers he describes as "practical theorists," who created informal theories designed to validate specific strategies for moving the camera.[19] By articulating an account of "technologies transformed by ideas," Keating is able to elicit the different models for thinking about the camera that were at play in the studio era, ranging from anthropomorphic treatments to claims that the camera is a form of mechanical vision that transcends human perceptual capacities.[20] In combining production history, visual analysis, and accounts of "practical theorists," Keating situates the moving camera historically while remaining flexible about the open-ended varieties of its uses.

Despite the importance of Keating's study, as well as the new surge in writings on camera movement, there remains a problem in the way camera movements are understood. The problem is not just that a failure to address camera movements has left a gap in the history of film theory. Rather, because there was never a moment to stop and systematically think about the assumptions that underlay how the moving camera was being talked about, key ideas, especially about the relation of spectator to camera, simply remained in place.

3 .

Throughout the fragmented history of thinking about camera movement, one core assumption is consistently present. This is the belief in the importance of point of view, or how we see the world on film through the camera. The answer for almost every writer is that the camera functions as our surrogate, our mode of access to the world. The way of framing this answer may take various forms: the camera can be a surrogate for our eye, it can be an anthropomorphic entity of its own, or it can attain a kind of machinic vision. What's common to each form of response is the view that we access the world of the film by way of our relation to the camera. I focus on point of view in this book, then, because of its centrality to thinking about camera movement. But I also do so because this topic reveals a methodological assumption that *the* critical problem to solve has to do with the place of the camera within the fictional world. From there, it is assumed, everything else can fall into place. No goal of this book is more important than showing how such an approach has prevented us from grasping the work that camera movements do and from coming to terms with the difficulties that camera movements pose for thinking about moving-image media more generally.

The idea that the camera is a stand-in for the viewer runs throughout writings on camera movement. Béla Balázs writes: "In the cinema the camera carries the spectator into the film picture itself. . . . [O]ur eyes are in the camera."[21] Or there is Irving Pichel's remark: "Most commonly, the camera is treated as an extension of the spectator's eye."[22] Herb Lightman, writing the same year as Pichel, asserts that the "camera is the 'eye' of the audience."[23] Bordwell writes: "Camera movement, I suggest, presents us with a constricted but effective range of visual cues for subjective movement. . . . [W]e can hardly resist reading the camera-movement effect as a persuasive surrogate for our subjective movement through an objective world."[24] Michael Snow, describing his own *La Région Centrale* (*The Central Region*, 1971), says that the connection between spectator and camera "is more mental than physical. . . . [I]t is as if you were the cameraman."[25] The idea is found in contemporary discussions as well. Bruce Bennett, writing on 3D films, claims that "the mobile cinematic eye . . . is an adventurer's eye" and talks about the fantasy of immersion that occurs by lining up camera movement with a character's point of view.[26] Slavoj Žižek wonders if "a camera [is] not our eye separated from our body, drifting around" the world of the film.[27] And debates about video games often assume the connection, as in Alexander Galloway's account of the emergence of the "first-person shooter" out of the subjective shot or Will Brooker's assumption that "the game 'camera' represents the player's point of view."[28]

The governing assumption that the camera functions as a stand-in or surrogate for the viewer also appears in less explicit forms. Take Tom Gunning's discussion of the famous camera movements in *Cabiria* (Giovanni Pastrone, 1914):

> Even in *Cabiria's* carefully constructed fictional world, camera movement in many shots does not create a character's point of view or act as a narrating agent revealing salient information. Rather it expands the basic visual role of the cinema: presenting a scene before us. *Cabiria* uses camera movement

to intensify the scene's three-dimensional aspects, showing that *one can peek around the edges of things*, as space becomes transformed before our eyes in a continuous manner.[29]

Notice the phrase "one can peek"; this is the moment when an implicit logic of identification with the camera takes place, suggesting that it takes up our potential position within the world of the film. This assumption allows Gunning to say that our "sense of being 'within the world of the film'. . . comes partly from shifting our orientation within space through the movement of the camera."[30]

I argue that this assumption has gone unanalyzed. In many ways, this is the result of two things. The first is the long-standing affinity between camera and eye, so much so that it can still function as an organizing chapter for a handbook on film theory.[31] (I address this affinity in chapter 3.) The second has to do with the emergence of phenomenology in film studies. Phenomenology's attunement to modes of being in the world, to forms of lived experience, for the first time privileged the moving camera as the central technique for theoretical modeling. Vivian Sobchack, for example, sees a clear affinity between her project and the moving camera: "We understand [the camera] and its projects in lived space as we understand ourselves in spontaneous motion and responsive activity to the world."[32] This "correlational" structure, in which the moving camera matches our own forms of movement in the world, becomes Sobchack's model for thinking about cinema more generally. The result is that there is, in a sense, no impulse to challenge the central assumption underpinning conceptions of how we relate to the moving camera.

To be sure, a correlational impulse is not unique to Sobchack. Bazin praises the long take for approximating the freedom of vision that governs our everyday looking.[33] And Bordwell argues that the moving camera demonstrates that spectators respond to visual cues in a manner similar to how they do outside the movie theater. Sobchack's argument, though, is that the moving camera can be treated as a genuine other: "The viewer intersubjectively and prereflectively recognizes and understands the camera as *sharing the manner of his or her own existence*."[34] Elsewhere, she focuses on the way that the apparent intentionality of the camera—that we see it as going somewhere, as having a project— subtends our recognition of it as a being like ourselves.[35] (This is a position akin to the account of Steadicam given by the cinematographer Larry McConkey: "My camera becomes like another person and the audience becomes connected through that person . . . more empathetic, more involved."[36]) Jennifer Barker develops this position further, emphasizing affinities between types of camera movement and the movements of the spectator's body:

> Our bodies' muscular empathy with the film's body emerges partly from experience. When the film swivels suddenly with a whip pan, or moves slowly with a long take or a tracking shot, or stretches itself out in widescreen to take in a vast landscape, we feel those movements in our muscles because our bodies have made similar movements . . . we can relate, having performed many of these basic gestures ourselves, in our own way.[37]

Phenomenological film theory presents a vision of a profoundly anthropomorphic cinema, built on the sense that the spectator moves with the camera as it moves through the world of the film.

For both Sobchack and Barker, the connection between spectator and camera—the idea that the camera functions as our surrogate—is inextricably tied to a belief in the camera's fundamental anthropomorphism. The link between these two positions, however, is by no means necessary, a separation that can be seen in the deep revision to the phenomenological model offered by Scott Richmond, who turns to a different theoretical tradition—ecological perception—to revise the affinity between camera and viewer. Richmond argues that the effect of camera movement results from "films' ongoing modulation of my perception of space, specifically my sense of my own position, orientation, and attitude in onscreen space."[38] This modulation does not follow the correlationist model that Sobchack and Barker posit. Richmond emphasizes the divergence of ordinary and cinematic modes of perception and isolates "the cinematic *illusion* of bodily movement."[39] We don't actually believe that we are moving through the diegetic world, but there are sufficient kinesthetic cues to make us feel that we are. This dual perception, of at once moving and not moving, is key to what makes cinema an *aesthetic* experience, an illusion capable of visceral and kinetic pleasures that in everyday life would produce a vastly different response. Yet even with this different approach, Richmond treats our relation to the film as defined by our relation to the camera. As he puts it elsewhere, writing with Elizabeth Reich, "the spectator identifies with the camera, as a technological perceiver of the world."[40]

Much of my argument, especially in the first part of the book, is aimed at undoing the core assumption of identification between camera and spectator. One way of clearing conceptual space is with examples. Jordan Schonig has observed that many theories of the moving camera are based on a specific kind of shot, that of forward motion. These theories do "not describe an essential condition of camera movement," he argues, "but rather an effect of particular ways of moving the camera—forward movements-into-depth—which strongly evoke the sense of an embodied mobile perspective." From Sobchack's interest in the subjective camera to Richmond's focus on flight, these are examples whose form of motion leads into the world of the film "as we project ourselves forward through space along with the unseen camera." Against this reductive tendency, Schonig points to lateral tracking shots, ranging from Walter Ruttmann's *Berlin: Symphony of a Great City* (1927), to Stan Brakhage's *The Wonder Ring* (1955), to Leos Carax's *Mauvais sang* (1986). Rather than emphasizing immersion, in these shots the movement of the camera makes us aware of the edges of the frame, serving "as a kind of paintbrush for generating two-dimensional screen phenomena."[41]

In that vein, one goal of this book is to open up a new range of examples to theory, to make the flexibility in the history of critical writings on camera movement speak against the tendency in more theoretical work to base arguments on a single type of shot. The shots I discuss range widely in the work they do. They include, for example, instances of attunement to characters within the frame, in which the movement of the camera is designed to express the psychological state of the character. These are the kinds of shots in which, as Joe McElhaney writes about Minnelli's *Two Weeks in Another Town* (1962), "the movements of the camera . . . do not simply follow the movements of the extras around the restaurant. They also follow an 'internal' movement here, that of Jack's psychological state. . . . The camera's tracking movement . . . [is] clearly intended to correspond to Jack's increasing withdrawal from the present situation."[42] How would a model focused around the position of the camera account for a movement that attunes us to the interior state of a character? Another type of camera movement is based on perceptual games, in which the assumption of an identification with the camera is played with or subverted. In *The Texas Chain Saw Massacre* (Tobe Hooper, 1974), for example, immediately after the first person has been killed in the house, the camera suddenly and swiftly glides up behind a woman sitting on a swing. The movement suggests that the camera is the point of view of an attacker, yet in fact no one is there. The theoretical puzzle is that as we watch the sequence, we can feel the way an implicit assumption of identification with the camera is activated—and then dissipated—as if the filmmaker were teasing our familiar habits of viewing.

Throughout this book, I use such examples to revise the logic of point of view, putting forward camera movements that resist, subvert, or lie beside an analogy between camera and eye.

Another part of my argument has a more explicit theoretical orientation. If reliance on point of view is fundamentally mistaken, if we do not experience images, even of the forward-moving camera, as if we are (necessarily) at the position of the camera, and yet we also—and often—believe that we watch moving images in this way, as the example from *Texas Chain Saw Massacre* suggests, what explains this? The way I account for our belief that we move through the world of the film with the camera is that it is a *fantasy*, a fantasy that camera movements might be able to place us within the world of the film itself, actually or virtually. More precisely, I describe it as an *epistemic fantasy*: one of being at a place we cannot be, a place we are ordinarily barred from inhabiting. Filmmakers, I argue, trade on an underlying *desire* we have to identify with the camera, to be with it as it moves through the world—whether or not the camera is also identified with the point of view of a character. Theories of camera movement draw out this feature, but they mistake it for a fact, an underlying and solid layer; this is what leads to their methodological flaws. What they take as conceptual bedrock is rather the expression of a deep epistemological fantasy.[43]

The explicit use of epistemological fantasies can be found in the openings of two films whose plots are themselves centrally concerned with problems of knowledge and knowing. Hitchcock's *Psycho* (1960) begins with a wide view of a city while titles give us place, day, and time ("Phoenix, Arizona"; "Friday, December the Eleventh"; "Two Forty-Three P.M."). All the while the camera pans across nondescript buildings, then starts to move into one, showing a half-shut window that it moves up to, pauses at, then passes through into the room where Marion and Sam are ending a lunchtime tryst (a hidden dissolve makes the transition possible).[44] Another example is Welles's *Citizen Kane* (1941), which starts with a close-up of a faded "No Trespassing" sign; the camera pauses, then begins to rise up the fence—a dissolve takes it higher up, still climbing, then another dissolve to a new section of the fence adds to the sense of scale, the enormity of the barrier. A third dissolve finally brings us to the top, where we see Xanadu in the distance, a single lit window drawing us in; the window remains in the frame across multiple shots until the camera winds up inside the bedroom and we are given an extreme close-up of Kane's lips uttering the word "Rosebud." It's worth noting that in both *Psycho* and *Citizen Kane* a window is used to incite epistemic desire, a suggestion of the presence of something hidden from us that we want to discover. The lure that leads us forward is likewise associated with an image of a barrier—the "No Trespassing" sign, the half-shut window—an almost ontological block that helps generate the fantasy that we will be given access to special, private knowledge. The effect is not a feature of the formal technique itself; John Farrow's *The Big Clock* (1948), for example, stages a similar movement across a city and toward a building, moving through a lit window to reveal where George, the protagonist, is hiding from the police, yet without raising such fantasies.[45] Rather, the effect involves an overdetermined investment in wishing the camera to go to forbidden places, one in which the movement of the camera is a necessary (but not sufficient) condition. Welles and Hitchcock thus create forms that play with, evoke, our desire to see where the camera is heading, to figure out the object of the camera's inquisitive movement.

4·

The assumption that the moving camera is the surrogate for the spectator's movement—whether that movement is seen as perceptual, virtual, kinesthetic, or illusory—has proved difficult to dislodge, and it continues to shape debates even in the age of digital cinema. Take one of the central ways that the rise of digital media has recently been described, as a rejection of a human-centered mode of perception. Where early theorists of the digital called for a new phenomenology, one that was attuned to the way that digital media allowed new aspects of human action to come into view, more recent theorists have emphasized the extent to which digital media sever a tie between image and body.[46] Hito Steyerl describes this new trend as involving a rejection of the terms of linear perspective, the recession into depth that Schonig identified as a central component of a phenomenological account of the perception of cinematic worlds. Steyerl remarks, for example, on "the decreasing importance of a paradigm of visuality that long dominated our vision: linear perspective. Its stable and single point of view is being supplemented (and often replaced) by multiple perspectives, overlapping windows, distorted flight lines, and divergent vanishing points."[47] Her argument harkens back to what Lev Manovich observed as the cornerstone of the digital: not an ontological grounding of the image but the proliferation of screens within a frame, like the windows of a computer.[48]

Shane Denson's work is exemplary of this shift, as he argues that new digital technologies of image production and manipulation operate at a speed that is beneath the level of human perception. What underlies contemporary cinema is not the human but the nonhuman, the sheer speed of computational processes demanding a new approach to old questions. (The spread of code that Michael Mann visualizes at the beginning of *Blackhat* [2015] is, in the capacity of the camera to move with it, already a slowed-down visualization of such processes.) Denson calls the new logic "discorrelation," the decoupling of the camera from the terms of the human subject. What emerges now are cameras that operate outside that constraint: "Cameras are irrational, neither subjective nor objective, incommensurate with human subjectivity and perspectives."[49] It's here that claims to importance for digital camera movements emerge. If we are moving with the camera through space, if we are there with it, then *how* it moves is directly connected to the way we experience the world it shows. Where Walter Benjamin talked about film, with its montage rhythms of shocks and shifts, as a training ground for the experience of modernity, newer technologies can be said to use camera movements as a perceptual attunement for a nonhuman world. From the microtemporality of computer processing to the planetary scale of the Anthropocene, everything seems to eclipse a human-centered understanding of the world. Changes in film style ought to be understood in relation to this new organization of the world.

While some of my arguments resonate with Denson's claim that post-cinematic modes "displace" the spectator, no longer situated as a "coherent subject in relation to a film," the form of my approach differs.[50] Part of the difference is that Denson treats phenomenology as *the* way to think about the moving camera, positioning Sobchack as the theorist whose work accurately describes and accounts for the moving camera before the onset of the post-cinematic condition. In so doing he takes on board the "camera as surrogate" model as his orienting point. Thus he can say that because camera movements now "fail to situate viewers in a consistently and coherently designated spectating-position," and that "they deviate from the perceptual norms established by human embodiment," a new theoretical program is not only needed but necessary—and the entire apparatus of twentieth-century cinema is inadequate to the twenty-first.[51]

However, as I argue here, the changes ascribed to post-cinematic filmmaking—that is, the displacement of the camera from its attunement to the human—have long been part of the basic grammar of camera movement. The sense that such discorrelation is new is a conclusion driven by the fundamental mistake of assuming that the moving camera once functioned (in a fairly uncomplicated way) as the surrogate for the spectator, however that relation was described.

We can see how this argument plays out by looking at a shot important to many recent discussions of camera movement: the opening, seventeen-minute shot of Cuarón's *Gravity*, which has come to be a hallmark of the uniqueness of the digital. Ryan Pierson argues that the terms of its movements around the protagonists, Ryan Stone and Matt Kowalski, create "a breathless freedom from exactly those laws of physics that are threatening [Stone]."[52] The shot's indifference to constraints suggests to Pierson a crisis about the identity of the camera and the failure of our ontological descriptions to account for what it does. Seizing on the same movements, Richmond sees in the camera's disconnection from stable forms of spatial organization "the dizzying, thrilling panic of movement beyond my control and according to an alien logic," a recognizable cinematic pleasure keyed to our submission of motor control to the technical apparatus itself.[53]

Yet beyond the virtuosic swirling and the rejection of familiar spatial coordinates, one moment in the shot stands out for the way it negotiates perspective. Kristen Whissel describes it as follows:

> The camera seems to follow Kowalski's look, turning as it displays the view of the rotating earth until it returns to Kowalski, who now appears at the other side of the frame. Digital camera moves combine with the earth's rotation and Kowalski's shifting position to undermine the optical cues conventionally used to anchor the camera's and the spectator's point of view.

Whissel argues that Cuarón uses "directions in motion . . . to dis-locate and disorient perception and perspective."[54] Denson also emphasizes this perceptual shift, but argues that it serves to undermine the very techniques that work "to correlate spectatorial subjectivity with cinematic images."[55] Note the differences in his description: "As the camera pans across this sublime (digital) image, the astronaut's vision is correlated with ours . . . [but] this apparent correlation is shattered when, at the conclusion of the camera's slow and lingering rightward pan, the apparent subject of vision appears again as its object."[56] This is, for Denson, the drama of discorrelation, an active strategy on the part of post-cinematic enterprises to undo the affinity between spectator and image.

Yet Denson passes over a basic thing: the kind of perceptual shift that *Gravity* effects, in which a character emerges from the frame in a place where they shouldn't be, has been a hallmark of narrative cinema for almost a century. As I argue in chapter 3, filmmakers have long employed such perceptual games to generate startling effects and to shift the alignment of spectators' relation to the world of the film. Indeed, it's so much a part of the basic cinematic vocabulary that Minnelli parodies it in *The Band Wagon* (1953). During the first performance of "That's Entertainment," Lester Marton walks off screen right, carrying a ladder, which stretches out behind him; Tony Hunter looks on in astonishment as the ladder keeps going and going and going, for an absurd amount of time. And then Lester walks back into the frame from the left (again), carrying the back end of the ladder and acknowledging Tony's perplexed look. What I want to emphasize with such examples, and they are legion, is that this kind of effect has always been a part of cinema, that filmmakers quickly realized that they could create unique effects and experiences by unsettling the spectator's intuitive belief in an identification with the moving camera.[57]

We can draw this point out in a slightly different way. Not least due to the legacy of Bazin, there has been a long-standing affinity between camera movement and the long take that emphasizes a refusal of trickery. John Gibbs and Douglas Pye summarize this position:

> The long take deals in the experience of unbroken duration, the continuity of real time, as opposed, for instance, to the synthetic continuity of time that is achieved in continuity editing. Continuity of time brings with it continuity of space—if the camera moves, it reveals space that extends beyond and around the static frame—and also continuity of action—what we see unfolds before us in the unbroken shot. . . . Such shots carried a sense of unarguable veracity.[58]

On this reading, the long take, with its implicit reliance on the moving camera as the primary technical means of conveying information, stands as a guarantor of truth: a preservation of the image's fidelity to the world. And it is precisely because the assumption of "veracity" has been connected to the long take that shots like the opening of *Gravity* stand out as examples of a new kind of cinema.

A rejection of the position offered by Gibbs and Pye, or by Bazin, is natural for theorists of digital cinema. The problem, again, is that the idea that no trickery can happen during a single shot in the predigital era, while intuitively appealing, is profoundly misleading. Not only do the oft-cited false cuts suture together the ostensibly continuous time in Hitchcock's *Rope*, but a range of other films use camera movements to bring multiple times into the same space. In Antonioni's *The Passenger*, for example, at one point the camera pans away from David Locke as he stands at a window and listens to a recording of an earlier conversation with Robertson; it circles around the room and finds him back at the same window—a hidden cut allows the transition to happen—but now in an earlier time, in the midst of the conversation we had heard the recording of at the beginning of the shot. Or there is *Notting Hill* (Roger Michell, 1999), in which Will Thacker walks through the seasons in his sadness: his movement to the right, tracked in a continuous shot by the camera, traverses a range of different times, an articulation of the emptiness of time, his indifference to its specificities. Or take this description from Jonathan Rosenbaum: "Consider the continuity of the camera movements in [Pere Portabella's] *Vampir-Cuadecuc* [1971], which typically proceed from the Count Dracula story being filmed by Jesús Franco to surrounding details pertaining to the actors, crew, and locations, thereby traversing centuries as well as the space between fiction and documentary."[59]

The point here is not to argue that theorists of the new have not properly understood history or to diminish the power and originality of new cinemas. Nor is it to deny the impact of digital technologies; the shot from *Gravity* is impossible to imagine in a predigital cinema. My aim, rather, is to undo a persistent argument about digital camera movements, and digital cinema more broadly: namely that the technology has changed to an extent that it requires an entirely new set of critical terms.[60] By contrast, I think we have *never* gotten a handle on the terms of camera movement, *never* figured out how to create a working model for thinking about the kinds of things it does and can do. We have been so struck by the intuitive force that the moving camera is about point of view, that the camera functions as our eye, that we have been unable to see anything else.[61]

Across this book, these topics ripple outward. They become central to how we think about technique and its implications, whether that involves antiperspectival strategies, the epistemic relation of the spectator to the image, or even the political implications of being absorbed in and immersed by the image. These topics become central to questions of cinema and its relation to social forces, whether that is negotiating modernity—not just its Western forms but also postcolonial situations—or the way style can have an ethical charge. They also, and not least, become central to how our thinking about the very thing we call a camera changes in the contemporary media world.

5.

The Lure of the Image is divided into two parts. In the first I attempt to engage, diagnose, and move beyond the assumption that the best way to think about camera movement involves the terms of point of view. Why has that belief been so persistent? How has it shaped an understanding, for filmmakers and theorists alike, of the possibilities of film style? Is there a better theoretical model? Chapter 2 discusses the basic assumption about spectators and the moving camera and shows some of its wider consequences. The chapter is built around an important episode in the history of French film criticism: Serge Daney's discussion of Jacques Rivette's famous criticism of the use of a tracking shot in Gillo Pontecorvo's *Kapo* (1960). Looking at the confluence of arguments surrounding "the tracking shot in *Kapo*," I argue that the case allows us to see a deep anxiety—one that extends to the contemporary moment—that comes with the belief that the moving camera carries the spectator along with it. It seems to Daney, I argue, that the effect of the camera movement is to make spectators unable to differentiate themselves from the positions, political as well as aesthetic, of the film, no matter how troubling they are. I describe this dynamic as "the lure of the image" and show how it exemplifies the political consequences not only of the intuitive account of the moving camera but of key assumptions of 1970s film theory. In chapter 3, I lay the foundation for a better way of thinking about the intersection between camera movement and point of view, an alternate—and more plausible—model for construing their relation. I show that rather than being understood in terms of identification, camera movements are best modeled through a logic of expression; that is, the moving camera expresses a point of view on the world it shows without trapping the spectator in the image. Replacing identification with imagination, I argue that our complex relation to the moving camera can be recognized as the ground for a wider range of aesthetic possibilities.

The second part of the book aims to develop this alternate model and so is comprised of a series of case studies that are varied not only in their historical context but also in what the moving camera does. Each case shows the importance of the model of expression for thinking about camera movements, and it does so by taking up the way camera movements are used to negotiate a relation between individuals and supraindividual forces—whether that is the movement of history, the imposition of social norms, or the very fact of modernity itself. Chapter 4 begins this project by looking at moments in the work of two directors, Fritz Lang and Guru Dutt, in which tracking shots along the line of a character's perception are used to bring the audience into a relation to the image that is *not* aligned with that character. Lang's interest, especially in his German films, is in exposing the hidden and collective unconscious drives that underpin a rationalized modernity; Dutt is concerned with the postcolonial nation-state and its responsibility to the people it claims to represent. Chapter 5 explores the virtuosic camera movements of Ophuls, seeing in them not so much ornament as an attempt to provide an ethical perspective on actions that the characters within the film's world are not able to achieve. Chapter 6 develops the terms of an antiperspectival aesthetic that fractures the assumption of a straightforward relation between spectator and camera. It examines how three films by Terrence Malick use the moving camera to create multiple viewing points within the film. Looking at the way this polyphony of spectatorial positions develops across *The Thin Red Line* (1998), *The New World* (2005), and *The Tree of Life* (2011), I argue that these camera movements enact an antiperspectival aesthetic of irony.

The final chapter returns to the theoretical debates from chapter 1 and the first part of the book, but with an explicit focus on new digital media. I canvas recent debates on digital camera movements, arguing that these writings fall into the trap of thinking that the central problem to be addressed is the way the digital camera creates qualitatively different, and hitherto impossible, kinds of movements. By contrast, I argue that a more significant conceptual problem is the increasing move away from the use of a single camera—the perspectival frame—to look out on the world. The new ways of looking include phenomena such as the separation of time and space in special effects sequences, such as "bullet time"; split-screen films and media works; and 3D experiments that use the two cameras to disorient familiar forms of perception. I conclude by turning to documentary cinema, working through how a persistent concern about the presence of the camera in the world gets resolved through an emphasis on its movement.

One of the frequent dangers in thinking about film is being trapped by the constraints of theories, guided by a picture that spells out what an element of cinema like camera movements can or ought to do. Films are not like this, nor are filmmakers; they are rarely gripped by theories in this way. Earlier, I suggested that theories of film have generally been based on the presumption that what they need to explain is the static shot. While some of that is due to a history of thinking about film organized around the polarities of photography and montage, the problem has a more general source. There is an understandable desire to think about film (or any other complex phenomenon) by focusing on what seem to be the simplest components. Sometimes this can be a good idea; not always. One of the attractions of thinking about camera movements is that they seem to be an element of cinematic style where complexity is primary, in which something important is missed in attempts that seek explanation by isolating a single orienting or grounding point. In working through the problem of the entwinement of point of view and camera movement and in articulating an alternate model, I've tried throughout to attend to and be guided by the way that films themselves explore and work through various possibilities and to construct an approach that can explain the full dynamics of these experiments. *The Lure of the Image* explores what such a shift in perspective allows us to see.

Part One

CHAPTER 2

The Lure of the Image

I.

Of the many myths, fables, and stories that film scholars have turned to in order to understand the effects of cinema, Plato's "Allegory of the Cave" is by far the most prominent. In a dark space, people are bound to their seats, next to one another but without interacting. They face a wall, and shadows are cast onto that wall from a light source behind them; sounds, too, are produced, and the people in the cave assume that the echoes they hear off the wall in front of them originate with the shadows they see there. As Plato tells the story, for as long as they are in the cave the chained people regard the two-dimensional shadows and projected sounds as reality. What could be more cinematic? Jean-Louis Baudry, in the midst of an essay on cinema's production of an impression of reality, notes that it is "curious that Plato, in order to . . . make understood what sort of illusion underlies our direct contact with the real, would imagine or resort to an apparatus that doesn't merely evoke but quite precisely describes in its operation the cinematographic apparatus and the spectator's place in relation to it."[1]

The appeal of the Cave, however, goes beyond descriptive similarities. For Plato, the allegory furnishes the baseline conditions that drive the discussion of education and knowledge that follows. For the people trapped in front of the shadows, it is not enough to "put education into souls that lack it, like putting sight into eyes that are blind." It is not a matter of content, of information. Real education has to do with the "craft" of turning away from the shadows and toward the light, that is, the good.[2]

The educative dimension of Plato's myth has been especially appealing to generations of politically inclined theorists, critics, and filmmakers. These thinkers, too, have held that it is not sufficient to simply show spectators new political content; spectators must, as Plato argues, be taught *how* to move away from the shadows they take for reality. Thus, in the polemics within French film theory and practice of the 1970s—of which Baudry's essay is a part—the rhetoric of education and pedagogy was frequently used to model a way to escape the power of images over viewers. Serge Daney makes the connection explicit in an essay on Jean-Luc Godard's films of the late 1960s and early 1970s, films that eschewed the pleasures of narrative cinema in favor of a didactic politics and a radical deconstruction of the very apparatus of cinema itself. Godard, Daney argued, held that "the movie theater is, in every sense of the word, a *bad place*, at once immoral and inadequate." As a result,

> one must learn how to leave the movie theater. . . . And to learn, you have to go to school. Less to the "school of life" than to the cinema as school. . . . School thus becomes the good place which removes us from cinema and reconciles us with "reality" (a reality to be transformed, naturally). This is where the films of the Dziga Vertov Group came to us from (and earlier, *La chinoise*). In *Tout va bien, Numéro deux* [1975] and *Ici et ailleurs* [1976], the family apartment has replaced the movie theater (and television has taken the place of cinema), but the essentials remain: people learning a lesson. . . . School . . . is the good place (where you make progress and from which you must move on) as opposed to the cinema (the bad place where you regress and never move on).[3]

This is a key fantasy of political cinema: the images on screen may be inherently dangerous, drawing audiences into an illusory world where they mistake shadows for reality, but films can correct these tendencies. The resources of cinema can turn the theater into a scene of instruction, thereby giving spectators critical distance from the images in front of them.

If the Allegory of the Cave is the dominant fable for film theory, another myth addresses a deeper worry about our relations to images. Plato allows for, even encourages, a way out of the situation he describes, but this is not the case with Ovid's telling of the myth of Narcissus. As Plato does, Ovid emphasizes the physical situation under which the act of viewing occurs, taking pains to describe the pool in which Narcissus sees his own image: "Its borders had no slime, / No shepherds, no she-goats, no other herds / of cattle heading for the hills disturbed / that pool; its surface never had been stirred / by fallen branch, wild animal, or bird. / Fed by its waters, rich grass ringed its edge, / and hedges served to shield it from the sun."[4] The pool is secluded, lacking the normal indexes of context; nothing disturbs or intrudes on its stillness. The rest of the world falls away, and the surface on which the image is thrown is invisible as a surface; there is only the image to be drawn into, to become absorbed in. This is the space of illusion, and is—like Plato's Cave—easy to see as a movie theater.

Narcissus, of course, is no simple narcissist. When he sees a face in a pool and falls into rapt contemplation, what he sees and loves is literally a reflection of himself. But that is not what he thinks he sees. The story is not exactly about the love of oneself so much as about the inability to distinguish oneself from another within an economy of desire.[5] Do I desire myself or another? In desiring another, am I in fact just desiring an image of myself? It's precisely for this reason that the myth of Narcissus is important for both Sigmund Freud and Jacques Lacan as they work out the ways in which the self emerges through encounters with others and with images of others.[6]

That legacy is well known and has been the primary way the myth of Narcissus has entered debates about film and other media (especially in psychoanalytically inflected theories). But there is another way of treating the myth, one that focuses on how Narcissus finds himself seduced by an image, in a position from which he cannot and does not want to escape. What Ovid draws attention to, over and over again, is Narcissus's inability to get outside the allures of the image: not even Echo's voice, reminding him that there is a world beyond the image— that he does not have to be wholly absorbed and consumed by it—can bring him back to awareness.[7] This is a myth, in short, about the power images have over us. Leon Battista Alberti, for one, saw in Narcissus a model for art: "What is painting but the act of embracing by means of art the surface of the pool?"[8] Plato's central problem in the Cave is the inability to distinguish illusion from reality; the prisoners take the shadows of reality for the real thing. These are the grounds for a criticism driven by a belief in the possibility of critical thinking. In Ovid's tale, by contrast, Narcissus is seduced by the image even when he knows that he is looking at an image. There is no anxiety over the confusion of reality and illusion, but rather a recognition of the power that illusion has over us despite whatever we might believe we know.

Roland Barthes's short and dense "Leaving the Movie Theater" may be the most sustained account of cinema that draws on these aspects of the tale of Narcissus. In it, Barthes describes the effect of the movie theater on the conditions of film spectatorship as one akin to a state of hypnosis. He does so in terms that follow Ovid's description, noting the importance of setting, the intersection of a physical and a social architecture, and even the particular moods people have in the theater: "vacancy, want of occupation, lethargy."[9] These dynamics produce a dream-like state; the viewer is absorbed in the image and loses their sense of self. In this context, Barthes suddenly wonders about what's on screen. "The film image," he asks, "is what?" And he answers: "A lure."[10] The image holds us; it draws us in. In being at the movies we are caught, drawn ever deeper into the film. We can't get out.

The image, as Barthes describes it, is not merely an attraction, something to be looked at; it is the source of a threat to our sense of self, the grounds on which we stand, our epistemic and ethical compass. He writes, "In the movie theater, however far away I am sitting, I press my nose against the screen's mirror, against that 'other' . . . with which I narcissistically identify myself."[11] This is the logic of the lure, to which both Narcissus and the movie viewer succumb: we become stuck on the image, unable to free ourselves.[12] Thus, when Barthes looks for ways in which spectators can "unglue" themselves, releasing themselves from the lure that has hooked them, he does not find resources in the film being watched, in the specific combinations of image and sound presented on screen. Rather, he urges a practice of looking away, "letting oneself become fascinated *twice over*, by the image and by its surroundings . . . the texture of the sound, the hall, the darkness, the obscure mass of the other bodies, the rays of light, entering the theater leaving the hall."[13] But for that to happen, one must already be off the lure; the image is too seductive to permit such distraction.

Plato to Ovid, Barthes to Baudry—what unites these accounts is the way they tie a perceptual and epistemological story to a set of ethical (and political) concerns, so that these wider stakes are inherent in the initial spectatorial situation. Indeed, it's not least the tightness with which these sets of concerns are linked in these accounts that helps explain their staying power. Yet they are, crucially, myths: stories of fears and anxieties about our relation to images. I take it for granted that as such they do not provide a sober, much less accurate model of this relation, but in their extremes they illustrate the intensity that attaches to it. This chapter, then, takes up the terms of these anxieties, the way that critics, theorists, and filmmakers have both relied on and worried about our inability to disentangle ourselves from the image we see on screen. I don't think this topic is simple, or that the answers to the questions that emerge from it will be straightforward. To work through them is to diagnose what can go wrong in our account of images, as well as why this has often led to a hyperbolic account of a loss of self in front of the screen.

Much of the writing on cinematic images has assumed that the problem of overinvestment arises because of the logic of the medium itself, whether that entails material fact or social institution. In what follows, I take a different starting point, moving away from analyses of the conditions that underlie general accounts of our attachment to images and toward an investigation of how specific techniques show things about that attachment. Rather than follow the Plato-Baudry line of thinking, my interest in the story of Narcissus lies precisely in the fact that Narcissus does not become enraptured by images as such; the specifics of the image matter.[14] If Barthes passes over this dimension of our relation to images, he nonetheless emphasizes that attachments happen in multiple ways, and that we need to pay attention to how complex forms of engagement operate on and with spectators. Taken together, Ovid and Barthes provide a genealogy of the power of images that encourages us to focus less on the apparatus and the medium and more on matters of style, look, and technique. What that enables, I argue, is an account of the responsibility of the spectator for the relation they take up toward the images themselves and of the perils of abdicating this capacity for critical judgment in relation to cinematic images.

I proceed by working through a specific debate over the role of camera movement—one that appeared at a crucial moment in the history of filmmaking and film theory, around 1960 in France—in order to offer a way to negotiate the lure of images. The focus here is on the belief that we move through the world of the film with the camera, tracing out the implications it has for the way we think about a range of questions that extend outward from models of spectatorship to the morals of film style. The case study, that is, shows the consequences for film theory, and for thinking about spectatorship, when the assumption that the moving camera functions as the surrogate for the spectator is left to stand unquestioned.

2.

The idea that style is intimately bound up with ethical matters has a long-standing, if idiosyncratic, history in French culture. It's found, for example, in the development of French moralism in the seventeenth century, when an intense concern with comportment, with style, resolved tensions between private, middle- and upper-class devotional practice and the demands of absolutism and state power. Rather than appealing to established doctrines or divine authority, moralists examined private conduct through the lens of public behavior. In La Rochefoucauld's terms, what mattered was a capacity for "discernment," the ability to see "into things" and discover "everything worth noticing."[15] Imagined public perception—one's appearance to others—would function as a guide. All this, La Rochefoucauld noted, could roughly be described as "character."[16]

When moralism was the basis for art, it involved a complex positioning: between characters within works, to be sure, but more importantly, for the audience in relation to the work and for authors in relation to their own products. (It's related to but not quite the same as the concerns with sympathy and spectators that preoccupied British thought in the eighteenth century.) Thus, when La Fontaine concludes his version of "The Oak and the Reed," he writes: "in the end / [The wind] uprooted the one that had touched the sky with its head, / But whose feet reached to the region of the dead." Rather than a moral lesson—you shouldn't always try to resist the force moving against you, but know when to give way—we're presented with a mode of seeing and inhabiting a world. A position, a metaphysic, or, if you like, a style. La Fontaine presents a worldview, which expresses the moral of the tale. When, a century later, Buffon continues this thought with the dictum, "Style is the man himself," he is working off an assumption, at least in the arts, that matters of formal style are intimately bound up with ethical claims on both artist and audience.

These concerns about style never disappear in French culture, but they emerge with a flourish in mid-twentieth-century debates about political commitment, art, and historical responsibility. There, we can discern two versions. The first holds that every work of art, style, or technique implies a broader world (and worldview); we find this in Jean-Paul Sartre's 1939 essay on William Faulkner (from *Situations I*), or in Maurice Merleau-Ponty's account of painting in "Eye and Mind." The second version, more directed, holds that every stylistic decision, and every broader stylistic pattern, carries moral implications. This is Sartre in *What Is Literature?*, where he collapses the distinction between aesthetic decisions and political commitment ("literature is in its essence the taking of a position"); it is also in Barthes's *Writing Degree Zero*, where he states that "writing . . . is essentially the morality of form."[17]

In this intellectual context, a debate about the stakes of style played out in French cinema, especially in the pages of *Cahiers du cinema*, where it took shape as part of that journal's increasing transition from cinephilia to politically oriented criticism.[18] This debate centered on tracking shots, as critics and theorists worried about the implications of the way the camera could follow a character, reframe an event or action, move between places, or provide an expressive gesture to reflect on the world of the movie.

One of the most important reflections on this period is a 1992 essay by Daney, "The Tracking Shot in *Kapo*." Daney, though not widely known in English-language film studies, is probably the most important French film critic after André Bazin. After beginning his career in the mid-1960s at *Cahiers du cinéma*, Daney became its editor from 1973 to 1981; later he founded the journal *Trafic*. "The Tracking Shot in *Kapo*," written shortly before Daney's death, recounts his education in cinema, how he came of age in—and lived through—the rise of modern cinema, and how the debates around it shaped his critical outlook.

As Daney recalls, the key moment for him was reading Jacques Rivette's 1961 review of Gillo Pontecorvo's *Kapo* (1960), which Daney treats both as emblematic of *Cahiers du cinéma*'s transition to political criticism and as the start of his own development as a cinephile and critic.[19] *Kapo* tells the story of Edith, a Jewish teenager arrested with her family in Paris during World War II and taken to a concentration camp. Her parents are killed, and a friendly doctor gives her the identity of a criminal to avoid extermination. Over time, she becomes hardened to her surroundings and to her fellow inmates, even taking on the role of a sadistic guard (the "Kapo" of the film's title). She is redeemed when she feels guilt for causing the punishment of a handsome male prisoner of war; they fall in love, and she eventually sacrifices herself so that others may escape (and, dying, rediscovers her Jewish identity).

Rivette's review, entitled "On Abjection," is a withering polemic. Pontecorvo, Rivette argues, produced a sentimentalized and voyeuristic film about a historical tragedy, succumbing to clichés about individual heroism and brutality while missing the larger implications of the events he was showing. As Rivette puts it in the review's opening lines, "The least that one can say is that it's difficult, when one takes on a film on such a subject, not to ask oneself certain preliminary questions; yet everything happens as though, due to incoherence, inanity, or cowardice, Pontecorvo resolutely neglected to ask them."[20]

What really infuriates Rivette, though, are the formal techniques Pontecorvo employs. His key example is a brief tracking shot roughly halfway through the film. The scene concerns Teresa, the most politically committed of the inmates, who has insisted that they retain human dignity and not become "animals." At morning roll call, it's discovered that she has stolen and eaten part of a roll being saved by another inmate. Edith takes her outside, cruelly mocking her beliefs: "You preached such fine words. Remember? . . . And now here you are, just like all the others. But it's only normal. All those things you said were only nonsense." As Edith talks, Teresa suddenly looks up with wide eyes, focused slightly to the right of the camera, as if in horror and shock at her own actions. Shaking free of Edith, she rushes toward the background, where lines of prisoners are forming near the camp's fence. A shot from the opposite side of the building picks up her movement, tracking with her as she runs along the lines of marching prisoners, still a look of shock on her face, the music rising in intensity. Another Kapo in the background notices her and begins to chase her. A sudden cut moves to a static shot outside the fence, looking in; the music stops, and voices saying "No, Teresa!" can be heard as she rushes toward the electrified fence. She grabs it; we see flashing lights accompanied by dramatic music. Pontecorvo then cuts to a close-up of Teresa, now dead, still clinging to the fence. And then he cuts again, moving back to show Teresa in a medium long shot and on a diagonal angle to her front and left, slightly below her; the prisoners continue to run behind her, looking at her body but not breaking their lines. The camera then rushes forward, moving toward her and twisting around until it frames her body, hanging on the fence, against the sky (see figure 1). The music dwindles, and we hear the yelling of the Kapos until everything fades to black.

Of this final ten-second shot, of which only four seconds actually have the camera in motion, Rivette writes: "The man who decides at this moment to track forward and reframe the dead body in a low-angle shot—carefully positioning the raised hand in the corner of the frame—deserves only the most profound contempt." Thirty years later, Daney isolates this sentence as the driving force behind his own understanding of cinema, the critical touchstone around which his judgment and viewing habits took shape.

As Laurent Jullier and Jean-Marc Leveratto argue, the phrase "tracking shot in *Kapo*" has become a common term of criticism in contemporary French media discourse, moving beyond the specialized zone of film criticism to enter the broader arena of political life.[21] Kick-started by

FIGURE 1. *Kapo* (Gillo Pontecorvo, 1960). The tracking shot.

Daney's essay, then buttressed by the resurgence of public debates over the representation of the Holocaust in *Schindler's List* (Steven Spielberg, 1993) and the spectacle of the television coverage of the Iraq War, the phrase has come to function as a go-to polemical putdown when an emphasis on the image feels at odds with the subject matter, when aestheticism threatens to overshadow—even cheapen—the seriousness of a topic. Following this usage, much of the writing on Daney's essay has tended to portray the problem as one of a mismatch between form and content.[22] But it's not clear, at least within the original texts of Rivette and Daney, that this is the right problem. A form/content mismatch is a notably slippery kind of criticism, and a failure to join "sober" form to "serious" content is constitutive of many works that critics praise, from the comedy of *To Be or Not to Be* (Ernst Lubitsch, 1942) to the highly aestheticized vision of *Kanal* (Andrzej Wajda, 1957).[23]

It turns out to be surprisingly difficult to pin down which problem the "tracking shot in *Kapo*" stands for. One temptation is to place it within the orbit of bad taste, one of the more interesting, and least analyzed, aspects of aesthetic judgment. There's some fit to this impulse: calling someone's taste "bad" has a deeper effect than praising it as "good," similar to the way we're more likely to respond strongly to being described as a "bad" person than as a "good" one. So we might think that Rivette sees *Kapo* as gauche, tasteless, shallow, vulgar, or the like, and that the harshness of his criticism has to do with the fact that this is a subject that needs to be treated with tact and taste. Yet if Spielberg may have shown bad taste by positioning himself at the end of *Schindler's List*, Pontecorvo is not being accused of that; indeed, given his palpable artistic intent, what Daney glosses as an attempt to make a "beautiful film," the problem may be that Pontecorvo has too much taste.[24] Perhaps it's more about tastelessness, but that better describes a later shot in *Kapo* that echoes a famous embrace between Cary Grant and Ingrid Bergman in *Notorious*; Pontecorvo places it in the public toilets of the concentration camp. Vulgarity, likewise, is about different problems, more about why Jerry Lewis's never-seen *The Day the Clown Cried* is treated with some trepidation (as is, to a lesser extent, *Life Is Beautiful* [Roberto Benigni, 1998]): humor of a certain sort doesn't belong to such a serious subject—another reason *To Be or Not to Be* is so astonishing an achievement.

Bad taste, more generally, involves the wrong dynamic. Its use is connected to a commonly held set of principles, to a cultural norm of what's appropriate.[25] And it would be odd to think of Rivette as objecting to a film because it had bad taste—not least because the French New Wave, and the *Cahiers du cinéma* group in particular, frequently embraced films for their display of bad taste or tastelessness. After all, one of their founding principles, articulated in polemics by François Truffaut and others, was to reject the "cinema of quality" in favor of the more "vulgar" products of the Hollywood studio system. Nor were New Wave filmmakers themselves innocent of bad taste: Godard's love of the vulgar and tasteless is well known, and certainly Rivette indulged in it as well. (The intersection between bad taste and artistic innovation runs deep.)

Another possibility, echoing concerns about matching form and content, has do with the question of representing the Holocaust: How should images be used to depict it? Should they be used at all? This debate, especially in the years since Claude Lanzmann's *Shoah* (1985), is too vast to engage here, but it's important to note that its kernel was already present by the time of the filming of *Kapo*. Alain Resnais's *Nuit et brouillard* (*Night and Fog*, 1956) was the central reference point, but so were the American documentaries of the camps—like the footage taken by George Stevens that would become central to Godard's own reflections on the topic in *Histoire(s) du cinéma* (1988–98)—and Georges Franju's allegory of the camps in *Le sang des bêtes* (*Blood of the Beasts*, 1949).[26] But Rivette, like the critical tradition from which he emerges, is not unduly exercised by such debates. Style, even excess, is not anathema to representations of the camps, or to representations of death in general. Even Bazin, for all his polemics against expressionism, defended its use in Alfred Radok's *Distant Journey* (1949)—a postwar Czech film about Theresienstadt—as a form of realism; the subject of the camps, he argued, for once justified the stylistic distortions.[27] And should we really think that Roberto Rossellini erred—or that Rivette and others thought he erred—in *Roma città aperta* (*Rome, Open City*, 1945) by giving a stylized presentation of Pina's death in the form of a *Pietà*?[28]

The problem with relying on these familiar terms of criticism is that what Daney and Rivette are saying is far stranger. The models clustered around bad taste, and around the relation of form to content, tend to treat the "tracking shot in *Kapo*" as a type, a particular instance of a general tendency. This is even the case for Jullier and Leveratto, who argue that the debate around the shot, if initially idiosyncratic, matters when it becomes something more generic, operating as "a metonymy to express the mutual incompatibility between art cinema and the entertainment film." That may be true about the afterlife of the polemic, but we aren't really going to understand the problem Rivette and Daney are interested in unless we can get a sense of what it is about *this shot* that's so troubling for both. It is, after all, a curious shot to be exercised by. The shot is certainly objectionable, but it's also quite brief, only a few seconds long and not even the most extensive camera movement in the scene. Other shots in the film could certainly be described as worse. So why single it out? Why does it mark the film as a whole, and indeed the filmmaker himself, as worthy of contempt? And why does the way Rivette describes it matter so much to Daney?

These questions, I argue, turn on two related things. The first is a fact acknowledged but underplayed by most writers on the topic: Daney's admission that, based on his having read Rivette's review when he was a teenager, he refused to see Pontecorvo's film, a refusal he steadfastly carried with him throughout his career as a critic.[29] This is quite simply stunning, especially given Daney's overall investment not only in cinephilia but also in difficult cinemas; he has, as he acknowledges, gladly seen films that are far worse and more morally objectionable than *Kapo*. The answer to this puzzle, I argue, has to do with the second thing: the importance of the moving camera, and the way that both Rivette and Daney—along with many other critics and theorists—believe that it pulls the spectator along with it in ways that threaten a sense of self. Indeed, Rivette's claim about the "tracking shot of *Kapo*" comes not in a vacuum but at a charged moment in the history of thinking about camera movement, and it takes place against a series of claims about the various uses to which tracking shots could be put. How the moving camera matters for these discussions of image and viewer is the more difficult phenomenon to grasp, but it's at the heart of these polemics over style and ethics. Daney's anxiety about the power of the moving camera, which he glosses as a form of seduction, places it at the heart of the dynamics of an overattachment to images.

3.

It is a striking feature of French film culture at this moment that camera movements were taken to matter greatly for a debate about style and ethics. For much of film history, such discussions revolved around montage. Montage allowed politically committed filmmakers to transcend the sheer givenness of reality in the film image, to create new combinations and juxtapositions, and to introduce viewpoints from outside the world they show. Depending on the filmmaker (or theorist), this was taken to happen in different ways. Montage could causally determine the viewer's response: "a tractor plowing over the audience's psyche," as Sergei Eisenstein once put it.[30] If done properly, there would be only one way to experience a shot, scene, or film (later critics in *Cahiers du cinéma* would describe this model as "terroristic"). Or montage could create the space in which a critical intelligence had room to operate; this is more the legacy of a Brechtian influence.

Tracking shots, by contrast, were framed differently. This context is somewhat lost to us, since the end of the 1960s saw a dramatic transformation in discussions of their use, not least of which was Godard's penchant for extended horizontal tracking shots—what Brian Henderson labeled a "non-bourgeois" style.[31] For other filmmakers, the duration of tracking shots furnished a counterpoint to the formal logic of classical Hollywood films, making time available in new ways; this is a trend that runs from the films of Miklós Jancsó in the 1960s to more recent accounts of "slow cinema" in the 1990s and 2000s.

The context for Rivette in 1961, though, is slightly—and importantly— different. Tracking shots had already been connected to the long take and its preservation of real space and time. This association emerged primarily from Bazin, who argued that the extended tracking shots of directors like Orson Welles and Jean Renoir, coupled with their use of deep space compositions, gave spectators the "freedom" or "liberty" to explore the image as they would ordinarily look at the world. Bazin's rhetoric of transparency can sound simplistic and naïve, a defense of visual and political neutrality that ignores the larger structural positions that define the cinema. But when he says that the camera movements in Welles and Renoir restore our freedom as spectators, it's not exactly an ethically "neutral" position about the subject. Against the legacy of montage, especially the Soviet model, Bazin advocated stylistic devices that returned the spectator to an arena of judgment and responsibility. This may have sometimes resulted in the defense of a relatively minimal model of subjectivity, but it set the stage for the more complex accounts of the relation between form and ethics that would emerge.

One can understand, simplistically but accurately, the dynamics of French film culture in the 1960s, and the various turns and twists it took, as working through the implications—the powers and limitations—of Bazin's positions and arguments. This is especially true with camera movement. Two famous claims, both from 1959—the year *Kapo* was filmed— have the quality of aphorisms. Luc Moullet, writing about Sam Fuller, declared that "morality is a matter of tracking shots." Several months later, Godard defended Resnais's formal experiments in *Hiroshima mon amour* (1959) with the line, "tracking shots are matters of morality."[32] Often equated, there is an important difference between them. Moullet argues that the morality of Fuller's films is expressed through their formal construction (the tracking shots simply are their moral content), an ethical defense of a filmmaker whose avowed politics were suspect. Godard, by contrast, suggests that the formal aspects of a film are open to moral assessment, that one could not treat matters of style in isolation from the larger ethical and political concerns of the film itself. Still, taken together they begin to articulate the stakes behind the subsequent discussions of tracking shots. In 2006, for example, Charles Tesson—another former editor of *Cahiers du cinéma*—brought the two lines together with Rivette's review in his "Little dictionary of the film critic's received ideas." Tesson's aperçu runs: "Tracking shot: Say it's a moral matter. Take for example the one in *Kapo*."[33]

Rivette's own indebtedness to Moullet and Godard is explicit, as he invokes them and then attacks critics who see in them only a reductive formalism.[34] Instead, he argues, Moullet and Godard are getting at a filmmaker's responsibility for the way the world of the film is created: "The point is that the filmmaker judges that which he shows, and is judged by the way in which he shows it." Now, the idea that we sense the existence of the artist, another being, behind the artwork is familiar enough. But Rivette goes further; the fact that we recognize what we see as being made means that its maker becomes available for assessment. As Jullier and Leveratto note, this is the discourse of the professional, looking at the image and thinking about what it means that it was made in a certain way. In Daney's words, "Imagining Pontecorvo's gestures deciding upon and mimicking the tracking shot with his hands, I am even more upset with him because . . . a tracking shot still meant rails, a crew, and physical efforts."[35] The shot is objectionable, that is, because it has to be planned and executed, because we can sense the effort that goes into its construction. Pontecorvo is necessarily implicated in, and responsible for, its form.

Sam Di Iorio has observed that Rivette wrote the review at a moment when he had become dissatisfied with the formalist critical practices of the 1950s, especially those focused on the idea of the "auteur theory," and was moving instead toward a criticism that sought to "consider modern cinema in terms of moral consequences."[36] Yet a new model had not cohered. Debates about the relation of individuals to broader apparatuses were beginning to gain prominence in French intellectual culture but had not yet found their way into film theory. Rivette is thus in a particularly unstable position within the discourse around the stakes of style. While moving away from the logic of the auteur, Rivette is still invested in the responsibilities of individuals—the filmmaker, the viewer—for what is being shown on screen. Di Iorio argues that this kind of position, and the language employed, comes directly from a history of "moral criticism" that had a major articulation in Jean Paulhan's *The Flowers of Tarbes, or Terror in Literature* (1941).[37] In words that evoke Rivette's denunciation of Pontecorvo, Paulhan notes that in modern criticism "it is less the work than the writer that is being judged, and less the writer than the man." Paulhan clearly does not view this as a good thing: "The chair is forgotten in favor of the carpenter, the remedy in favor of the doctor. Skill, knowledge, and technique, however, become suspect, as if they were covering up some lack of conviction."[38] Rivette writes from this background; indeed, he even says that one of his aims is "to reclaim Paulhanien terminology." He is concerned with the moral evaluation of the individual who makes the film while also aiming to analyze the technique being employed—the zone Paulhan labeled as rhetoric—and the significance of the way it is being used within the film.

Much of the language in Rivette's review relies on a belief that the viewer of *Kapo* will (necessarily) become aware of the constructed nature of the image, especially with the tracking shot. This is no trivial thing. Based on a Brechtian legacy, there is a tendency to argue that any sense of the "constructedness" of the artwork has a positive ethical and political valence.[39] It is said to reduce the viewer's investment in the film's world, providing a kind of critical awareness of the illusory nature of what the viewer is being presented with—and in general decreasing any absorption in the film's world. If the terms of Rivette's criticism echo the Brechtian logic—sensing the madeness of the film object opens the filmmaker up to judgment—the result he desires is neither inherently positive nor negative. One needs to take into account what's being done, in what form, and for what end.

This reading is sharpened by an implicit comparison. When Rivette condemns Pontecorvo's use of tracking shots to aestheticize the dead body in *Kapo*, the contrast is with Resnais's *Nuit et brouillard*, a film that extensively uses tracking shots but does so in a very different manner. *Nuit et brouillard*'s famous opening shots begin by showing us the untarnished countryside, the world of everyday life that seems far removed from death and deprivation. In the first two shots, the camera then begins to pull back, and as it does so it reveals that it is in fact situated within the boundaries of the camp, looking out from behind the barbed wire. The direction of movement is crucial here. The camera does not cross a boundary to move *into* the space of the camps (although it does so in later shots); instead, it shows that it was already there, that there is no line separating it from the camps.

This clarifies our sense of Rivette's objections. In *Kapo*, the camera moves up to Teresa from the outside, staying on the far side of the fence; it views her at safe distance from the world she inhabits, treating her as a spectacle—almost an artwork separated by an ontological barrier—rather than an inhabitant of its own world. Pontecorvo, that is, absents himself from the world of the camps, denies that he is a part of it; the tracking shot proves that he evades responsibility for the world he shows. He is judged by the way he judges what he shows.

It's at this point that Daney recognizes something in *Kapo* that Rivette does not quite see, and recognizes it within Rivette's own prose. ("I haven't seen *Kapo* and yet at the same time I have seen it. I've seen it because someone showed it to me—with words."[40]) What's at stake in *Nuit et brouillard*, after all, is not just Resnais's own relation to the camps but that of the spectators of the film, and not only spatially but ethically. When Resnais's camera pulls back to show that it was already inside the camps, it implicates us as well: we were there all along, even if we didn't know it; the work of the film is to make us aware of this fact, that we cannot escape these boundaries. This is what Daney means when he says that *Nuit et brouillard* showed him that he lived in a world defined by the camps. Pontecorvo, by contrast, leaves the spectator outside, interested in spectacle and pathos—a world separated from us by the absolute boundary of the fence.

It's in the analysis of such moments that discussions that emphasize the primacy of the role of the cinematic apparatus in structuring the position of the viewer fall short, and why the idea of a lure—an aestheticized object whose form entices us—provides a better model. In a defense of the tradition of apparatus theory, Nico Baumbach argues that it is interested in "metapolitical questions . . . preliminary to any analysis of specific films."[41] If apparatus theory sets out some of the conditions under which a form of attachment happens, the practical means by which attachment takes place occurs only within the film—as a matter of technique or, better still, of *style*. This is what Barthes has in mind in his discussion of the "lure" when he speaks of being seduced "twice over."

Style may seem like a peculiar term here, since it's often used to isolate formal attributes that can then be employed to ascribe a given film or set of films to a broader tendency, movement, or period.[42] But there is another lineage, reflected in the way we talk of adopting a style, having a style forced on us, being in style, and so on. When we watch a film, we are imaginatively inhabiting its world in a particular way: our mode of access to the world, our position within it, is shaped by the form of its presentation, its broad point of view. We adopt its style (or refuse to do so). This means, then, that style is not (or not just) a value-neutral set of attributes that describes a technique, film, or group of films, or even something that marks out the personal characteristics of a filmmaker.

Style is what grabs us, shapes us, and holds us. And as such it is thoroughly imbricated with matters of ethics and politics.[43]

What the example of *Kapo* shows might be described as the dark side to style, the danger in its address to the viewer. We are, after all, responsible for our reactions to a film.[44] When we watch a film and respond to something inside it, we are not simply making a judgment about a world, or a moral or political position, that's shown from outside. Nor are we wholly enraptured by the world of the movie. A stylistic feature brings us in, but without the metaphysical condition that, according to myths (and theories) of cinema, precludes our capacity to retain our sense of self. This is the charged force behind Daney's reading of Rivette's response to *Kapo* and his choice to act on the basis of his recognition. Daney's refusal to see the film comes from the belief that camera movements, especially forward moving ones, implicate viewers in the film's world; that the moving camera would leave him unable to respond ethically to the image he sees; and that it would leave him no choice but to be implicated in and by the way *Kapo* presents its world. And he would then be responsible for the position he is made to take up.

4.

We can see why the moving camera might pose a problem of entanglement by looking at a film made around the same time as *Kapo*: Alfred Hitchcock's *Vertigo* (1958), a film that stages a particularly fraught relation between image and narrative, one in which the dynamics of absorption are at stake. *Vertigo*'s plot is notoriously shabby. Among other far-fetched scenarios, we have to believe that Gavin Elster decides on perhaps the most elaborate (and unlikely) murder plot in movie history to kill his wife, Madeleine. His scheme, after all, requires Scottie, a retired police detective, to fall in love simultaneously with Madeleine—or rather, the woman pretending to be her—and the dead women she is pretending to channel. He must also then be counted on to suffer from his vertigo at the precise moment in the bell tower when he could have exposed the crime, and, moreover, to have no interest in continuing up the staircase after he believes that Madeleine has thrown herself to her death. The problems continue; I won't go into them here. We are required, as spectators, to fail to notice the flimsiness of the plot even as we are drawn into its labyrinthine dynamics.

To achieve this act of willful ignorance, Hitchcock works hard to create forms of attachment, not just for us but also for Scottie. And the point around which *Vertigo* swirls, the driving engine behind its logic of fascination, is the way the image—as both a general phenomenon and a specific thing—can shape a viewer's world. This is how Scottie comes to be enmeshed in the plot in the first place. He agrees to follow Madeleine not because of an argument presented to him, or because of any of the reasons he asks for when he initially speaks to Elster. Rather, he simply sees her, framed in green against the deep red backdrop of Ernie's—and immediately becomes enraptured. (Elster depends on this: "Look, we're going to an opening at the opera tonight. We're dining at Ernie's first. *You can see her there.*") Throughout the first half of *Vertigo*, Madeleine is presented almost as a pure image. Partly this has to do with her silence—more than forty-five minutes elapse before she says a word—but mainly it has to do with the way we gain views of her. Scottie repeatedly observes her through frames: in the flower shop, for example, where he sees her—and we do as well—through the opening of a half-shut door. Or as he drives through the streets, and Hitchcock is careful to ensure that our views of Madeleine are through the frame of the car's front windshield.

Not only is Madeleine presented as a framed image, a picture; it is at times unclear whether she is anything but an image. She appears in a window in the boarding house, available for view, but there is no evidence to be found that she was in fact there. Even more evocatively, at times Hitchcock lights her so that she gains a hallucinatory air, not quite a physical being: her walk through the Muir woods, Judy's emergence from the hotel bathroom made over into Madeleine. Her image-like quality becomes explicit in two moments that deal with painting. One is when Midge tries to undo the spell that Madeleine has on Scottie by painting herself into the *Portrait of Carlotta*, substituting her own face for Carlotta's. She fails in her efforts—"No, that's not funny, Midge," Scottie says as he gathers his hat and leaves—but she gets what's going on. Earlier, when he had dropped Midge off at her apartment and told her about the case, she asked him: "Is she attractive?" "Who? Carlotta?" he replies, muddling the identity of the person he's following. Midge says, "I guess I'd better go see the painting," and after she gets out of the car Scottie immediately takes out the museum catalog and flips through it until he comes to the *Portrait of Carlotta*. He is more enraptured by an image than he is by a person (more precisely, he is enraptured by an image that he believes Madeleine believes is of her former self). The image functions as a lure, attracting him until he is unable to let go.

The key scene for this aspect of *Vertigo* takes place as Scottie follows Madeleine through various parts of San Francisco, looking to see where she goes during the day. One of the places she visits is The Palace of the Legion of Honor, where she sits in front of the *Portrait of Carlotta*. Scottie walks into the room and stands somewhat behind her in medium shot; he refocuses his attention slightly, and Hitchcock cuts to a close-up of a bouquet of flowers on the bench beside Madeleine. The camera then moves up from the flowers, tracking forward toward the painting until it reveals a similarly arranged bouquet being held by the figure in it. After a pause, Hitchcock cuts back to Scottie, whose gaze shifts slightly. Another cut moves behind Madeleine, this time emphasizing the spiral of her hairdo; the camera tracks toward her, framing this aspect of her coiffure in close-up, then moves over her head and toward the painting, eventually coming to rest on a close-up of that figure's hair and showing it to be arranged in the identical manner (see figure 2). Hitchcock ends the brief sequence by cutting back to Scottie, who turns to ask a museum guard for the name of the painting.

These shots show Scottie's increasing fascination with Madeleine, his growing sense that something is going wrong—and that this has to do with her relation to Carlotta Valdez. But Hitchcock could have equally, and more directly, conveyed this information by using a series of static shots to show Scottie making the connection between Madeleine's appearance and the details of the painting. So why use camera movements?[45] The answer no doubt involves timing, the way the temporally extended yet directed movement of the camera reflects Scottie's growing absorption in the puzzle before him. But it also has to do with an effect Hitchcock wants to produce: to make *us* fascinated by this discovery, to feel the dawning of awareness as we are pulled into an ephemeral world in which past and present are coming together. In that sense, he relies on us as viewers to feel that we are "at" the position of the camera as it moves through the world of the film, that this movement aligns us with the camera's investigative mood.[46] Scottie is thus not the only one who discerns an affinity between Madeleine and Carlotta; as the camera moves, we feel that we discover for ourselves—along with the camera— the visual affinities that reside in the painting. For a moment, we are within the world of the film, just as surely as Scottie is.

This is how the image functions as a lure: it holds us, traps us, won't let us go. The movement of Hitchcock's camera, and the way it binds us to Scottie's own fascination, makes sure of that. *Vertigo* shows the danger of being hooked, of being unable to step outside the image, and

FIGURE 2. *Vertigo* (Alfred Hitchcock, 1958). Discovering affinities with the camera.

it does so by making us identify with a character who is trapped in that position; we can't stay outside, but are made to participate in his vision. Scottie can't let go of Madeleine (and his image of her), and as we become wrapped up in his quest, neither can we. It takes Judy's confession (which she tears up, though not before we hear it) to wrench us off the lure so that we can see the devastation of the attraction—and Scottie's own realization of how he was hooked. Yet even the realization that he has been hooked does not in the end allow for his—or our—safe release.

Hitchcock is working within and off a line of anxieties about spectators and film worlds. Both Béla Bálazs and Walter Benjamin, for example, turn to a myth of a painter who creates a landscape so compelling that he steps into it, never to return. Benjamin's brief description notes: "A man who concentrates before a work of art is absorbed by it. He enters into this work of art the way legend tells of the Chinese painter when he viewed his finished painting." Bálazs is more expansive:

> There is an old Chinese legend that tells of an old Chinese painter who has painted a landscape. A beautiful valley, with mountains in the distance. The old painter likes the valley so much that he walks into the painting and disappears into the mountains, never to be seen again. . . . For that was the belief at the time: things just are as they appear to be. A picture is no longer a picture; it is a reality that can be entered into."[47]

This, Bálazs and Benjamin say, is the model of the film spectator (akin to what Michael Fried calls the "supreme fiction" of absorptive painting).

These are of course more myths, fantasies of how we engage films, but they matter for an understanding—by both critic and artist—of how images work. I have been arguing that they can be regarded as *epistemological fantasies*: fantasies of being at a place we cannot be, a place we are barred from inhabiting, of having a special or unique form of knowledge. And the kind of camera movements I'm discussing are able to achieve their effects in part because they are deeply bound up with and help contribute to such fantasies. They are part of an underlying *desire* we have to identify with the camera, to be with it as it moves through the world—whether or not the camera is also identified with the point of view of a character within that world.[48]

It's this kind of analysis that theories of cinema as an apparatus or institution often preclude: the form of attachment to the image that's at stake is not a given of the technological or social formation around the film, nor is it based on a universally given account of the way we engage with images (or the world). It is instead about the contingent ways that specific cinematic techniques work with and make use of our fantasies—not just what we actually feel but also what we want to feel. The lure is organized around a precise intertwining of viewer with image, a desire to latch onto *this* thing, that the logic of the apparatus fails to model. The shot in the museum from *Vertigo* depends on seduction at the level of technique. To escape, we don't need to undo the entire apparatus of the cinema, only to be able to negotiate the subtle—but no less powerful—ways in which we are trapped by images. (Hitchcock's trick is to shift the structure of our investment at the moment we are let off the hook, so that we seamlessly become intensely invested in the question of whether Scottie will discover [what we now know to be] the truth. We believe we are free from our seduction, from our illusion, but we have really just shifted objects.) The forward-moving camera is built around a *fantasy* of losing oneself in its movement.

5.

It is this aspect of camera movements, their ability to generate epistemological fantasies, that worries Daney when he thinks about the "tracking shot in *Kapo*," though he does not know how to phrase it. When the camera tracks in toward Teresa, its movement pulls the viewer along with it, into the world of the film; the viewer is made to inhabit the camera's position (just as, with *Vertigo*, the viewer shares Scottie's own growing absorption in the puzzle in front of him), to identify with its way of showing the world. The connection is just too close for Daney's comfort. The camera, he says, is "putting us in a place we did not belong. Where I anyway could not and did not want to be . . . forcing me to be part of the picture." There is, quite simply, not enough distance between spectator and screen.

The source of Daney's rejection of *Kapo*, then, is not the belief that it is an exceptionally bad film, that it is sufficiently degraded as to warrant a refusal to see it. On the contrary. We can understand Daney's fear as the worry that he might *not* respond to *Kapo* with moral horror, that he would be enthralled—or, as he puts it twice in the essay, "seduced"—by the image he sees on screen.[49] (As he remarked in a 1992 interview, "I've always nestled against the screen."[50]) Despite what he knows and believes—and precisely because he sympathizes with Pontecorvo's general politics—he fears he will find himself identifying with the position in which *Kapo* places him. And this in turn will tell him something he doesn't want to know about himself, will mark him as capable of a

FIGURE 3. *Ugetsu monogatari* (Kenji Mizoguchi, 1953). The death of Miyagi.

position—imaginative and ethical—he does not want to know himself to be capable of. This may be a worry common to many films, with varying degrees of seriousness. But Daney isolates Pontecorvo's use of a tracking shot—one that, in its forward movement, draws us in—as a technique that makes this blurring much more likely, seemingly inevitable. Based on Rivette's description, Daney believes that the camera's movement would give him no choice but to occupy its position—hence the position of Pontecorvo, the position from which the showing of the world is judged. The deck is stacked; he, too, will then be deserving of contempt.

It's telling that when Daney is looking for a good object to contrast with *Kapo*, he turns to a different technique: a pan from Kenji Mizoguchi's *Ugetsu monogatari* (1953), the celebrated shot in which Miyagi is stabbed by two starving soldiers fighting over the meager ration of rice she is carrying for her child. Throughout this encounter, the camera stays back, observing the action at a distance. Indeed, the actual killing of Miyagi—the soldier stabbing her with a spear—is so quick and almost incidental that we might miss it (see figure 3). (It's this fact that allows us to briefly suspend our disbelief at the end of the film, when we hope, along with Genjuro, that Miyagi is somehow there in the hut cooking dinner and tending to the fire.) Daney thinks that Mizoguchi gets it: the "fear and trembling" with which death should be approached is reflected in the shot of "little men hacking each other apart for some feudal virility. It's this fear, this desire to vomit and flee, which issues the stunned panoramic shot."[51] Unlike in *Kapo*, the camera does not pull us into the events in front of it. We are not so overtly implicated in that world, and it provides the security from which we can witness and judge the nature of the violence we see.

Daney wants to preserve the fantasy of distance, what he calls his "real situation as a spectator-witness," which he sets off against the immersion generated by the tracking shot in *Kapo*.[52] In a sense, Daney is suggesting that forward-moving tracking shots of the kind he imagines in *Kapo* preclude the spectatorial space necessary for judgment. But the contrast with *Ugetsu monogatari* is puzzling, and it's not clear that Daney fully grasps its implications. It's true that *Ugetsu monogatari* is a better film than *Kapo*, that it has a more subtle and sophisticated understanding of death (and of most other issues, too). But that's a more contingent assessment than Daney makes it seem. One could say, after all, that the distance Mizoguchi maintains means that he treats Miyagi's death with a kind of sublime indifference: one death among many (it's war, after all). That wouldn't exactly be "fear and trembling." Or that Mizoguchi's eschewal of involvement amounts to a denial of responsibility for the horrors of the Second World War, one of *Ugetsu*'s allegorical frames: if (Japanese) spectators can stand outside the events and judge the violence, are they no longer implicated in it? One could also read the tracking shot in *Kapo* differently. Earlier in the film, a prisoner is hanged for sabotaging the factory at the concentration camp; all other prisoners are required to watch, and when one woman attempts to turn her head away, she is forced to look directly at the hanging. Might we think of the "tracking shot in *Kapo*" as operating according to a similar logic, forcing us to look even when we'd rather not, bringing out our implication in seeing this death as spectacle—a position the film marks as being that of the camp inmates themselves? Alternatively, Pontecorvo's decision to place the camera outside the fence might be taken to suggest a kind of release. If Theresa can't escape, can't get beyond the boundaries of the camp, the camera can; it could be taken to respond to, acknowledge, and provide the embodiment of the desire she cannot herself make actual.

My point is not that any specific interpretation is right: that Mizoguchi is evading the "meaning" of death, for example, or that Pontecorvo's shot should be redeemed. Rather, I want to draw attention to the ease with which alternate readings can be generated, since it reveals something important about Daney's anxieties. He latches onto Mizoguchi and the fixed camera too quickly, too unequivocally—and this with a director renowned for his use of a fluid, moving camera. Daney makes an absolute claim in a fluid field of interpretive possibilities. The tracking shot in *Kapo*, he seems to believe, will simply bring him too close to what he sees, so that he will be unable to resist the viewpoint of a film he knows (from Rivette) to be "worthy of contempt." Yet in rejecting the dangers of the tracking shot and seizing on Mizoguchi as the way out, he also eschews the responsibilities of style, the requirements of judgment—or of discernment. He seems to believe that judgment is only possible without potentially dangerous attachments, that one must be free from temptation in order to be reliable (ethically and aesthetically). This is a fantasy of purity, of being able to be *only* a witness, neither complicit nor responsible.

At issue in this line of thinking is a familiar position, one that sees critical distance from the film—the freedom from investment—as necessary for acts of judgment. This position loosely draws on Brecht's rejection of traditional forms of emotional involvement in favor of a spectatorial position that allows for disinterested contemplation, argument, and evaluation. Daney endorsed this model in his essay on Godard's radical filmmaking, in which he describes most films as involving "the accumulation of images, hysteria, carefully-measured effects, retention, discharge, happy ending: catharsis."[53] The point, Daney argues there, is to replace the seductions of entertainment with the clarity of political pedagogy. What the example from *Kapo* shows, however, is that this fantasy of a pure critical distance is precisely that: a fantasy. Daney is searching for a way out of entanglements that, simply by virtue of being a spectator, he cannot help but be caught up in.

I don't mean to treat Daney harshly. The anxieties he presents are real, and serious; certainly we should take them seriously. What his essay reveals, however, is that it's not possible to escape the necessity of judgment or the responsibilities that engagement with cinematic technique and style imposes. The pan does not make him wholly secure, perhaps only less vulnerable. To an extent, he knows this—"always," he remarks on the "tracking shot in *Kapo*" in 1977, "the idea of risk."[54] Daney makes it clear that a turn to montage, the last redoubt of politically committed theorists and filmmakers, does not provide a way out of the dilemma. This is not just a matter of counterexamples: the parallel editing at the end of *Birth of a Nation* (D. W. Griffith, 1915) that leads us to identify with the Klan—a short circuit of our own beliefs—on the basis of which Eisenstein would argue that parallel montage necessarily generates a certain ideology, pitting good against evil in the form of two distinct personages.[55] Daney argues that it's a far deeper matter, in which cinema makes the zone of moral judgment "a living question again."[56]

At the end of his essay, Daney takes up the contemporary legacy of the "tracking shot in *Kapo*," and the example he chooses turns precisely on the question of montage—and with it, the uses of new technology. The only thing he can think of that's as bad as *Kapo* is the music video for the song "We Are the World" (1985), written by Michael Jackson and Lionel Richie and performed by a range of celebrities as part of a charity drive for African famine victims. "Here we have, I thought, the present face of abjection and the improved version of my tracking shot in *Kapo*."[57] The song makes a claim on its listeners that they are global citizens, hence responsible for suffering outside their immediate context (a responsibility that can be discharged by giving money). The music video bears out that message, using the singers as a conduit for the viewer's identification. But it also does something more. Daney writes, "The rich singers . . . were mixing their image with the image of the starving. In fact, they were taking their place, replacing them, erasing them. Dissolving and mixing stars and skeletons in a kind of figurative flashing where two images try to become one."[58] The video thus performs what he calls an "aesthetic seduction," using montage to fuse two images into one.

Here, too, Daney thinks that recognizing the production of the images matters for our understanding of it. But in contrast to Pontecorvo's careful planning, something else is going on with the making of the video:

> I have more trouble imagining the movements of the person responsible for the electronic dissolve of "We Are the World." I imagine him pushing buttons on a console, with the images at his fingertips, definitely cut off from what or whom they represent, incapable of suspecting that someone could be upset with him for being a slave to automatic gestures. That person belongs to a world—television—where, alterity having more or less disappeared, there are no longer good or bad ways of manipulating images. . . . And this world, which no longer revolts me, which provokes only lassitude and uneasiness, is precisely the world "without cinema."[59]

Again, the constructedness of the image is highlighted, and it is something that is felt (Daney thinks) in the very way we watch these moving images. And again this is not given a positive spin, but rather read for its indifference to what is being shown. Yet rather than being an affront to the principles of cinema, aesthetic and ethical, Daney suggests that new technologies have rendered such principles irrelevant: the gestures are too automatic, the images too weightless, for any meaning to inhere in specific techniques. Daney almost longs for Pontecorvo here, seeing the "tracking shot in *Kapo*" as emblematic of a moment when *cinema* mattered, and when decisions about how to position or move the camera, or how to cut from one image to another, carried serious weight. What Daney calls "television" has ended that legacy.

The hope Daney sees lies in the activity he is undertaking: a recounting of what cinema meant, an account of a sensibility—personal, social—shaped by cinema. This project, he thinks, is best represented by Godard's *Histoire(s) du cinéma*, the massive video project about the history of cinema and the history of the twentieth century being made at the time Daney was writing his essay, and in which Daney appears as an interlocutor. Daney writes, "What was the meaning of Godard's formula if not that *one should never put oneself where one isn't nor should one speak for others?*"[60] It's one of the signal virtues of *Histoire(s) du cinéma* to refuse the lure of identification with the film worlds it shows and to demonstrate the inescapability of judgment in montage.[61] When Daney writes of the music video that it "dissolves and mixes stars and skeletons in a kind of figurative flashing where two images become one," we can hear in this description the antithesis to Godard's practice. Over and over again, Godard juxtaposes—moves between, superimposes, flashes, and so on—multiple images from the history of cinema, the history of painting, the history of the twentieth century; there are also texts, voices, citations from music and film scores, and so on. These elements do not "fuse," do not seek—as Daney says of "We Are the World"—to "become one"; they are held up against one another as an index of Godard's judgment, his sense of the connections that can be made between events.

Two things are worth noting here. First, Godard's practice of montage contains no necessary or intrinsic relation between the juxtaposed elements. In episode 3A, for example, he juxtaposes images of Second World War bombers with the attack on the schoolchildren from *The Birds* (1963). The effect is to make us see Hitchcock's film as a response to aerial bombardment, to see it as the traumatic memory of the London bombing. But the connection, if it works, only emerges in the actual comparison itself, in Godard's montage. The two images thus become legible in terms of one another, but they do not thereby dissolve their specificity. We see them *and* the results of their combination. In the terms that Godard employs, in these instances, his videographic practice exercises the capacity to *judge*: it determines what's important in the historical events it shows and, from there, how best to preserve and make them public as an image. This mode of judgment is what cinema calls thinking, what defines it in his terms as *"une forme qui pense."*

Second, this model helps explain the curious image of Godard standing in his study, a shot that appears in various guises across the episodes. Generally, he looks offscreen to "face" an image from out of his memory or on a screen in front of him: he pulls out a book and reads a passage, recites a name or line he is reminded of, or, more frequently, summons up further images. When Godard does this, he identifies his position within the world of the *Histoire(s) du cinéma* as that of its "first viewer," and the shape of the video as it develops is, according to this conceit, his response to what he sees. He sees affinities, and then he makes a judgment—one that is expressed in the video. But then it is up to us to judge for ourselves: to judge that what Godard shows us is "right," that the connections hold true. The central feature of Godard's practice—and one of the hardest to keep in mind—is that there are no grounds outside our contingent ability to discern and judge the logic in the juxtaposition of images, texts, and sounds that can justify the arguments and connections being made.

If we follow Daney in thinking about films and film worlds and the dynamics of our relation to them—or perhaps more aptly, if we follow Godard as Daney sees him—the conclusion is simple yet far-reaching: We cannot escape the task of judgment, a task that is ethical as well as—and precisely because it is—aesthetic. And so Daney writes, "And then I see clearly why I have adopted cinema: so it could adopt me in return and could teach me to ceaselessly touch—with the gaze—that distance between myself and the place where the other begins."[62] The dangers of "We Are the World" and *Kapo* are that they work against this constitutive distance; the limit of Daney's essay is that he cannot figure out a way to negotiate the fear that such distance might disappear at any point. And without a secure distance, situated instead in a position where he can be lured and seduced by images, Daney believes he could no longer enact a form of critical judgment. If he shows himself aware of the claims that style makes upon a viewer, that he knows what the stakes of style are, he finds the threat too great to risk.

6.

Daney's essay is located in a curious space. Already looking ahead to the rise of digital and electronic media, it is also stuck in the past, unable to let older debates go. It is a gap that is at once theoretical and technological. The appeal of Rivette for Daney seems to be that Rivette is writing at a moment when there's no clear formula in place for dealing with questions about the stakes of style, about modes of viewing and attachment—but also when these questions are newly in play. This is what Daney sees and is drawn to, and he turns back to Rivette precisely at a moment in the early 1990s when the emergence of new media technologies had begun to unseat familiar assumptions about how media work. Indeed, in an essay written around the time of "The Tracking Shot in *Kapo*," Daney defended television on the grounds that its small size and location in the home allowed the viewer to exercise a degree of agency and responsibility: "You must never be where the television expects you to be," he writes in a maxim worthy of a moralist.[63] In that essay, as with his reflections on Rivette's review of *Kapo*, Daney uses a meditation on technique *and* technology—that of cinema, that of television—to understand not just our responsibility toward the images we encounter but also the kinds of claims these images make on us. I've been arguing here that the dual focus is key to Daney's position. As Paulhan said about literature: "We have, to all intents and purposes, given up on knowing what literature *owes* us. We are thrown before it, defenseless and without any method for proceeding, completely disoriented."[64] In response to this situation, Daney uses Rivette to turn to the question of technique, to a way of thinking about matters of style that implicates the actions of filmmaker and viewer alike. Daney's essay is an attempt to return his readers—and film and television viewers more broadly—to the messy grounds of judgment, to the value of individual films and works of art, and to the complexity of the entanglements of viewers with images.

Even more significant for Daney than the new technologies of image production and distribution was the rise of Theory in film studies (and across the humanities more broadly) during the 1970s. Wielding an array of methodological models, scholars sought to excavate and reveal the underlying conditions that governed the effects and powers of cinema. Daney's early career was part of this movement, but he would eventually work to move *Cahiers du cinéma*—and by extension, a wider culture of writing on film—away from theorists who sought to explain cinema per se and toward something like a critical cinephilia. "The Tracking Shot in *Kapo*" is organized by a self-conscious logic of return, a longing for the moment when Rivette's review could be written—a moment that anticipates but is not yet part of the theoretical waves that would come to dominate French film culture.

As Daney was well aware, the critical debates that emerged around and out of the events of May 1968 saw an increasing politicization of debates about cinema. Much of this concerned what Deleuze called the processes of "subjectification," the ways in which various institutions and apparatuses created subject positions.[65] These debates would culminate in broader theoretical analyses of the notion of a *dispositif*, a term Foucault introduced in the mid-1970s to map out more complex lines of social force than the more straightforward logic of control implied by the use of "apparatus."[66] Within the domain of film theory, figures like Baudry argued that the basic question that needed to be answered was how viewers were brought to believe in the basic reality of what they were watching on the screen in front of them. Arguing against those who looked for ideology in individual films, he turned instead to the way the cinematic apparatus, operating as a *dispositif*, created subjects within its organization.[67] Within this framework, the project of a counter-cinema was to produce a "knowledge effect" (rather than a "cinema effect") that would unbind us from the positions that had been artificially created for us.

The various challenges to apparatus theory are well known: some took aim at the premise of a general theory; others questioned the underlying theoretical models; while others focused on the actual spectators in theaters, drawing attention to the differences among empirical spectators that apparatus theory assumed (if implicitly) to be white and/or male. Still other responses sought to undo the structural position of the spectator as specified by apparatus theory, what Will Straw characterizes as "an immobile spectator caught in a fixed relationship to the screen."[68] Baudry famously treated this as an effect of the construction of the image on the terms of a perspectival grid:

> But this much, at least, is clear in the history of cinema: it is the perspective construction of the Renaissance which originally served as model. . . . Based

on the principle of a fixed point by reference to which the visualized objects are organized, it specifies in return the position of the "subject," the very spot it must necessarily occupy.[69]

I return to the role of perspective in chapter 6, where I indicate the centrality of this assumption for wide swathes of film theory (especially in the 1970s).[70] For now, it is enough to note that Baudry treats the moving camera as exemplary of a subject deprived of a body, its movements ensuring that what he termed the "transcendental subject" is fixed at the position of the camera.[71] Later theorists, however, would argue that it was precisely in its movement that the camera generated a connection to the spectator's own body—a rough phenomenology—and an unsettling of the rational and perspectival organization of the image. Bordwell explicitly pitched his interest in camera movement as working against Baudry's model, looking at the way visual cues are activated across a field of perceptual interests.[72] Anne Friedberg defended a model of "a 'virtual mobility'" that engages concretely, and in often-fraught ways, with the spectator's own sense of embodiedness.[73] Using a genealogy of mobile viewing forms, including the camera in the world of the film, Friedberg grounded her account of cinematic spectatorship in the body's engagement with the world of the film.

Daney's essay, with its faults and fissures, is a salutary lesson for both apparatus theory and the phenomenologically inclined response. He offers something like a dialectical move away from universalizing theory and toward a more flexible model, looking at the dynamics of film form while being attuned to theoretical problems. The approaches, after all, share a central belief about the way individual spectators relate to images, a guiding assumption that our primary relation is an identification with the camera.[74] Daney's "The Tracking Shot in *Kapo*" shows the danger of that assumption when it comes to the moving camera, while also revealing how difficult it is to get away from it. He clearly does not want to subscribe to something like Baudry's deterministic account of spectatorial positioning. Yet even when he turns to a technique, suggesting that the moral and political stakes of cinema are based at that level, the failure to move beyond the view that we are with the (moving) camera ends up trapping him within the very frame that apparatus theory would adopt as an account of cinema itself. Focusing on Daney's anxieties, I've been arguing that camera movements make evident a necessary stickiness to film worlds that shows us to be responsible for our reactions to them. That's why the contingency of judgment in Daney's arguments matters so greatly, even if he is himself sometimes loath to acknowledge it, and why it is necessary to go through the intricacies of critical exchanges over form if we are to learn what it is to engage with—to be stuck on—images. The exchanges are what provide us with the contours of an ambition to go beyond the given conceptual framework, even if Daney himself remains wedded to an understanding of the camera that holds him with its movement.

CHAPTER 3

Where Are We?

This chapter directly tackles problems that emerge from thinking about the relation between the moving camera and the logic of point of view. Two initial examples delineate their scope. The first comes from *The Shining* (Stanley Kubrick, 1980): the famous Steadicam tracking shots that follow Danny as he rides his Big Wheel through the rooms and corridors of the Overlook Hotel. These shots, repeated several times in the film, are deeply unsettling—not just because of what we see, and the increasing aura of fear and dread that surrounds the family, but because of the nature of the camera's movement. It moves smoothly behind Danny but is never quite in sync: it falls back and then catches up; it hesitates briefly as it turns corners and then accelerates across more open spaces. The absence of perfect following suggests the presence of some kind of agency—a spirit, the hotel itself—that occupies the position of the camera and is trailing Danny through the corridors, never letting him out of sight and implicitly promising malevolent actions.[1]

The reason for this uneasiness is not initially evident. After all, the experience of a camera imperfectly following its subject is certainly not unique to *The Shining*. It is a common feature of nonfiction films, from the famous shot that follows Kennedy through a crowd in *Primary* (Drew Associates, 1960) to the innumerable GoPro videos that populate YouTube. The difference here involves fictions. With nonfiction films,

FIGURE 4. *Amator* (*Camera Buff*; Krzysztof Kieślowski, 1978). Aligning points of view.

we know that the camera is in the world with the people it follows, and the imperfections of its following indicate authenticity; the filmmakers could not anticipate the movement of their subjects. With *The Shining*, the camera isn't in the world with Danny, yet the quality of its movement makes us feel it as a presence there. This is what Kubrick relies on. The camera both does and does not exist in the world of the film, and the effect of the film centrally depends on Kubrick's ability to maintain such uncertainty.

The second example is from an early scene in Krzysztof Kieślowski's *Amator* (*Camera Buff*, 1979), in which Filip is trying to visit his wife in a hospital in order to film their newborn daughter. A doctor is indifferent to his pleas until Filip mentions the camera he's carrying with him; suddenly displaying interest, the doctor takes up the camera, stands up, and opens the curtain behind him to reveal the interior of the hospital in the background. As he bends over the camera as if to film the view, Kieślowski's own camera moves forward, coming over the desk and past the doctor to look out onto the hospital (see figure 4). In so doing, Kieślowski aligns his camera with the diegetic camera held by the doctor, an alignment that effectively grants Filip entrance into the hospital.

What happens here is a familiar kind of perceptual game, which operates by playing with or shifting between viewpoints (such a game, as we'll see, can take a variety of forms). By the end of the shot in *Amator*, we read the image as an expression of the doctor's point of view even though it's clear that it isn't really that—not least because the doctor is visible at the side of the frame for a while. We see the shot, that is, as simultaneously belonging and not belonging to the doctor, and it is the movement of the camera that allows us to move into (or, as happens in other versions of the perceptual game, move out of) his point of view. We believe both that the camera is and is not in the world, that we are moving both with the camera (an outside perspective, as it were) and with the doctor.

If different in form and creepiness, the examples from *The Shining* and *Amator* operate on a similarly puzzling logic. Both shots require that we believe something that seems conceptually incoherent: for *The Shining*, that the camera can be felt as present within a fictional world in which it does not exist, and for *Amator*, that the camera can come to occupy a character's viewpoint in the midst of a shot while also remaining separate from it. At the same time, what we're being asked to do in each case is ordinary, an instance of something we do all the time with films. Because of this, theoretical models interested in questions of camera movements and point of view ought to be able to deal with these kinds of shots. It turns out they can't. What causes trouble in both cases is how the moving camera operates.

My question, then, has to do with the reasons why types of shots that are ordinary elements of fictional cinema can pose serious problems for the theories that ought to be able to explain them. In what follows, I draw on a range of cases like those of *The Shining* and *Amator* to show how these aspects of cinematic form pose problems of and for theory. I focus especially on point of view in part because this topic insistently arises when thinking about camera movements. But I also focus on point of view because the relation of viewer, camera, and world at the heart of debates around point of view is central to many familiar film theories. That is, while the problems I'm interested in here are specific to camera movement and point of view, they have wider theoretical implications. I argue that both theories of point of view and theories of camera movement overvalue epistemic questions about how the viewer relates to the world of the film, and that this results in a methodological assumption that *the* critical problem to solve has to do with the place of the camera within the fictional world—and our relation to it. From there, it is assumed, everything else can fall into place. As I show, the limits of such an approach are at the heart of the difficulties that camera movements pose for thinking about film.

I offer here a positive as well as a critical argument. Moving away from privileging questions of epistemic access leads to a more open and flexible approach to the way camera movements negotiate our relation to the world of a film, one that more closely matches the kinds of things that camera movements actually do. I argue that camera movements, as part of film style, work by expressing a perspective on the film world, and that how we experience that world is shaped by the form this expression takes. This does not mean that theories of point of view and camera movement are irrelevant; despite their limitations, they track aspects of the way we experience films and capture what I have described as *epistemological fantasies* that are exploited by films for various ends. A central purpose of my argument, then, is to open up an approach that allows us to see the complexity and uncertainty, but also the power, of the way camera movements involve us in the world of a film.

2.

It makes a good deal of sense to think that the puzzles generated by the examples from *The Shining* and *Amator* can be resolved through inquiry that centers around point of view. While debates about point of view in cinema cover a wide range of topics—narration, character identification, language, attitude, and so on—they generally revolve around our relation as spectators to the world of the film. In Jean Mitry's classic formulation, there is a fundamental tension in this relation:

> I know that I am in the movie theatre, but I feel that I am in the world offered to my gaze, a world that I experience "physically" while identifying myself with one or another of the characters in the drama—with all of them, alternatively. This finally means that at the movies I am both in this action and outside it, in this space and outside this space. Having the gift of ubiquity, I am everywhere and nowhere.[2]

A place to begin is with a common intuition: for any given shot, we occupy a particular vantage point within the world of the film, and this position can be specified as the place of the camera. The dynamics of offscreen space help explain this: not only does space extend beyond the four boundaries of the frame, but it is also behind us—people and things can emerge into the frame from behind the camera—and as the shot from *Amator* shows, from behind objects in the frame as well.[3] The camera, then, resides within a spatial world that extends all around it, and this allows us, as viewers, to experience the world of the film as if we were at a position within it.

Such a view runs across the history of film and film theory. It's in Dziga Vertov's fantasies about the "kino-eye," not just the eye/lens fusion at the end of *Man with a Movie Camera* (1929) but his description of the experience of cinema as placing the viewer in the location that the camera is filming from: "You're walking down a Chicago street today in 1923, but I make you greet Comrade Volodarsky, walking down a Petrograd street in 1918, and he returns your greeting."[4] It's also in Orson Welles's proposed screenplay for *Heart of Darkness*, a project to be filmed with the camera standing in for the position of Marlow. As Welles imagined it, the film would begin with a shot of the inside of a movie theater. The narrator would say that the audience should seem to be "entirely made up of motion picture cameras" looking at the screen. Then: "A human eye appears on the left side of the screen. Then an 'equal' sign appears next to it. The capital 'I.' Finally the eye winks and we dissolve."[5] We are the camera; the camera is us. This view is also implicitly present in Walter Benjamin's description of the experience of film in breaking apart the fabric of the world: "We can set off calmly on journeys of adventure among its far-flung debris."[6] More prosaically, there are innumerable characterizations of the filmic apparatus as akin to the human perceptual system, with the camera usually figured as the eye. The list could go on; the examples are numerous.[7] Each moment presents a version of an understanding of the viewer as occupying the position of the camera within the world of the film.

This intuition remains the dominant way of modeling the relation between spectator and camera. Christian Quendler observes: "As a concept and a guiding technique, the camera eye has served as a poetic metaphor that lies at the core of virtually every aesthetic movement and film-historical period"—and, we can add, of film theory as well.[8] It's the basis, for example, of Christian Metz's distinction between primary and secondary identification in cinema. Asking the question "*with what*, then, does the spectator identify during the projection of the film?," he answers: "The spectator can do no other than identify with the camera."[9] And after working through the difference between this relation and how we identify with characters, Metz returns to the basic formulation: "I am the camera."[10] It's also central to Kaja Silverman's account of the camera as an apparatus. Though aiming to emphasize "the difference between the eye and the camera/gaze," she nonetheless takes as primary the assumption that we engage the world of a film by way of the camera.[11] And it's found in Kristen Whissel's description of war reenactments in early cinema, as she remarks on how one film "places the camera/spectator in the trenches," a fusion of the two terms into a single entity.[12]

Yet as with many intuitions, this view has serious shortcomings. If I am watching the attack on the gas station in Alfred Hitchcock's *The Birds* (1963), I may say that I see Melanie Daniels react in horror at the explosion, then that I see more birds hovering in the sky above the town—Hitchcock's play on a bird's-eye view—then that I see Melanie rushing out from the restaurant. I don't imagine that I am really there, that I am threatened by these events. What seems to be the case is a more measured version, in which I identify with but am not the camera, and it positions me so that I see characters and events *as if* I were at its location. What we see is fictional but is nonetheless "directly" seen from the vantage point of the camera; the camera functions as a surrogate for our apprehension of the film's world.

A set of debates within studies of point of view has tried to develop more subtle models for such sequences. Gregory Currie, for example, argues that the intuitive view is generally false to the experience of watching a film:

> Do I really identify my visual system, in imagination, with the camera, and imagine myself to be placed where the camera is? Do I imagine myself on the battlefield, mysteriously immune to the violence around me, lying next to the lovers, somehow invisible to them, viewing Earth from deep space one minute, watching the dinner guests from the ceiling the next?[13]

Currie sees the key problem as involving montage. In the sequence from *The Birds*, should I think that I am at one moment outside the restaurant, looking in, the next moment high above the ground, and the next back by the restaurant once again? Does my position in the world of the film change that rapidly? The changes, moreover, are out of my control: I am moved through the world but am myself unable to effect such displacements, a radical dissociation of cinematic point of view from ordinary forms of perception. The conclusion of such reflections is usually that we cannot take ourselves as seeing the events in a movie directly, as if we were present at the position the camera inhabits. When we watch a fictional film, we are not—actually or virtually—at the place where the camera is. That is not to deny that we are given a specific position from which to see, or look at, the world of a film. But as George Wilson emphasizes, "it does not follow that if a person *imagines* seeing a scene from a certain perspective, then he thereby also imagines being at a place which offers him that view."[14]

Although the positions of Wilson and Currie diverge, we can discern a shared (if implicit) assumption: the paradigmatic case to analyze, the basic unit of film construction, is the static shot, the immobile frame. The appeal of this assumption is evident. If the most basic model for how the viewer relates to the film world can be solved, then everything else about the role of point of view ought to follow from that.

This is where the moving camera causes problems. We can see this in one of the few places where camera movement does come up in discussions of point of view, a brief mention in a footnote in Wilson's *Seeing Fictions in Film*. Discussing several arguments made by Noël Carroll, Wilson is trying to make clear the intersection between the visual perspective of a shot and the fictional vantage point it establishes. He then comments:

> [My] formulation makes the simplifying assumption that the shot in question involves no camera movement. Of course, this is a gross oversimplification, but I do not think that it significantly alters the issues presently under discussion. A formulation that dropped this restriction would quickly become extremely complicated.[15]

There is a deep disconnect between the second and third sentences. Wilson goes from a brief dismissal—incorporating the moving camera into his analysis wouldn't really change anything—to an acknowledgment that including it would make the discussions too complicated for a consistent and coherent theory to emerge. There is an almost palpable anxiety in his prose.[16]

The problem that Wilson discerns, if only implicitly, is that it turns out to be much more difficult to dislodge the intuitive sense of an affinity between eye and camera once the camera is put into motion. As the examples of *The Shining* and *Amator* suggested, and as I've been arguing throughout the book, we tend to feel that we are "with" or "at" the camera when it moves through the diegetic world of the film. The simplicity of the static shot may be appealing as a ground for thinking about point of view, but camera movement threatens to undo basic claims about where we are when we look at a movie.

An example shows the contours of the problem. At the beginning of *Friday the 13th Part II* (Steve Miner, 1981), Alice wakes up from a nightmare about Pamela Voorhees attacking her. What follows is a shot lasting almost three minutes. It begins as she sits bolt upright in bed, and then the camera follows her as she walks out of her bedroom and into the bathroom, where she splashes water on her face and tries to get out of the memories of her nightmare. The Steadicam apparatus creates a smoothness of motion as the camera follows her through her house to answer the phone. After a short fight with her mother, she hangs up the phone and retraces her steps through the house, winding up in the kitchen, where she looks at an expressionistic drawing she made of Voorhees. It's here that the camera first breaks from its logic of following, moving downward to track her gaze onto the drawing—before going back to Alice's face again.

All this is fairly conventional, with the use of Steadicam flaunting what was then a still-new technology. The shot is largely external to Alice, and we read her state of mind through her actions rather than through anything the camera itself does. Indeed, it's only when the camera moves down to follow her gaze that it achieves what Mitry calls a "semisubjective image": an attunement toward a character's state of mind without actually occupying their perspective.[17]

A change happens when Alice returns to her bedroom. The camera now stays outside her (open) door, looking in at an oblique angle. We can hear the rustle of clothing and surmise that she is getting undressed—the camera is positioned so as to imply nudity without actually showing it—and then articles of clothing are tossed onto the bed. A slight movement of the camera begins to suggest something new: the jostled frame indicates that there is movement independent of Alice's actions, as if the camera were settling in to watch. It has, in a sense, begun to treat her as an object to be viewed rather than a subject who is pulling the camera along with her. When she walks out of the room in a robe, the camera pans with her. But it is a pan, not a track; it does not go with her but instead remains separate. Alice walks through the hallway and into the bathroom, from which we can hear the sounds of a shower curtain and then the water being turned on.

It's at this moment that the camera begins to move forward. What is remarkable about the movement is that without anything else happening in the shot, we feel that we are now moving as a character, that we are likely at the point of view of the killer who is approaching the defenseless—unseeing, unhearing—Alice. (The opening few minutes of Jen Proctor's *Nothing a Little Soap and Water Can't Fix* [2017] trades on the feeling of such shifts.) Adam Hart calls this type of shot the "Killer

POV"; what *Friday the 13th Part II* shows is that nothing more than the timing of the movement of the camera, and the way it moves, is necessary to make us feel that we are with an autonomous subject moving through the hallway.[18] Nothing has changed, yet everything changes. The camera turns the corner into the bathroom and approaches the shower curtain. Echoing Hitchcock's *Psycho*, and hence increasing our certainty that we are at the killer's position, the curtain fills the screen as the camera keeps moving forward. Suddenly there is the screech of the curtain being drawn open, pitched at the same frequency as Bernard Herrmann's violins in Hitchcock's film. But the joke turns out to be on us; Alice is pulling the shower curtain open to go answer the phone (which is suddenly ringing). It's a clever twist on the logic of disavowal by which (male) spectators displace sexual and deadly thoughts onto the presumed villain; the camera, hence the villain, turns out to have been us all along.

3.

In light of such examples, it's not surprising that theories of camera movement often emphasize precisely this closing of the gap between viewer and world; the moving camera, they hold, effectively places the viewer within the world of the film. Even Katherine Thomson-Jones, who approaches camera movement from the debates on point of view, argues that "we are meant to imagine ourselves moving through the world of the film" along with the camera.[19] In such accounts, the camera serves as a kind of perceptual anchor or surrogate for the viewer. Yet though these theories pick out an important feature of camera movements, like theories of point of view they prove inadequate to phenomena they ought to be able to explain.

There are several versions of this approach. One, articulated by David Bordwell, looks to perceptual psychology to argue that camera movement makes us feel as though we are ourselves moving through the space of the film's world. As the spatial arrangements of the film change in response to the changing position of the camera, we receive visual cues in the way we do when we move through three-dimensional space of our own volition. He writes:

> [W]e can hardly resist reading the camera-movement effect as a persuasive surrogate for our subjective movement through an objective world. Under normal circumstances it is virtually impossible to perceive those screen events as merely a series of expanding, contracting, labile configurations. The

cues overwhelmingly supply a compelling experience of moving through space. . . . [C]amera movement operates in that zone between the spectator's "look" and the camera's "look," perceptual cues serving to identify the two.[20]

Bordwell emphasizes that a physical camera is not required for the effect of camera movement to be generated; any kind of "kinetic depth effect" will work (which covers animation, composite effects, and digital technologies). Once such an effect is generated, the distance between camera and viewer is overcome.

A second version draws on a tradition of phenomenology to posit the moving camera as an independent subject within the world of the film, arguing that the moving camera functions as a surrogate for the viewer. A foundational link between phenomenology and movement is present in Maurice Merleau-Ponty's *Phenomenology of Perception*, in which he repeatedly argues that it is only by paying attention to the body in motion that we can understand how we perceive and inhabit the world.[21] This principle is isolated by Vivian Sobchack as the cornerstone to a broader account of cinematic experience. Movement, she argues, gives us the sense of a three-dimensional world and the objects that populate it, allowing us to express projects and intentions as we move through it. Because of this, it is the movement of the camera that best describes a cinematic version of this conception of experience, as its path through the world permits us to attribute to it the full range of capacities we claim for ourselves. When we watch a camera movement in a film, we are in fact watching through the eyes of another subject, a mobile and lived perspective that already processes the film's world for us.[22]

Others describe the effect in slightly different ways. Noël Carroll argues for an affinity between the movement of the camera and "the way in which our perceptual system works," a connection that allows filmmakers to more "automatically, even naturally" guide our attention through a fictional world.[23] Arthur Danto suggests that "when the camera moves the experience is of *ourselves* moving," from which he makes a further claim: "The kinetification of the camera goes some way toward explaining the internal impact films make upon us, for it seems to overcome, at least in principle, the distance between spectator and scene."[24] Edward Branigan, surveying a range of writing on film, argues that thinking of the camera as a human-like subject is part of our basic experience of the cinema.[25] Branigan argues both that film theory should be responsive to this baseline experience and that much of the historical discourse about camera movements—largely found in texts of film criticism—endorses this experiential claim. More recently, Vittorio Gallese and Michele Guerra draw on research into mirror neurons to argue that camera movements—especially Steadicam—produce mental responses that "reduce the distance between viewer and screen"; as we mentally replicate or simulate the camera's forms of movement, this activity grounds a sense of being in the world of the film.[26] As a result, they argue, "the involvement of the average spectator [in the world of the film] is directly proportional to the intensity of camera movements." We become "participants" rather than mere observers.[27]

There is an immediate payoff to an emphasis on the way camera movements close the gap between viewer and world. It highlights those moments when the camera pulls us along, when it functions as our surrogate within the world of the film. More emphatically, this model helps us say how, in cases like *Friday the 13th Part II*—or the scene from *Vertigo* discussed in the previous chapter—the effect of a shot or sequence is predicated on getting us to feel that we occupy the place of the camera itself. The moving camera positions us in the world of the film not as a spectator but as a participant.

Difficulties arise, however, and not least because camera movements rarely function in the way that human motility and vision do. In the shots from *The Shining*, *Amator*, and *Friday the 13th Part II*, for example, the camera glides over the ground in ways that are profoundly nonhuman, evincing a smoothness and fluidity we do not possess. Or there are cases like the opening of *Moulin Rouge!* (Baz Luhrmann, 2001), in which the camera moves at variable speeds, often hyperbolically fast, through the urban spaces of an imagined fin-de-siècle Paris. Camera movements can also constrain our perception by establishing limits to what we can see, a fixed form of vision that traps us within a frame. Indeed, taken together these are some of the reasons camera movements are so prominent in horror films. *Evil Dead II* (1987), for example, uses an inhumanly fast-moving camera to suggest the presence of a supernatural agency. In an early example, *The Cat and the Canary* (Paul Leni, 1927), the camera moves through the hallway of a house as if from some unknown point of view. Patrick Keating argues that the shot generates a formal and thematic uncanniness by displaying "the not-quite-human perspective of a ghost who might not exist through the means of the not-quite-human movements of another being that is not supposed to exist in the fictional world," namely the camera.[28] The lack of fit between human vision and the movement of the camera creates a tension that often drives the formal and experiential uneasiness of the genre.[29]

There are still more problems. When theories of camera movement hold that the gap between viewer and world is collapsed, they conflict with the basic principles of thinking about point of view in the cinema. This is no accident. Where Wilson asserts that camera movements change nothing about debates over point of view, Sobchack is indifferent to the very idea of point of view: there is "no such thing as *point of view* in the cinema"; it is "a purely theoretical phenomenon" answering a mechanical description of the film apparatus rather than the lived experience of film viewing.[30] Yet this position reduces the complexity of the way that camera movements work, since the logic of point of view, including the gap between viewer and camera, remains part of their basic operation. After all, in *Vertigo* we don't just see the *Portrait of Carlotta* ourselves, filtered through the camera to us; we are aware that Scottie is looking at it, that Madeleine is, and—less explicitly—that the whole situation is part of a film, itself a work of art (the perspective of the museum guard is present, too, serving as an anchor for the scene). We don't see the hospital in *Amator* solely as our view, through the camera, but also as belonging to what we know is the viewpoint of the doctor. Points of view, in other words, can be stacked within a given shot, and hence involve more than simply thinking about the position of the camera within the film's world can explain. As Branigan notes: "It is even possible for several (perhaps incompatible) points of view to be expressed simultaneously."[31] Each case entails a more complex dynamic than an emphasis on "camera as surrogate" allows for, and if point of view isn't sufficient to explain the complexity of these sequences, it is nonetheless necessary if we are to account for them.

We can bring these dynamics into clearer view with a shot from Welles's *The Magnificent Ambersons*. George Amberson Minnafer has just learned from his aunt that people are gossiping about the love between his mother and Eugene Morgan. What follows is a short scene in which George confronts the person he takes to be responsible for these rumors, his neighbor, Mrs. Johnson. Welles begins with a shot of a door that appears to be from George's point of view: Mrs. Johnson opens the door and addresses the camera, which moves forward through the open door and into the living room, a viewpoint we believe to be aligned with George's position. Suddenly, as the camera moves forward, George walks into the frame from behind and to the left, as if he were moving past the camera. We are suddenly no longer "at" his position within the film.[32]

A related example comes from *The Amazing Transparent Man* (Edgar Ulmer, 1960), which tells the story of a bank robber, aptly named Joey

Faust, who is broken out of jail by a deranged ex-major from the US Army. The plan is to have a captured German scientist turn him invisible with stolen uranium in order to allow him to steal radioactive material, which will then be used to turn an army invisible and thereby take over the world. At one point, as the members of the plot stand around the workshop, they realize that Faust—who is now permanently invisible—has entered the room. The camera begins to track forward, moving toward the major; as it reaches a medium-long shot, he recoils as if he's been struck by a blow, tries to reason with Faust, and is then strangled and pushed up against a wall. While the camera has remained at a distance from this, now it draws closer as Faust says: "If I choke you hard enough, you'll bring me back!" The camera approaches the major, who has been released from Faust's grip, circling until it winds up in front of him. We hear Faust say, "You're showing how badly you need me," and the major turns and looks at the camera.[33] As a result, we feel as though the camera has taken up Faust's viewpoint, fully identified itself with him.

As Faust continues to berate the major, the camera tracks in, and the major keeps his eyes fixed on roughly the same spot. The conversation continues, with Faust claiming a higher price for his services, but the camera now starts to back away—and the major begins slowly walking forward, still facing the camera and looking in its direction. He stops, although the camera continues to move; Faust says, "Shall we talk it over in private? Downstairs?," and the camera pans quickly to the left to show a short staircase down to a door. The camera comes to a halt, and Faust says, "Over here, major. I'm waiting"; the major then enters the frame, coming to the top of the staircase. As he gets there, suddenly the door opens below and they exit through it; we were not with Faust after all. Based on the movement of the camera, the disembodied voice of Faust, and the reactions of the major, we assumed that we were looking at the major through Faust's eyes. The camera had a definite and localized position within the world of the film. But then Ulmer pulls the rug out from under us, leaving us unmoored—and accents his evident amusement at his trick through a brief trill of a flute on the soundtrack.

At the beginning of this chapter, I described such moments as amounting to a "perceptual game" that films play with their viewers. As the camera moves and the character whose eyes we thought we were looking through comes into view, our sense of where we are within the (fictional) world becomes unstable, our relation to the intersection of camera and character less certain. If theories of point of view have trouble explaining how the initial impression arises at all—the peculiarity of our sense of

being "with" the camera—theories of camera movement run into difficulties with the second part. George's entrance into the shot *does* change
how we relate to the camera, a shift similar to when Kieślowski's camera
in *Amator* moves into the point of view of the doctor. To the extent that
theories of camera movement explain something important about this
perceptual game, they have difficulty incorporating the broader matters
of film style and form that equally drive it.

4.

There seems to be an impasse, as each theoretical approach accounts
for a key feature of the problem while failing to deal with others. While
we might have an impulse to tinker with the given theories, either to
fix one or to combine both, that will not resolve the problem. Not only
are theories of point of view and of camera movement fundamentally
at odds with one another, they have gone wrong at a much deeper level.
Both theories take the central question that needs to be answered as
having to do with the epistemic relation between viewer and film world
and with how the camera gives the viewer access to it. Once this is
determined, everything else is taken to fall into place. The two theoretical approaches may conflict, may contradict one another, but they are
essentially two sides of the same coin: the epistemology of (fictional)
cinematic worlds is the question on which everything else supervenes.
It's this assumption that so severely limits their explanatory power in
the cases I've been discussing.

It's easiest to recognize the assumption in theories of camera movement, since one of their striking features is that they tend to privilege
moments when the camera is ostensibly at the viewpoint of a character,
moving with them through the world. This generates a conflation of
camera, viewer, and character that smooths over the epistemic gap that
fictional worlds entail. We see it especially in Sobchack's emphasis on
moments in films when a "subjective camera" (or "subjective shot") is
featured, ranging from her discussion of the opening of *The Piano* (Jane
Campion, 1993), to an analysis of the vertigo effect in *Vertigo*, to a
more extended treatment of *Lady in the Lake*. For Sobchack, the subjective camera matters precisely because it ensures that everything depends
on the place of the camera in the world. By eliminating additional perspectives within the frame—there is no separation from the character
with whom we identify, as in over-the-shoulder shots—the subjective
camera serves as a model that contains within itself the answer to the

basic epistemic question. The only position we can occupy within the film is that of the camera.

Again, it's important to be alive to the ways that such shots fail on their own terms—namely, as an attempt to approximate human vision, our way of looking at the world. Joris Ivens, reflecting on his own early experiments with an apparatus designed to reproduce human vision—what he dubbed the "'I' film"—recalls that "the result on the screen looked as if the shot had been taken by a drunken cameraman drifting down the street in a rowboat."[34] Sobchack acknowledges such problems and does focus (for example) on the ways in which *Lady in the Lake* fails to capture our way of being in the world.[35] Yet she sees these perceptual problems as essentially practical in nature, mainly involving the limits of technology. In that case, it is worth noting that advances in camera technology over the past several decades—whether in size or stabilization—have not resolved them. This is true even for the most ambitious recent attempt to use a subjective camera, Gaspar Noë's *Enter the Void*—a problem Noë implicitly acknowledges by motivating the technique through the diegetic presence of hallucinogenic drugs.[36]

A deeper problem, as James Conant has argued, is that the very idea of a subjective shot quickly dissolves into incoherence. Conant notes, first, that the logic of subjective shots ignores a distinction between what it means to see events in a film's world from a particular character's vantage point and what it means to see through a character's own eyes. If we did "see" from the position of a character—that is, as if we truly saw with their eyes—our vision would be informed by views, beliefs, imaginings, dreams, and so on; sight alone is not enough to account for how we perceive the world.[37] Second, Conant argues that the underlying logic of the subjective shot relies on an opposition to an untenable notion of an "objective" shot, a fantasy of being able to take "a view from nowhere" that ignores the camera's (implicit position) within the world of the film. A shot is always taken from a specific viewpoint; the idea of a subjective shot, and its conflation of point of view as a whole with the viewpoint of a character, misses this distinction.[38]

Perhaps the most serious limitation, though, is that subjective shots are simply a minor percentage of camera movements and cannot be the ground for theoretical models of camera movements more generally. Indeed, the vast majority of camera movements do not involve identification with a character's point of view (however defined); they reveal a new part of a scene, follow an action as it moves through space, and so on. This is the domain of mobile framing, from Hollywood to art films to experimental cinema—Marie Menken's *Arabesque for Kenneth Anger* (1955) is an example of the latter—where the movement of the camera opens up the film's world without any relation to the vision of a character. Moreover, even when we are led to imagine ourselves as moving through the world roughly with the viewpoint of a character, rarely is it the case that there is an attempt to strictly identify the camera with the perspective of the character. A shot early in *The Half-Naked Truth* (Gregory La Cava, 1932), for example, follows a customer through a crowd at a carnival; while attentive to his movements, it is not thereby identified with his viewpoint. In an astonishing moment early on in Allan Dwan's *East Side, West Side* (1927), John Breen is fighting a gang in the Lower East Side ("I ain't never seen anyone so tough this side of 14th St.!"). As he beats them up, one antagonist starts to stagger toward the camera—and the camera begins to pull back at the same speed. As this continues, we notice two things: first, that other members of the gang are beginning to stagger in the same direction, and second, that different people are running from behind the camera into the distance. The shot attunes us to their psychology but also suggests the idea of the camera as a boat, drawing people along in its wake while others are brushed by. If subjective shots involve such evident complications, incoherencies, and inadequacies, their appeal for theorists—and at times for filmmakers—has to lie in the fact that they offer a straightforward solution to the epistemic question of how viewers gain access to the film's world. But the ease of that solution is not sufficient to compensate for its costs.[39]

Theories of point of view fare no better, likewise emphasizing an epistemic question to the detriment of their explanatory ability. Kendall Walton can serve as a representative of this position, since his account of fictions as games of "make-believe" informed many of the subsequent discussions of point of view. As part of an attempt to account for our capacity to have emotional (and other) responses to fictions—that is, to things, people, and events that aren't really there—Walton describes an imaginary scene from a horror film:

> Charles is watching a horror movie about a terrible green slime. He cringes in his seat as the slime oozes slowly but relentlessly over the earth destroying everything in its path. Soon a greasy head emerges from the undulating mass, and two beady eyes roll around, finally fixing on the camera. The slime, picking up speed, oozes on a new course straight toward the viewers. Charles emits a shriek and clutches desperately at his chair. Afterwards, still shaken, Charles confesses that he was "terrified" of the slime. *Was* he?[40]

Two features of Walton's description are puzzling. First, sound and music are missing from it, as is the role of the camera and other aspects of style. These elements, some of which are nondiegetic, play a central role in creating the response that Walton ascribes to narrative and diegetic events (and is a reason horror with the sound off can easily turn into parody). Second, the scene Walton describes is rare: the slime (or the monster, or what have you) rarely turns to attack the camera. Most responses of fear are when we witness a character within the film being attacked, when we are afraid, in a sense, on their behalf. And this kind of experiencing of emotion at a remove is a different thing than Walton emphasizes, one that reaches outside the constraints of fiction—as when I wince in pain when you cut your finger with a knife, or when I am moved when I hear of your suffering.[41]

What gets Walton into trouble is that he takes the epistemic relation of viewer to fictional world as the central question that needs to be resolved. Once he has given an account of that and has the idea of make-believe up and running, matters of style and presentation do not trouble him. Of course, Walton is aware that we identify with the position of characters within the world of an artwork and have our emotional responses shaped by them, and that matters of style are present and important. But the belief that the epistemology of fictions has primacy means that these features are relegated to the margins. And this leads him to somewhat bizarre arguments, like the claim that the brushstrokes of van Gogh's *Starry Night* (1889) inhibit our psychological participation in the work because they complicate games of make-believe.[42]

Walton thus illustrates the underlying problem for the range of theoretical approaches I've been discussing: the belief that the aim is to figure out our relation to cinematic worlds *by way of* a consideration of our relation to the camera. This assumption persists throughout debates over point of view and cinematic fictions, and it limits the explanatory power of these theories in helping to think about camera movement (among other things). If we are to be able to recognize the complexity of how camera movements function in ordinary as well as virtuosic instances and to provide a model for our ability to do so, we will need a different approach.

5.

Curiously, the beginning of a solution can be found precisely at the place where theories of camera movements founder: the troubled notion of subjective shots. A number of recent films stand out for their use of stunningly complex and virtuosic camera movements, usually digitally created or modified, pegged to sequences of flight. The fantasy of such sequences, as Scott Richmond describes it, is that "I feel *myself* moving through space"—even though I know I am seated in a theater.[43] Richmond emphasizes moments of flight, such as the Stargate sequence in *2001: A Space Odyssey* (Stanley Kubrick, 1968):

> The perceptual effect of this movement is immersive, visually and viscerally overwhelming. . . . I do not feel *disorientation*, quite, but rather a sort of heightening of orientedness, a drawing out, roughening, and thematizing of an embodied feeling of not quite flying through space. Thus I find myself caught up in one of the purest examples of the illusion of bodily movement in the history of the cinema.[44]

More generally, sequences of flight claim to give viewers new kinds of visual experiences, moving them through a fictional world in a way that is unencumbered by the burdens of gravity or the limits of the human body. Freed from the constraints of the physical camera, new technologies emphasize the visceral experience of moving through a three-dimensional space. If subjective shots were unable to form the basis for a wider theory of cinematic engagement, here the intersection of new technologies, narratively motivated instances of extreme movement, and an interest in the direct solicitation of the viewer's participation seem to promise a new form of immersive experience—a new kind of "phantom ride," as it were. These sequences aim, as the tagline for *Avatar* (James Cameron, 2009) puts it, to have us "enter the world" of the film.[45]

Despite this promise, sequences of flight rarely use the camera in a subjective shot or as a straightforward surrogate for the viewer. Instead, they position a figure at the center of the frame, thereby ensuring that our relation to the camera's movement through the world is predicated on our relation to that figure. This feature is found across a range of films, including *Avatar*, *Spider-Man* (Sam Raimi, 2002), *How to Train Your Dragon* (Dean DeBlois and Chris Sanders, 2010), *Red Cliff* (John Woo, 2008), *Men in Black* (Barry Sonnenfeld, 1997), *Spirit: Stallion of the Cimarron* (Kelly Asbury and Lorna Cook, 2002), *Gravity*, 2012 (Roland Emmerich, 2009), and *The Curse of the Golden Flower* (Zhang Yimou, 2006). The presence of figures within the frame complicates any appeal to a direct engagement between viewer and world.

An initial account of these sequences might say that while contemporary films aim to create new kinds of experience, they also want to avoid the problems of earlier experiments with a subjective camera. And so they give us a character, group of characters, or object that serves as a focalization for viewers' attention, allowing smoother access to the world of the film. In this vein, Sara Ross argues that the feature helps "mut[e] the perceptual experience of forward motion" and "anchor the flying effects to character experience."[46] We have new spectatorial experiences, but with less disruption: a familiar story about the way narrative film reinvents itself.

A more far-reaching account is given by Richmond in an essay on *Spider-Man*, in which he argues that such figures matter less as an anchor for perceptual experience than for the way they generate a complex interplay around our position with respect to the fictional world. Discussing several such shots, Richmond argues that they show that our relation to the onscreen world exceeds the terms given by the presence of the camera and its (fictional) position within that world; our engagement is predicated instead, and more emphatically, on our identification with onscreen bodies. As he observes with respect to *Spider-Man*, scenes with emphasized camera movement work to bind viewers to the transformations—physical and mental—the hero is undergoing. This does not mean straightforward identification, a belief that we are in the position of Spider-Man himself. What emerges, Richmond argues, is a dynamic relation between viewer and character—"two bodies, onscreen and off"—so that we are "less in the position of Spider-Man/Peter and more in the position of a dance partner, in a kind of superhero pas de deux."[47]

Richmond gets something right when he moves away from the primacy of epistemic questions, but in its place his solution turns to and isolates a different dynamic of identification, especially the viewer's identification with bodies on screen. While this move does change the terms of analysis, in the end it winds up substituting one determining feature for another while keeping the same logic in place. Both positions impose artificial limits on what the moving camera does, generalizing too readily from a specific kind of case to a more general explanatory model.

What is needed instead is a broader account of how camera movements create ways of experiencing the world they show. This is not a problem to be solved by building a new theory or by seeking a different, alternate theoretical approach. Rather, it requires moving from the ground up: recognizing the complexities involved in the intersections of camera movement and point of view and thinking about them in a way that avoids the methodological dangers of taking one or another feature of cinema as having primary explanatory authority.

We can get at a more supple way of treating the perspective of characters within camera movements, and the relation between camera movements and point of view more generally, by picking up a distinction Richard Wollheim draws between "internal" and "external" spectators in paintings—a shift in medium that, not least, removes the camera from initial consideration. Wollheim's argument is initially straightforward: the external spectator marks the position that we take up outside the world of the work of art, the position of the viewer with respect to the image itself; the internal spectator, by contrast, picks out a viewing position within the work and the "virtual space" it creates. Importantly, Wollheim emphasizes that the internal spectator is not a figure in the painting but is rather marked as a position so that "he can see everything that the picture represents and he can see it as the picture represents it."[48] This means that the internal spectator is not, as we might think, the figures in Caspar David Friedrich's paintings with their backs turned as they look out at the world, paintings such as *Two Men by the Sea at Moonrise* (ca. 1817) or *Cliffs of Rügen* (1818–1820). Instead, Wollheim turns to a series of landscapes by Friedrich—for example, *Landscape with a Rainbow* (ca. 1810) and *Meadows Near Greifswald* (1822)— that contain no represented figures but are felt, by virtue of the way the image is constructed, to be from some person's or agency's view. The "unrepresented" viewing position is that of the internal spectator, and Wollheim argues that our relation to an internal spectator is not based on identification but on imagination. We do not believe we are there, that we *are* the internal spectator—or even at such a position—but we come to *imagine* what it would be like to occupy that position and what an experience of the depicted world would be were one to be in such a position. (The distinction between identification and imagination is crucial to Wollheim's project.[49]) From here, the relation between style and content opens up. Wollheim emphasizes that the internal spectator is not a neutral position but colors how we parse the fictional world being shown. Friedrich, for example, "aims at showing us what the internal spectator sees, but he also aims at showing us the expressive manner in which the internal spectator views what is before him."[50] This is a matter of visual form: "The only way in which an artist can endow an internal spectator with experiences, or, more fundamentally, with a repertoire, is through the way in which the artists depicts whatever it is . . . that this spectator confronts."[51] The internal spectator thus serves as a point of reference for understanding the world of the painting, a way of recognizing alternate modes of viewing and inhabiting the depicted world that are different than the mode that we are given from our position as an external spectator. The *way* the image is painted suggests a mode of experience, an argument that depends on a dynamic interplay between visual organization and spectatorial imagination.

Wollheim does not think an internal spectator is present within every, or even within most, works of art; this is not a general theory of painting. Once the structural logic of an internal spectator is established, however, we are led to treat the construction of the image at least in part as an expression of that viewpoint.[52] Wollheim acknowledges that internal spectators can be very close to the position of the external spectator, even difficult to distinguish at times. But they can also be, and often are, far more complex. Many of the debates about Velazquez's *Las Meninas* (1656), for example, could be described as having to do with the relation between internal and external spectators.[53] More to the point is a painting like Manet's *The Railway* (1873), which shows a woman and a young girl in front of a trellis behind which steam from a train is rising. It's not just that an internal spectator, on Wollheim's terms, would have this visual experience. By positing an internal spectator, we are able to inhabit the painting in a more open and flexible way, drawing on the different possibilities of inhabiting the world that both figures—the woman facing us and the child turned to look through the iron bars—offer. Looking at it through the woman's distant air gives the image a degree of melancholy, a sense of vague disquiet that colors the picture. (Is the girl her child? Is there a larger story taking place? Is it a lament for lost leisure?) By contrast, attending to the child inclines us toward wonder, the way her world is closed off, operating on a different plane of existence from the woman; the steam behind the trellis is alive with fleeting fascination. Manet's achievement lies in bringing them together, in offering both shadings as ways of inhabiting the world being shown. The postulate of an internal spectator allows us to experience this world through the woman and the child *even though* we do not share their points of view.

We can see this sort of effect in a scene from William Wyler's *Wuthering Heights* (1939), when Cathy and Heathcliff spy on a party happening inside the Linton's mansion. The camera, starting behind them, gradually moves forward and passes over their heads—they are crouched in front of a large glass window—until it presents a clear view of the dancing inside (see figure 5). It frames a beautiful image, a picture of the world of society and excitement they long to join (made more poignant by its repetition later in the film, when Heathcliff returns to discover Cathy married to Linton and the camera tracks back out the window, a barrier

FIGURE 5. *Wuthering Heights* (William Wyler, 1939). Internal spectators.

forever introduced into their world).[54] As the camera moves over Heathcliff and Cathy to show the ball through the window, we look at it as they do. The construction of the shot—the rapidity of the camera's progress picking up their excitement and its halt at the window marking their exclusion—*expresses* their emotional relation to the events, which in turn shades our apprehension of and engagement with the scene. The camera responds to them as, in effect *it creates them as*, internal spectators. We can imagine what it would be like to see as they do, because this is expressed by the movement of the camera.[55]

Even on an initial pass, the logic of the internal spectator provides a better way to understand the recurrent presence of characters within camera movements. Rather than increasing immersion in the world of the film or securing identifications in it, this construction establishes positions from which we can imagine how that world is being experienced. The model is based on the intersection of expression and imagination, the way the artist shows the world and how we grasp that act of showing. Importantly, Wollheim is not isolating a specific technique or tendency but making an argument about the formal logic of images. The internal spectator is a structural position that an artwork creates and from which *we could imagine* perceiving the scene depicted.[56] The position does not even have to remain static; writing about Manet's *Mademoiselle V . . . in the Costume of an Espada* (1862), he observes: "The internal spectator circulates, up and down, backwards and forward, in and out of the various encumbrances which, littering the space around the central figure, embody the difficulties that he has in effecting the encounter on which he has set his heart."[57] The way we see the fictional world largely has to do with the way the image as a whole *expresses* a

viewpoint from within that world, a viewpoint that Wollheim emphasizes as containing an "affective and emotional contribution" to a scene
that is "at least as important as the perceptual contribution."[58] Established by a painting's style and mode of expression, the internal spectator shapes our experience of seeing the world it shows.

Wollheim's account of internal spectators joins questions of pictorial representation to a tradition of thinking about the imagination and
whether we have to be a part of our own imaginative acts.[59] It's a tradition that Wollheim explicitly invokes, emphasizing "a distinction easy to
miss, but not hard to hang on to when caught, between my remembering
an event as I experienced it and my remembering it as experienced by
me—between my remembering the event in the way I experienced it and
my remembering it as something that I experienced."[60] What he calls
"acentered perception," in which we can imagine—or remember—an
event from a point of view that is not our own, is crucial to the logic that
he develops in relation to visual imagery. If there is a mode of perception
that does not require me to be the centering point, then there is no reason to assume that how I relate to an artistic world must be determined
by the visual (or perspectival) viewpoint that I am forced to occupy. In
this vein, Richard Moran argues that "to picture [a] scene from some
point of view or other"—a necessary fact of both representational art
and imaginings—"is not, however, the same as to say that part of what
I imagine is that I *witness* [the scene] from this point of view."[61] If this
distinction is familiar from theories of point of view, Moran draws a
different conclusion, arguing that optical point of view is not necessarily
tied to meaning. Discussing an imagined case from *Macbeth*, he writes:

> Presumably, if he had had proper suspicions in time, Duncan himself could
> have imagined, visually and vividly, that he might be murdered in his sleep.
> He might, then, visualize this from some point just above his sleeping figure
> on the bed, perhaps from the point of view of one of the murderers. But this
> would not mean that it is part of what he (incoherently) imagines that he
> sees himself asleep from some point of view above his own body. On the
> contrary, a crucial part of the emotional tone of his imagining would be his
> sense of fear and outraged at the idea of being attacked while completely
> defenseless *and unaware*. . . . [E]motional aspects of imagination, such as
> imagining something with apprehension or regret, should also be seen as
> part of a *manner* of imagining and not as something that must belong to the
> content of what is imagined.[62]

This point is bound up with Wollheim's attempt to disentangle the
notion of imagination from that of identification: the former, Wollheim

says, involves a mode of presentation, a way of showing something, rather than a conflation of my position with that of another person—or, we might add, with that of a camera.

Recently, Christopher McCarroll has transposed these debates to the phenomenon of "observer memories": memories of something we did, or that happened to us, but in which we see ourselves from the outside. One of McCarroll's aims is to show that observer memories, although they are not how we experienced the initial event, can in fact be genuine memories (though, like all memories, they can be misleading). "Visual perspective *alone*," he writes, "cannot help one determine if a memory is genuine or not."[63] But McCarroll also wants to figure out how to understand the position, the point of view, we occupy when we observe ourselves from the outside. He argues that while we do not have to imagine ourselves—or anyone—as occupying the position from which we see our memory, point of view is neither irrelevant nor neutral. Drawing on Sartre, McCarroll argues that "the image is a form of consciousness, a way of thinking (imagistically) about an object or event . . . the image reflects one's knowledge (implicit and explicit)."[64] The position from which we remember an event informs us about what we believe about that event, about how it matters to us, and about how we understood it when it took place. Viewpoint is not neutral.

Part of McCarroll's argument is that observer memories are not necessarily retroactive constructions. If I remember an event from the outside, we might think, it must be because I later added content to my initial experience. Against this view, McCarroll uses experiments in perceptual psychology to show how observer memories may be created at the moment of the event itself. They may be facilitated by moments in which we are aware of ourselves being perceived from other positions (teaching, performing, playing sports, etc.). But they can also occur when we are engaged in highly kinetic activities; "self-generated movements" can cause, or be translated into, "a representation of the self in the visual modality. Spatial information may be generated internally and a body image forms the representation of the self."[65]

This suggests a way to think about camera movements. As the camera moves, it prompts us to imagine how the world of the film ought to be seen, much in the way the establishment of an internal spectator opens up the way we can experience the image. The mistake theorists of camera movements make, then, is to assume that any such content has to be tied to the position of the camera itself. McCarroll cautions against this: "The point of view may be internal, as if one were seeing the action through the eyes of one of the characters, but other internal modalities—such as emotional or kinesthetic—need not neatly align with the internal perspective."[66] The moving camera is enough to generate an image of the world, but the way the shot is organized need not revolve around an identification with the position of the camera.

Wollheim's model, buttressed by McCarroll's work on imagining and remembering, provides a path around the centrality of epistemic questions—as well as those based on identification—in debates about camera movement and point of view. The internal spectator creates a refraction of sorts, splitting the beam that connects the viewer to the film world into different spectatorial positions dispersed within the image. We are not necessarily, or even primarily, "at" the viewpoint established by the camera, nor even at that of a character. Instead, we are able to simultaneously inhabit multiple positions within the world of the film. We see "imaginatively" from these multiple positions, *as if* we could have the view of the world expressed through the position of an internal spectator. We imagine what it would be like to see the world in such a way, and as with the observer memories McCarroll describes, learn something about what we see from the way in which we see it. If this resembles the logic of point of view, the difference is that what matters is not the fact of being shown something, and the position from which the showing takes place, but rather the construction of the shot itself, the manner of the showing.

Because this model operates without grounding in the position of the camera or in identification with characters, it extends to a much wider range of cases. John Ford is certainly not renowned for his virtuosic use of camera movements, yet they play a key, if subtle, role in many of his films. In *Fort Apache* (1948), Colonel Thursday, taking over an outlying fort, repeatedly states that despite his penchant for regulations he is no martinet. He's lying about this, but he's also far worse: a man driven to rectify the stain on his reputation and return to the formality of the East by doing something of great importance. The film chronicles the cost of this decision, but it also gives an alternate vision of life in the sprawling O'Rourke clan—not that there's no order there (the rules and social standing of the military still apply), but it's inflected and shaped by personal bonds. Throughout the film, Ford uses a select number of camera movements to describe a community of equals, to integrate community and society; in a sense, he uses the camera to bring people together.

The key moment comes at the noncommissioned officers' ball. Thursday and Mrs. O'Rourke are required to dance together, something

Thursday views with profound distaste but which he recognizes as a social obligation. They begin dancing back and forth, the camera barely bothering to pan with their movements. As they continue, however, Ford cuts to a closer shot, the camera now panning more swiftly with them. And then something changes. Thursday and Mrs. O'Rourke dance off into the middle distance, and suddenly the whole tenor of the dance is different: it becomes more open, freer, less an obligation than a shared pleasure. It's absolutely clear that this happens, but why are we aware of it? Partly it has to do with the performance, the way that Mrs. O'Rourke's pleasure in dancing slowly infects Thursday's reticence, as if his body is unable to resist the appeals of movement and rhythm. But this is vague, uncertain: How much can we infer with certainty by observing their movements in the middle distance? We are inclined to read all this into their actions because the shift in the dance occurs when the camera starts, for the first time, to move on its own, to follow the pair in their patterns and to articulate a spatial arrangement around them. It's as if the camera is caught up in the new mood of the dance—or that the camera, suddenly dancing, enables the dance to begin in earnest; everyone else now joins in. The camera's movements convey to us, attune us to, the shifting emotions in the scene, a range of visual expressions that (assuming we read them rightly) seem pegged to the characters' inner states. This logic of expression continues a minute later, after the end of the official dance, when we see Thursday's daughter and O'Rourke's son, very much in love, dancing together away from the fuss of the party. The camera moves toward them, subtly rocking back and forth with their dance but remaining at a respectful distance—an expression of a knowing intimacy. In both cases, the camera's movement produces a stylistic evocation of an emotional register that defines the terms of community within the fort.

The appeal of the approach I've been articulating, one that is buttressed by the line of thinking that Wollheim and McCarroll represent, lies in the way it makes questions about the relation between viewer and camera, and between camera and world, not primary determinants of meaning but secondary phenomena. Nor is a relation to characters necessary to compensate for the absence of epistemic grounding through the camera. Instead, it's only once we determine the particular manner in which we are being shown something—an investigation particular to each film, even to each shot—that we can begin to answer questions about point of view. Emerging from the logic of internal spectators, this approach nonetheless articulates a more general way of proceeding. It gives us a way of thinking about camera movements that accounts for the ground level of phenomena, the details of films and their stylistic expressions. "We experience and interpret the world," McCarroll writes, "from a variety of points of view: internal/external, field/observer, visual perspectives, embodied perspectives (e.g., kinesthesia); emotional perspectives, and cognitive (e.g., evaluative) perspective."[67] What we discover is that visual point of view is simply part of the larger expressive strategy of the work, and that expression is at the heart of meaning.

6.

With this model in place, we can now return to the problems raised by the examples with which this chapter began, cases in which the movement of the camera makes us feel (paradoxically) present within the world of a fiction film and in which the moving camera suddenly takes up—or rejects—the point of view of a character. These are moments when films depend on our capacity to feel that we are moving with the camera even though we know that we are not, versions of a "perceptual game" that filmmakers have long enjoyed playing. Instances of this game range from *Peter Ibbetson* (Henry Hathaway, 1935), when Peter returns to his childhood home, and what looks like a point-of-view shot of the house swivels right to take in grounds, as if following his gaze, then swivels right again to show Peter and his companion only now arriving; to the animated short *Little Match Girl* (Arthur Davis and Sid Marcus, 1937), in which the animated camera moves with a girl on a swing, and her second swing allows the camera to take up her point of view as she goes over and looks at the ground underneath her, then on the next swing continues in the direction of her movements to leave her point of view and move up into the clouds; to Hitchcock's *Rebecca* (1940), in which Max's recounting of Rebecca's movements in the boathouse causes the camera to move across the room as if it were in her position—a form of a shot he repeats in *Rope*, when Rupert imagines what must have taken place during the murder of David and the camera follows his attention across the empty spaces of the room; to Max Ophuls's *Le plaisir* (1952), when the camera moves forward to take up the position of the spurned lover as she rushes up the stairs to throw herself out a window; to Toshio Matsumoto's *Funeral Parade of Roses* (1969), when the camera moves through a crowd as if from the (impossible) position of the now-blinded Eddie; to John Carpenter's *The Thing* (1982), when the camera, apparently occupying the position of the alien/dog, tracks through a hallway before the creature itself enters the shot; to Haile Gerima's *Sankofa* (1993), in which the camera appears to be moving from the perspective of the castle guard until he steps into the frame; to *10 Things I Hate about You* (Gil Junger, 1999), when Patrick enters the club and the camera swivels around to take up his point of view before, as we arrive at the concert, he walks back into the frame; to Justin Lin's *The Fast and the Furious: Tokyo Drift* (2006), in which Sean looks out the window of his car as he "drifts" around a curve, and the camera, as if inhabiting his view, moves out past the edge of the cliff to stare down into the abyss before snapping back inside the car to show his successful negotiation of the turn.

These perceptual games have not gone unrecognized. In chapter 1, I discussed the opening shot of *Gravity*, whose play with perceptual expectations has been debated. Warren Buckland describes a shot from *Wings of Desire* (Wim Wenders, 1987) in which Daniel descends from the top of a circus tent, noting that the shot "is initially internally focalized" so that it reads as a point-of-view shot, but "when the camera reaches the ground level, we then see Daniel enter the shot."[68] Ofer Eliaz finds this play in Mario Bava's *Black Sunday* (1960), where a character "unexpectedly *steps into the shot* that had begun as his point of view."[69] Keating also notices it in the opening number of *Gold Diggers of 1933* (Mervyn LeRoy, 1933), which starts with Ginger Rogers singing "We're in the Money," then moves across an array of similarly costumed singers "until the camera reaches the end of the line, where, to our surprise, Fay re-appears."[70] Branigan notes "a camera movement in *Dial M for Murder* ([Alfred] Hitchcock, 1954) [that] moves around and behind an unsuspecting victim to end as the murderer's POV."[71] As Bordwell remarks of such cases, "It is a permissible play with convention to have a character enter a shot which has been initially established as her or his point of view."[72] Indeed, it is in part because of the generality of these perceptual games that they can be found outside mainstream narrative and art cinema. Hart has observed the way that Maya Deren's *Meshes of the Afternoon* (1943) plays with ostensibly subjective shots, in which the handheld camera appears to be from Deren's position but then, sometimes with the help of whip pans and hidden cuts, she steps into the frame. The result, he argues, is a blurring of the very difference between modes of vision, experience, and subjectivity.[73]

There are of course some films that make these games their structuring principle. *Vampyr* (Carl Dreyer, 1932) systematically creates expectations about the spatial organization of the world and then subverts and undermines them.[74] Early on, as Allan Gray knocks on the door of the inn, Dreyer cuts inside—we see Gray through the glass door in the middle distance—and then begins to move the camera toward him. The sense of physical presence, that the camera is moving with a character—*some* character—is strong. But this is dispelled when Gray backs away from the door and looks up; evidently, no one was there after all. Dreyer then cuts to a shot of the roof of the inn, with the camera—positioned in a plausible location for Gray and following a familiar shot/reverse-shot formula—panning across and then tilting down to show a ground-floor window. Gray suddenly enters the shot, revealing our belief that we were looking from his point of view to be mistaken. Soon thereafter, Gray is let in by a woman—an action intercut with ambiguously located shots of a figure with a scythe getting on a boat—and walks through the foyer/bar at the front of the inn. The camera pans with him, and as he moves through a doorway it begins to track quickly behind him, moving around corners to keep him in the frame. Because the woman is not visible in the frame, we assume that the camera reflects her movements; after all, it's plausible that she would follow Gray through the rooms. But then the camera turns a corner and we see her already in an alcove folding linen. (How did she get there? Wasn't she just opening the door?)

Dreyer generates a virtuosic set of variations on the perceptual game that camera movements allow. Shots repeatedly begin as if the camera were at the position of a character, a belief that is often confirmed by the additional formal device of a shot/reverse-shot structure. Then, as the camera moves, the character through whose eyes we thought we were looking comes into view; it's an effect that produces a jolt, a surprise, a moment of deep uncertainty. It's not that we are somehow ejected from the world of the film, made to feel an ontological gulf. The effect is more prosaic, but also more powerful. As spectatorial possibilities separate, we recalibrate our sense of the shading given to the scene by the camera, and the expressive content of the shot shifts or changes accordingly. The uncertainty of viewpoint, moreover, fits the film's broader concerns, a foreshadowing of the ontological and epistemic disturbances to come. We learn that nothing is stable, not even the line between the world of the film and the world in which it was made; the frequency with which Dreyer employs variations on the perceptual game leads to a sense of all-consuming doubt. Again, emphasizing point of view or camera movement alone won't give us this. We have to recognize and account for how the camera's movements *express* something about the world of the film. *Vampyr* does this by creating multiple viewpoints that in turn provide a shading (and shaping) of our experience of the world's fuzzy parameters. (This is partly what it means to call it an expressionist film.)

To be sure, point of view is still here. So, too, are camera movements and the closure of the gap between viewer and world. Indeed, the effectiveness of perceptual games in a film like *Vampyr* depends on their presence. But the explanatory scope of these theories is now recalibrated. The example of Dreyer, and the various camera movements analyzed throughout this chapter, provide a way to describe how the force of camera movements carries us into the world of a film without coming up against the strictures of point of view. The crucial point is to recognize that many of the shots that contain perceptual games with camera movement depend on the presence of what I've been describing as epistemological fantasies. We are not with the camera in the world of the film, but we *want* to be with it, and the way films incite the desire to be at the position of the camera, to be moving with it, allows us to believe in something that is not, strictly speaking, possible for us to do.[75] To consider these features as fantasies means taking intuitive claims—about viewpoint, about the camera, about identification—and treating them not as facts but as temptations, aspects of our relation to moving images that can be used and exploited by films for various ends.

Late in *City Lights* (Charlie Chaplin, 1931), Charlie is standing on the staircase outside the apartment of the flower girl he's in love with. He has just looked for her at her usual place on the street and failed to find her there; now, he looks inside her room and sees a doctor's tools—but nothing more. Charlie repositions himself on the rain barrel outside her window to get a better view. There is a cut back to the doctor's tools, but this time the camera tilts up to show the girl's grandmother standing at the head of a bed. We can only see the railing of the bed; the rest is blocked off from view by a wall. The camera begins to move forward toward the grandmother and then, remarkably, swivels around the wall to show the flower girl lying in bed, with a doctor sitting beside her and talking to the grandmother (see figure 6). A cut takes us to a view of the trio in profile, as an intertitle gives the doctor's diagnosis of her fever and illness. The film then goes back to Charlie, stunned by the news, who climbs back onto the staircase and mournfully sits down.

City Lights is a film about the intersection of sound and vision, speech and sight—and not just because it was made in the aftershocks of the transition to sound. Throughout the film, Chaplin is concerned with what

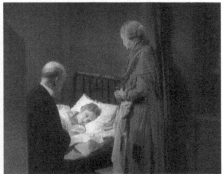

FIGURE 6. *City Lights* (Charlie Chaplin, 1931). The camera taking up Charlie's gaze.

it means to see another person, and to see them in a way that recognizes them for who they are. The question is at stake in the interactions with the millionaire: when drunk, he recognizes and befriends Charlie; sober, he can only see a tramp unworthy of his concern. It is even more central in the relation between Charlie and the flower girl, who falls in love with him based on his voice, his actions, and her own mistaken assumption about what they signify. The film's final pair of shots, after her vision has been restored, tests the quality of her sight: Can she see in this tramp the man who saved her, and whom she mistakenly believed to be wealthy? There, Chaplin forestalls our discovery of the result, leaving the film hauntingly poised on a series of close-ups. In the earlier scene, however, it is Charlie who is only capable of hearing—he's in her position, as it were—blocked by the wall that obscures the bedridden flower girl from him. The extraordinary aspect of the scene is that the *camera itself* takes on the burden of his sight; it enacts his, and our, desire to look at a scene that's behind a partition, to move around a barrier, to be an observer of a private moment (perhaps to overcome the condition of being at a movie). It is as beautiful and moving an example of the intertwining of perceptual games, expressive viewpoints, and epistemological fantasies as exists.

Part Two

Part Two

CHAPTER 4

Object Lessons

The Variable Dynamics of Point of View

I.

Few things in the history of film and film theory are as conceptually overdetermined as the point-of-view shot. When it is explicitly present, point of view is taken to be the central feature in determining what a shot means or how it works. Point of view is also one of the most effective ways of generating the enduring fantasy that we are in the world of the film at the position of the camera. This fantasy drives psychological theories of the "natural" function of cinematic techniques, from Münsterberg to Bazin to Reisz to Bordwell, in which the camera stands in for our look within the film. But it doesn't end there. Take Laura Mulvey's "Visual Pleasure and Narrative Cinema," which builds its argument by distinguishing three different "looks" in classical narrative cinema: the look of the audience at the screen, the look of the camera at the scene, and the look of characters at the diegetic world. As Mulvey famously argues, "The conventions of narrative film deny the first two and subordinate them to the third," creating situations in which a male character becomes "the bearer of the look of the spectator."[1] The camera binds us to the view of that character and sees the world as he does.

Mulvey's analysis was of course important for its account of the gendered construction of the point-of-view structure in classical Hollywood cinema, but the assumption about point of view behind her argument, that we are at the position the camera occupies within the world of the film, runs throughout writings on film style. This chapter explores a curious wrinkle in point-of-view constructions: shots that use a moving camera to embody a character's look, yet do so in ways that undermine—or perhaps better, displace—identification with the character doing the looking. Revising the terms of the subjective shot, these shots draw on our sense of attunement to a character only to create forms of connection to other individuals, to objects in the film world, and to broader social communities and formations. I describe them as "object-defined" camera movements, shots that are organized by a point-of-view structure that the viewer experiences not as the expression of the character doing the looking but as that of the person or thing being looked at. Guided not by the look of the subject so much as "the logic of the object," these shots create a tension between the familiar way in which we are used to understanding point of view and the creative deployment of a technique.[2]

The idea of a shot (or scene) being guided by an object is by no means uncommon and can be used for a range of expressive purposes. Robert Bresson's *Une femme douce* (*A Gentle Woman*, 1969), for example, frequently builds scenes out from close-ups of objects, moving outward from their material facticity to the social and interpersonal relations in which they are imbricated. The film's first flashback thus begins with a close-up of a gilded ring in the palm of a hand, a shot that is held for about five seconds—during which all we can do is look—before we are given information to place the ring in the midst of a pawnshop, its worth being decided by the man holding it. This economic transaction leads to the first encounter between the man and the woman, the pawning of a ring not only foreshadowing the marriage between them but suggesting that its terms will be primarily economic: contractual rather than personal.

Camera movements are often involved in such shots. Marie Menken's *Visual Variations on Noguchi* (1945), for example, responds to the sculptor's works by panning and tilting—often with a handheld camera—to convey their formal properties, the different ways in which Noguchi's objects inhabit and create space. The camera might trace out the lines of a sculpture; it might move out from behind an obstruction to catch a glimpse as if in passing; it might simply hold steady in relation to what's in front of it. Each of these gestures, each of these forms of movement, responds directly to the object in front of the camera, to what's being shown to the viewer. Or take the scene in Roberto Rossellini's *Viaggio in Italia* (*Voyage to Italy*, 1954) in which Katherine encounters a series of statues at the Museo Archeologico Nazionale. With each statue, the camera moves in relation to it, sometimes panning across while at other times tracking in to indicate her interest in its form. The most virtuosic encounter between camera and sculpture involves the Farnese Hercules. Starting on the figure's right and slightly to its front, a framing that captures its bust, the camera swivels around in a crane shot to a position behind and above the statue, thereby also framing the guide and Katherine looking at it. The camera then slowly pulls back and settles into a stationary position, its overall movement tracing the massive dimensions of the figure and investing it with a physical sensuousness that mirrors her exclamation, "Oh, it's wonderful!"[3] It's no coincidence that films about artworks often use the camera to articulate the encounter between viewer and object as structured by the object itself.

The form can also occur within narrative contexts, as with the treatment of the ring that Uncle Charlie gives to Young Charlie toward the beginning of Alfred Hitchcock's *Shadow of a Doubt* (1943). After she declares that she knows there's something secret about her uncle—the camera tracks in to Cotton's face at that moment, which has gone deadly still—he pauses and then asks for her hand. The camera moves toward their clasped hands as he puts a ring on her finger, as if to seal a marriage between them. When she holds it up, there is an extreme close-up—following her gaze—to show the engraving of another person's initials on the inside of the ring. Later in the film, when Young Charlie finally realizes that her uncle is the "Merry Widow" murderer, she does so by matching the initials of his most recent victim to the engraving on that ring, information she discovers when looking for the missing pages of a newspaper in the library. Hitchcock marks her realization by a track away from the ring she is holding in her hand, a shot that moves back up into a high angle, the smallness of the ring signaling its loss of value to her—confirmed a little later when she gives it back to her uncle, placing it on the table between them as if it were merely any other object. Finally, when Young Charlie decides to let her uncle know that she has found out his secret, she does so through the ring. Patrick Keating notes that the camera's movement toward the ring on her finger represents "Uncle Charlie's subjective experience without representing his optical experience."[4] In these scenes, the camera's attentions are shaped by the power the ring holds.

Another ring. In Peter Jackson's *Lord of the Rings* trilogy, the intertwining of object-defined shots and a subjective camera is already present in the prologue to *The Fellowship of the Ring* (2001), which narrates the fight of the Elves and Men against Sauron and his army of Orcs. "Victory was near," the voice-over tells us, and then the music pauses as Jackson cuts to a series of characters suddenly looking up with expressions of shock and awe. He cuts to Sauron in black armor, the glowing ring on his finger, as the narrator observes that "the power of the ring could not be undone." There is a cut to Sauron towering over the assembled army as they look at up him, then a shot that tracks in on his hand and moves closer in order to bring the ring into close-up, so much that the fiery elvish script is clearly visible on its surface. This shot is from the point of view of one of the characters and is understood as their perspective, but what it indicates is not their interest but the intrinsic power of the ring itself: its capacity to draw any gaze toward it, to overwhelm whatever tries to confront it. Time and time again, Jackson uses a variation of this shot to indicate the ring's power. A character—Bilbo, Frodo, Gollum, Boromir, and so on—will look at the ring, and then the camera will be pulled toward it. These are point-of-view shots that serve not to define the characters looking but rather the object they are looking at.

This type of bondedness of the camera to what it shows can also be deployed with people. A familiar kind of camera movement toward a character's face often functions as an expressive gesture to elicit, depict, or express their inner state. In *Miracle Mile* (Steve De Jarnatt, 1988), a sequence of shots involves slow tracks in toward Harry as he struggles to come to grips with the consequences of his own actions and the possibility that he has sounded a false (and destructive) alarm about a nuclear attack on Los Angeles. The camera's movement reveals his increasing panic—as well as his refusal or inability to step outside his own view. Indeed, this kind of movement, often done at moments when a character sees something unusual or intense, is a kind of cinematic cliché. The ending of *Waltz with Bashir* (Ari Folman, 2008) is an extreme variation, as the (animated) camera performs an extended track in toward the main character's face at the moment he witnesses women fleeing the massacres of the Sabra and Shatila refugee camps. The moving camera may not be aligned with his point of view, but it expresses his position all the same.[5]

What I focus on in this chapter involves a further complication, shots in which the moving camera takes up the optical point of view of a character but expresses the terms of what they see. This chapter explores two filmmakers—Fritz Lang and Guru Dutt—who have little in common: different national cinemas, different generations, different genres, different preoccupations. Yet I bring them here in dialogue because each deploys camera movements that interweave the formal perspective articulated by the position of the shot and the perspectives expressed by the way it unfolds. The perspectival tension they generate is then used to trouble what they see as the increased rationalization of their worlds—interwar Germany and the developing Indian state—by introducing new ways of inhabiting its spaces and by producing new kinds of appeals to its inhabitants. The camera movements are an explicit instance of the need to move beyond the belief that we identify (only) with the position of the moving camera within the diegetic world.

2.

Lang is a peculiar figure to include in a study of the moving camera, since of all the things that come to mind when we think about his German films, especially those from the silent era, camera movement is not high on the list. The images that have been burned into our minds are by and large still: Peter Lorre framed within the reflection of knives in the window from *M* (1931), the giant machine turning into the god Moloch in *Metropolis* (1927), and Mabuse's head superimposed on the empty floor of the stock market in *Dr. Mabuse, der Spieler* (*Dr. Mabuse the Gambler*, 1922). There's a good reason for this. Relative to his contemporaries, Lang uses few camera movements; in some cases, there are shockingly few. Across the entirety of *Die Nibelungen* (1924), for example, there is only one shot that moves: early in *Siegfrieds Tod* (*Siegfried*), the first view of the dragon includes a tilt down as it takes a drink from the lake. No other shot in the next four and a half hours changes its initial framing.

This does not mean that there is no movement in these films—far from it—but such movement is largely contained within the frame. Think of the crowds surging through spaces in *Kriemhilds Rache* (*Kriemhild's Revenge*) or *Metropolis*, the revelry of Carnival in the Italian episode of *Der müde Tod* (*Destiny*, 1921), the carefully orchestrated actions of the bank robbery in *Die Spinnen* (*Spiders*, 1919), or even Haghi's stately but stunning movement when he rises up and walks out of the room toward the end of *Spione* (*Spies*, 1928). In each of these cases, the movement within the shot works in conjunction with the shot's overall construction, helping to define what we generally think of as Lang's visual style and thematic preoccupations. In this vein, Lotte Eisner emphasizes the "ornamental design" that guides both image and narrative, noting how in the second part of *Die Nibelungen* the "epic slowness of *Siegfried* . . . has given way to an intense acceleration of destiny, a thundering crescendo that sweeps those responsible for Siegfried's death to their destruction."[6] The stationary camera seems intrinsically tied to this account of Lang, creating the basic template within which these dramas can play out. The rigidity of the frame, that is, establishes the sense of control that is reflected in and emphasized by the images and narratives Lang presents.[7]

Even when camera movements are present, they don't form a significant part of his style until *Metropolis* in 1927. An initial question would be why it takes Lang so long to begin to use camera movements. It's certainly not the case that German cinema, despite contemporary French complaints of excessive theatricality, was static: F. W. Murnau and E. A. Dupont, and even Ernst Lubitsch as well, created a mobile cinema, but Lang seems to have been unwilling to try to better them at their own game. One possible explanation is the cameraman. Is it significant that Lang's cinema became more mobile and fluid when he replaced Carl Hoffmann with Karl Freund for *Metropolis*? No doubt Freund was important to Lang's changing visual style, but it's worth noting that Hoffmann worked on Dupont's *Varieté* (1925) and Murnau's *Faust* (1926) in the years following *Die Nibelungen*, two films that feature extravagant camera movements. Or was it Lang's trip to America in fall 1924, where he not only had his vision of New York but spent time in the Hollywood studios and learned of their new techniques?[8] *Die Nibelungen*, after all, seems to mark Lang's final attempt to create an "authentically German" style of his own. Whatever the reason, *Metropolis* contains Lang's first systematic use of camera movements, and by *Spione* and *Frau im Mond* (*Woman in the Moon*, 1929) basic devices like reframing finally become part of his visual grammar. Indeed, his two sound films—*M* and *Das Testament des Dr. Mabuse* (*The Testament of Dr. Mabuse*, 1933)—use camera movements more extensively than do any of the silent films.

If infrequent, Lang's camera movements in his German films are nonetheless extraordinarily rich and interesting, especially the way that they employ complex articulations of narrational perspective and point of view. Not only does he use camera movements to negotiate complex subject positions within the films, but these camera movements also create more open, fluid spaces—all of which creates a generative tension with his broader themes of destiny and design.[9]

One of the most striking features of these camera movements is the way they are defined by the object they show, especially when they show a person. Two examples from early in *Metropolis* demonstrate this tendency. In the scenes in the pleasure gardens, Lang shows a medium shot of Freder embracing a woman in front of an ornamental fountain, roughly facing the camera (she is a courtesan of sorts, instructed to serve his pleasures). As they move together, the camera pans with them, keeping them centered as Freder whispers into her ear; the shot creates a kind of intimacy, a knowing and sympathetic response to the emotional connection of the two characters. Although this is elegant, it is also fairly conventional, a case in which the form of the shot matches and accentuates its content.

A more intriguing example comes when Freder descends into the machine rooms of the city to see how his "brothers" live. In one of the film's most celebrated sequences, a worker is unable to contain the pressure of a control station and the entire machine explodes, leading to Freder's vision of the machine as Moloch. As the explosion starts, Lang does something curious, cutting to an extreme long shot of Freder standing close to a large wall. Freder then rushes toward the camera, hand outstretched—it seems partly to help the fallen worker, partly to ward off the force of the explosion—and the camera starts to move toward him, reducing the intervening distance. The camera's movement is quick and not entirely smooth, perhaps mounted on a swing of some sort.[10] As Freder comes into long shot, he stops and begins to recoil backward, raising his arms over his face (see figure 7). He staggers back, the camera almost pushing him against the wall behind him.

While the previous shots contain dynamism within their frames—not just the explosion but the images of the workers in synchronized movement—this is an instance of an interplay between movement within the frame and the moving frame itself. An initial reading would be that the shot functions as a visual emphasis, a visceral response to the power of the explosion. Eisner, for example, says that the movement of the camera means that "the spectator seemed actually to have experienced an explosion."[11] In this reading, the camera is centrally oriented around a kind of material presence in the world of the film, both for itself and—by extension—for us as well. Yet while the camera's movement may be a reaction to and embodiment of the physical power of the explosion, it is also an expression of *Freder's* response to it. That is, while the camera creates an experience for us of the explosion, it is also shaped

FIGURE 7. *Metropolis* (Fritz Lang, 1927). The force of the camera.

and defined by what it shows. The shot is constructed so as to display Freder's mental state at this moment, not just *that* he responds but *how* he responds—the movement of the camera allows us to grasp his interior condition.[12]

Such an interplay of perspectives is complicated enough, but Lang adds a further wrinkle—one with important consequences for these matters—in a type of shot he employs in both *Dr. Mabuse* and *Metropolis*. This is my focus here: the camera is positioned at the optical perspective of one character, a "subjective shot" that tracks in toward another character, yet is defined *not* by the point of view of the character who is aligned with the camera but by the character who is the object of the gaze. We experience the shot as an expression of what it shows, as being defined by its object.

I want to spend a bit of time with the form of this type of shot, drawing out both the conceptual problems it presents and the possibilities it affords. I begin with its first appearance, in *Dr. Mabuse*, with a shot that is in fact the first camera movement marked as significant in any of Lang's films—and the last camera movement to be given emphasis as a camera movement until *Metropolis*.[13] The shot comes midway through the first part of the film, as Attorney Von Wenck searches illegal gambling houses for the mysterious card player(s). Sitting down at a table, he takes out a wallet and bundles of cash; an old man across from him—Mabuse in disguise—haltingly searches for his spectacles and begins to fiddle with them, an action that causes light to reflect off their lenses. Von Wenck looks up, and Lang cuts back to a medium shot of Mabuse, this time with the frame blacked out except for the area around the spectacles. Von Wenck seems stunned. Lang cuts to a close-up of the spectacles, then to a close-up of Von Wenck, who says, "But these are Chinese spectacles." Yes, Mabuse replies, "from TSI–NAN–FU!!" There is a cut back to Von Wenck as his eyes briefly roll back; he looks around, then a cut shows us a long shot of Mabuse about to deal. Lang now cuts to Von Wenck, the camera placed on Mabuse's side of the table, and begins to close the frame around him: Von Wenck is framed within a narrow band between the two blacked-out sides of the frame. A cut to an extreme close-up of Mabuse's eyes—they concentrate and close—is followed by a return to the previous shot as Von Wenck visibly staggers. After Von Wenck gathers his cards, Lang cuts to a shot of the cards from his point of view, a feature of the shot confirmed when their number and suit change to the phrase "TSI NAN FU." After a return to

FIGURE 8. *Dr. Mabuse, der Spieler* (*Dr. Mabuse the Gambler*; Fritz Lang, 1922).
Mabuse's power.

the shot of Von Wenck, Lang cuts to a long shot of Mabuse and then
gradually blacks out the image except for Mabuse's head, which itself
grows larger and larger, filling up the screen (see figure 8).

   This sequence leads to the first direct struggle between these antago-
nists, as Von Wenck refuses the order to "take" despite the magic words
on the table in front of him. It is, in other words, a narratively significant moment. But I'm more interested in the shot that tracks in toward
Mabuse's head, the moment when Von Wenck is most directly threatened by the hypnotic spell being cast. The intuitive reading, I take it, is
that the shot gives us Von Wenck's view of Mabuse, that it reveals how
he sees Mabuse at that moment. But Lang has a number of other ways
to indicate that we're looking at the world from the eyes of a character,
including shot/reverse-shot patterns based on eyeline matches, superimpositions, and the narrowing of the field of vision by blacking out
portions of the frame.[14] This is not one of those cases. Rather than seeing the world from Von Wenck's perspective, and thereby identifying
with him as he struggles to maintain control over his own mind, what
we see is the visualization of Mabuse's efforts to usurp that point of

view. The shot is defined by the character it shows, not by the character whose vision it is aligned with.[15]

The logic I'm proposing runs in contrast to how we normally think of a "subjective shot," which binds the look of the camera *and* the look of the audience to the look of the character. Even George Wilson, who is generally skeptical of the view that "veridical POV shots" count as "subjective"—he argues that viewers generally see material from a character's visual perspective without imagining themselves as occupying that character's position within the diegesis—holds that visual (and, presumably, aural) effects can lead us to believe that we are seeing a character's field of vision:

> [A] range of the visual properties of the shot are supposed to represent subjective enhancements and distortions of the character's field of vision at the time. For instance, when the character is drunk, dizzy, or otherwise perceptually disoriented, then special effects of focus, lighting, filtering, or camera movement may be employed to depict the way these psychological conditions have affected the character's visual experience.[16]

It's this added visual emphasis that is present in *Dr. Mabuse*, as Lang appears to use both the movement of the camera and the increasing isolation of Mabuse's head from the rest of the scene—gradually blacking out everything else—to mimic Von Wenck's increased absorption in the attempted hypnotism.

In subjective shots, everything should supervene on the delineation of point of view. But Lang shows that meaning is not reducible to a determination of the field of vision of the character into whose position we are being placed.[17] In the shot from *Dr. Mabuse*, we see Mabuse from a perspective that is identified in several ways as that of Von Wenck: the spatial layout of the scene, the context of the shots that immediately precede (and follow) it, and the visual effects within the shot. Yet we do not experience the shot as being put in the position of Von Wenck's gaze or as sharing *his* increasing hypnotic fascination with Mabuse. We experience Mabuse's hypnotic power directly. The shot expresses not the attitude of the character whose look is identified with the camera—and, at least structurally, with the look of the audience—but rather the object of the shot. We don't just see Mabuse as the central object of our attention; we sense his own engagement and interaction with the world of the film. We see him, that is, as both object and subject.

Of course it's true that we readily grasp or understand the state of mind of characters when we don't see through their optical point of view. Narrative cinema as we know it depends on our ability to identify with the viewpoint of characters who are within the frame and whose optical point of view is not shown by the camera. What's different here is the use of the subjective camera, since its presence means that we're overtly cued to read the shot through the perspective of the character who shares the position of the camera. Lang's virtuosity lies in his ability to combine this background assumption with an awareness of the state of mind of a character being seen by the character whose point of view we inhabit—and to apprehend this directly, without first identifying with the character who is doing the looking.

Our sense of the orientation of the shot is intimately linked to its meaning. If we think that the shot is primarily about Von Wenck, that the binding of the camera to the perspective of a character trumps all other considerations, then we'll read the shot as having to do with his struggle to maintain focus and concentration. If we treat the shot as focused around Mabuse, however, then we'll see the episode as having to do with his attempt to assume power. Curiously, most discussions of the shot have (implicitly) read it this latter way. Rudolf Arnheim says that the shot works "to demonstrate the power of the mysterious man," while Siegfried Kracauer adds that it clarifies the "relation between Dr. Mabuse and this chaotic world . . . a creature of darkness, devouring the world he overpowers."[18] Or, as Tom Gunning puts it, the "shot expresses all the power Lang places in Mabuse's gaze. [. . .] The camera's movement follows the trajectory of the gaze, giving it an almost ejaculatory power."[19]

One reason we tend to treat the shot as being about Mabuse is that he is looking directly at the camera, so his spell of hypnosis is as much about asserting control over *us*—since we are looking at him, too—as it is about forcing Von Wenck to gamble recklessly. Both Arnheim and Kracauer, for example, emphasize that the shot is directed toward the audience: "Mabuse's face gleams out of the jet-black screen, then, with frightening speed, rushes to the foreground and fills the whole frame, his cruel, strong-willed eyes fastened upon the audience."[20] This is not an effect that can be achieved through the relay of Von Wenck's gaze—as if our identification with him determined our relation to the shot—but rather comes about through the direct encounter between audience and screen, between us and Mabuse.

There is a further twist. Although the fact that the shot is taken from Von Wenck's point of view is not, as I've been arguing, its centrally defining feature, it is also not irrelevant to the ensemble. Both Noël

Burch and Gunning argue that a struggle between viewpoints plays out across *Dr. Mabuse*: the film's narrative arc is defined by which character has control over the logic of the film at any given point.[21] With this tracking shot, however, we have a case in which two characters are simultaneously in possession of this power. While the camera is locked into the perspective of Von Wenck, what it shows is the expression of the gaze of Mabuse; from a different direction, we are looking at the hypnotic power of Mabuse but still recognize that, fictionally speaking, it is Von Wenck who is doing so. We are aware of both at once, albeit in different ways. It's as close as Lang comes in the film to something like genuine ambivalence, a moment of struggle between the characters in which the destiny machine (or fate) hangs in the balance.

While Lang moves away from camera movements in *Die Nibelungen*—part of his effort to create what Kracauer calls "the complete triumph of the ornamental [or monumental design] over the human"—he begins using them again in *Metropolis*, and once more becomes interested in shifting subject/object relations.[22] In a certain sense, this is Lang's central indebtedness to and work within the terms of expressionism, and its interest in the ways in which the objective world can express internal states. Think of the painted backgrounds in *Das Cabinet des Dr. Caligari* (*The Cabinet of Dr. Caligari*, Robert Wiene, 1920), which expose the states of mind of the characters—even the aspects of their own minds that they are themselves unaware of. Or *Von morgens bis mitternachts* (*From Morn to Midnight*, Karlheinz Martin, 1920), in which the pools of darkness and light pull out the hidden tensions and disorientation in the clerk's movement through a set of nightmares and fantastic episodes. Lang's contribution to expressionist aesthetics, I'm suggesting here, comes in the way he allows a tension to emerge in the point-of-view shot, so that how we see is in fact an expression of the inner state of what we see—part of the project one contemporary critic describes as the creation of an "image with its thousand tiny displacements."[23]

Perhaps the purest example of these "object-defined" camera movements comes in *Metropolis* when Rotwang chases Maria through the catacombs, eventually forcing her up into his house, where he will create the robot—the "false Maria"—in her likeness. The sequence begins after Freder and Maria part from each other, and she recovers from her romantic swoon to pick up a candle to guide her way out of the catacombs. Rotwang begins his pursuit by dropping a rock from his hiding place; Lang swiftly cuts from the rock hitting the ground to a medium shot of a startled Maria turning around, eyes wide with terror and framed within an ambiguous black space. She looks around, as if to reassure herself that no one is there, and begins to walk out—only to be brought to a halt by the shadow of Rotwang looming on the wall in front of her. After she enters a new room, with skeletons visible in the distance, a close-up of the candle shows Rotwang's (black-gloved) hand emerging from offscreen space to snuff it out. Lang cuts back to the room, which is now dark, as Maria flees backward. A new round of terror starts as Rotwang begins to play a light across her body and the space around her, illuminating the skeletons in the walls—objects the camera follows by panning with the movement of the light. As Rotwang raises the light up Maria's body, Lang finally cuts to a shot that allows us to recognize Maria's vision of him: the light is at the lower part of the screen, Rotwang's face in close-up behind it.

Maria races off, moving up stairs and through caverns, pursued by Rotwang and trapped each time by the light he shines on her. Lang then introduces two shots that vary this pattern. The first is a long shot, showing Maria in the foreground and a tunnel stretching into the background, though it is blocked at the end. Maria rushes down the tunnel, away from the camera—Rotwang's light is still shining on her from a position behind the camera—and Lang suddenly moves the camera toward her. The movement is calculated, direct, and feels handheld. The camera closes in on her as she comes up against the back wall and then recoils in recognition that her path is blocked.

The second idiosyncratic shot comes shortly afterward. Lang cuts to a medium close-up of Maria pressed against a wall—the camera still seems handheld, moving slightly to keep her roughly in the center of the frame—as her face contorts in terror before she races off screen to the right and up a staircase to an opening above. A new shot shows her entering a cellar, with several doors embedded in the walls. Maria rushes toward them, and Lang cuts to a medium long shot in which the camera pans with her as she tries (and fails) to open each in turn. Eventually, the light returns to frame her in its beam, and then the camera begins to slowly track in toward her, again shaking slightly. As it reaches a medium shot, she turns around to face its gaze, and there is a quick axial cut to a position farther way, showing Rotwang half-emerged from the floor and shining his light on Maria. The scene fades to black.

On an initial pass, the sequence has a feel familiar from horror films. We watch a threatened woman fleeing from a male pursuer, and our point of view by and large accords with that of the pursuer. In these cases, we feel a kind of dominance or power, or perhaps a sense of the helplessness of the victim—our orientation, that is, is with the figure whose point of view we inhabit. And except for the one shot in which we see Rotwang's face over the light, *Metropolis* seems to be doing something similar, confirmed by the camera movements at the end that feel as if we were physically moving through space along with Rotwang. The handheld camera only further secures our connection with the pursuer, serving as a marker of a bodily presence moving through space.

The problem with this way of thinking—and once again, with the assumption that optical point of view secures meaning in and for the film—is that we experience this sequence very differently than that general model would imply. We experience not a feeling of power but one of terror, not of dominance but of fear. Our way of looking at the scene, along with our sympathies, is emphatically with Maria. So how does this happen?

The shift has to do with Lang's use of point of view. Adam Hart has emphasized the prevalence of shots in horror films that delimit the camera to the ostensible point of view of the killer. Yet because we rarely get a reverse-shot, Hart argues, "the only emotional cues we are offered come from the object of the look, with a radical separation between the viewer and the person through whose eyes we are looking."[24] The result is a separation between point of view and identification that allows us to feel for—and *with*—the person who is being threatened even when we are seeing them through the eyes of the attacker. The failure to recognize the distinction that the films themselves elaborate has, Hart argues, "prevent[ed] the genre's critics from exploring the possibilities for sympathy."[25] This failure has also led to an inability to grasp the complex formal patterns that constitute object-defined camera movements.

We can get a handle on why this might be the case by recalling the conceptual distinctions from chapter 3, in which I argued that how we understand what we are shown is centrally determined by style (manner of presentation) rather than perspective, that the way we see the scene is central to our understanding of it, and that point of view is a matter of the form of expression. In this way, we experience the sequence from *Metropolis* as an expression of Maria's fear of (what is to her) an unknown pursuer chasing her through haunted spaces. In a sense, it doesn't even matter that we know Rotwang is pursuing her; the structure of the camera movements is enough to give us a sense of her terror of being alone in the dark and belief that she is being pursued. (This is why it doesn't shake us when we realize that the camera's movement toward Maria in the cellar does not in fact correlate with Rotwang's own movement.) Nor does it matter that we rarely see from her point of view. When Lang employs a handheld camera to track in on Maria, *even though* it reads as being from Rotwang's point of view, it effectively serves to express her fear.[26]

To a large extent, the sequence reads this way because of the narrative context into which Lang places these camera movements. The first indication of the struggle between Rotwang and Maria is when the former drops the brick to startle her. I take it that our identification here is with Maria, with her hearing of the sound, something Lang confirms when the next several shots follow her reactions: her initial startle and fear, her exploration of the uncanny spaces of the catacombs, and so on. This identification carries over into the rest of the sequence, as we see the events colored through the physical enactment of her response. The camera may identify with Rotwang's viewpoint, but this is one place in Lang's oeuvre where seizing control of the enunciatory power of the apparatus doesn't drive the film.

A different scene makes clear the precision of Lang's structure. Maria will be pursued by Rotwang a second time, toward the very end of the film when he has lost his mind and believes her to be the living incarnation of his lost love, Hel. Although the danger is probably more acute, we do not experience the sequence as creating equal terror. To an extent, this has to do with the way Lang films it, part of a generic chase and rescue that serves to demonstrate Freder's heroics and far from the dark and uncanny spaces of the catacombs. But it is also, if not more, due to the fact that Lang introduces the sequence by giving us a sympathetic picture of Rotwang's mental state, his breakdown and insane fantasies. We see the final sequence, that is, less through Maria's terror and more through Rotwang's delusions.[27]

The lesson here is not just that point-of-view shots can provide us with multiple perspectives in a given shot, though that is certainly the case, but that the moving camera creates a different way of experiencing those perspectives. A pair of scenes from Hitchcock gives a sense of this, both of which show women looking at men lost in the grip of describing their own private (and deadly) passions. The first sequence is from *Shadow of a Doubt*, from a dinner after Young Charlie has begun to believe her doubts about her uncle. Asked to give a lecture to Emma's friends, Uncle Charlie agrees and approvingly notes that these (female) friends keep busy and draws a contrast with increasing bitterness: "In the cities, it's different; the cities are full of women, middle-aged widows, husbands dead, husbands who've spent their lives making fortunes, working and working. Then they die and leave their money to their wives." On this last phrase, Hitchcock cuts to Young Charlie, staring intently offscreen to her left at her uncle; a cut brings us to a profile of the right side of his face that appears to be from her position, and the camera starts to slowly track in as he continues: "These silly wives. And what do the wives do, these useless women?" Uncle Charlie continues his harangue against the widows, now gazing vacantly forward, as he continues his misogynistic monologue: "Horrible, faded, fat, greedy women." Throughout this speech, the camera is getting closer to his face, until the top of the frame is just above his eyebrows. Young Charlie's voice suddenly comes in offscreen, frantic: "But they're alive! They're human beings!" Hitchcock, importantly, does not cut here, but stays with the shot as Uncle Charlie slowly turns toward the camera, looking just above and to its left as he responds, "Are they?" A cut goes back to Young Charlie in a medium shot, and the tenor of the sound changes along with the camera distance; the closeness and intensity start to dissipate.

The slow camera movement is vital to the effect of the scene. It moves along the line of Young Charlie's gaze, yet the effect is to draw us in to what Uncle Charlie says, to his perspective. We don't get a sense of her increasing discomfort; rather, we are given confirmation of the power of his voice and personality. The camera's movement, that is, displays *his* power; it gradually draws us in until we are too close for comfort. It is a seduction, in which the camera is putting us in an uncomfortable position, precisely the kind of formal technique that produced so much anxiety on the part of Serge Daney when he thought about "the tracking shot in *Kapo*." The camera seems to make us inhabit a point of view we do not wish to think of ourselves as being able to inhabit. And its power is deep: not even Young Charlie's horrified "They're human beings!"—a reaction we undoubtedly share—breaks the spell.

Like many of the techniques Hitchcock deploys, he revises it in a later film. The parallel here, as William Rothman has observed, is with *Psycho*, where an echo of the relay between niece and uncle occurs in the conversation between Marion Crane and Norman Bates in his parlor. The moment is Norman's aria, which details what he describes as his "private trap."

> You know what I think? I think that we're all in our private traps. Clamped in them. And none of us can ever get out. We scratch and we claw, but only at the air, only at each other. And for all of it, we never budge an inch.

As we are drawn into the rhythm of Norman's words and the fears he speaks, the camera remains static, moving between differently framed shots of Norman and Marion. We are not seduced into unsettling positions by the moving camera. Instead, Hitchcock lets us observe as if we were spectators, as if we were Marion: sitting and watching, and recognizing ourselves (with dawning awareness) in what's being said. Where *Shadow of a Doubt* needs us to bypass our habitual moral compass, Rothman nicely remarks that "Norman pictures entrapment as a universal condition of human existence," and Hitchcock's formal choices seem to suggest that we will find Norman's speech compelling in and of itself.[28] Nothing else is needed to constitute its power.

Lang's interest is different, but we can pick out the seductions of object-defined camera movements when Freder and Maria meet for the first time and his plea for her love plays out across a curious set of shots that articulate a complex series of looks. As Maria moves toward the exit, Freder stretches out his arm in appeal, and she responds by placing her hand over her heart. After several more exchanges of looks, she begins to walk toward him, which we see from his point of view, a shot that tilts down to follow her progression down a staircase. Suddenly, Lang cuts to a shot tracking in toward Freder's upturned face. Clearly it is from Maria's point of view, but what we register is less a reflection of her emotional state than the way that Freder's desire, writ large upon his face, draws her toward him. His emotions capture the attention of both the camera and Maria.

Curiously, these kinds of shots largely disappear from Lang's formal vocabulary over the next several years. As he moves toward a more straightforward "American" style in *Spione* and *Frau im Mond*, no longer working for UFA but for his own collective production company, he increasingly uses editing patterns to specify character relations, and camera movements—especially in the form of reframings and pans— become more frequent. All the same, there are still some moments when this use of point of view recurs. In *Spione*, the initial encounter between Jason and Agent 326 is interrupted by a shot of Haghi in his headquarters, where we see him examining a sheet of paper showing 326's fingerprints and photos. The camera tracks in toward the sheet, an act of enlargement aided by the magnifying glass, then holds on one of the photos. The look of the camera is here pegged to Haghi's vision, but then Lang suddenly cuts from the enlarged photo to 326 and Jason as they (incorrectly) congratulate themselves on having escaped detection. The shot introduces an ambiguity into what we just saw, suggesting that it might have been the imagining by Jason and 326 of what would have happened if they had not been successful. As with *Dr. Mabuse*, rather than promoting one reading over the other, Lang creates a kind of ambivalence: we read the sheet of paper as both Haghi's point of view and the duo's imagining of what Haghi's point of view might be (a point of view they know exists but whose author eludes them, which Lang acknowledges by withholding a view of Haghi's face). This uncertainty will become thematic for a film whose plot revolves around questions of surveillance and the ability to discern the hidden plans of others.

In the work with the dynamics of point of view and camera movement, something of the peculiar power of Lang's films becomes visible. Lang's deployment of character psychology in his silent German films—the relations between Freder and Maria, 326 and Kitty, or even Siegfried and Kriemheld—is not exactly complex and subtle. Unlike the psychological investigations in expressionist or *Kammerspiel* films, Lang readily resorts to familiar types and idealized depictions of love. At the same time, an extraordinarily subtle affinity is created between the mental states of characters and the formal techniques used to portray them.[29] The character psychology Lang creates, as far as it exists, is less a function of anything the characters do or say than of the formal means used to present them to us. Object-defined camera movements are one example of this, as Lang takes up the tendency of narrative film to isolate point of view as the determining factor and subtly works to complicate it. It's a strategy that cuts the relentless structure of design and destiny, a structure closely tied to the enunciatory logic of his films. It's what allows Lang to flesh out a more human world in counterpoint with the films' overarching narrative logic and ornamental visual design.

3.

As Lang's style develops over the course of the 1920s, he goes beyond object-defined camera movements oriented toward another character and begins to use the technique in relation to broader social structures. We see intimations of this in Mabuse's (formal) assertions of control over the forces that attempt to ensnare him. But it really only becomes prominent in *Metropolis*, which breaks with Lang's earlier German films in its use of the moving camera. For the first time—and really for the only time in his silent films—Lang begins to create larger patterns and rhythms out of camera movements in order to develop thematic resonances across a film.

One such example is when Freder comes back from witnessing the explosion in the machine rooms; his father sends Josaphat to get the details and begins to console his son, who wants to tell him about what he saw. They stand, touching one another, and begin to walk toward the camera, which in turns starts to track backward, keeping them in long shot as they move through the vast office. It's a shot of familial intimacy, a son seeking to work through a difficult experience with his father, and Lang's camera responds by moving in concert with them. Of course, their connection will soon be broken by Freder's shock at his father's heartlessness, but this early emotional detail is central for indicating the deep affection between them—reestablished at the film's end—and for giving this particular formal technique a distinct association with intimacy.

The association recurs in Lang's later uses of backward tracking shots. The first instance is when Freder descends with the workers into the catacombs to see Maria. As they enter the large, cavernous chapel, the camera tracks back and moves out into the open space, a camera movement that prepares us for the quasi-romantic, quasi-familial relationship that will soon develop between them. Lang further draws a connection between this type of movement and the idea of familiar intimacy when Freder and Maria rescue the children in the workers' city from drowning. As they walk through the water, each carrying a child in their arms, the camera tracks backward with their movement—as if to transpose the intimacy between the couple to their care of the children, moving from romance to family. Finally, the last appearance of the shot is when Freder, Maria, and Josaphat lead the children to safety. As they climb gingerly out of the staircase, the two men supporting the woman between them, the camera again pulls back with their movement until they pass through a door and the children swarm around them in gratitude. The sense of familial connection established early on between father and son has now been fully transferred to the relation between son and the people—adults, children—he's drawn around him. A new kind of family has been created (he is the mediator, after all).

Although Lang does not employ such patterned uses of camera movement in either *Spione* or *Frau im Mond*, he returns to it with a vengeance in *M*. When Elsie Beckmann leaves school on her fatal walk, she is bouncing a ball in front of her, moving to the right; the camera follows from the street, showing her in profile and keeping her roughly centered in the frame. Eventually, she walks up to a kiosk and begins bouncing her ball against a sign stating the reward for catching the murderer, the camera tracking in to show the details. It's a gesture that summons up

Beckert, or at least his shadow and voice, as he bends into the frame and greets her. And it's here that point of view returns to the dynamics of Lang's use of camera movement.

The connection between the camera and Beckert, the sense that we are in the position of the murderer looking at a potential victim, recurs each time Lang shows a child who may be in danger. Take the brief comedic moment when we realize that a beggar, despite the sign proclaiming blindness that he wears around his neck, is not actually blind. As he looks out, Lang cuts to a tracking shot of a man—he has roughly the silhouette of Beckert—walking arm and arm with a child. Although formally couched as an eyeline match, the shot is not directly from the beggar's point of view; the camera is already moving to the left, parallel to the duo, and is clearly positioned in the middle of the street. It ends as a false alarm, the man embracing the child at the door of a school. Several minutes later, however, we see Beckert become fascinated with the image of a girl reflected in a shop window—both he and the girl are framed by ornamental patterns of knives—and begin to pursue her. Again, Lang positions the camera in the street, moving to the right as the girl strolls down the street and around a corner. This time, we hear Beckert's whistling growing loud and insistent before the tension is again deflated when the girl runs forward to greet her mother. They walk back to the left, the camera retracing its movements, and we see Beckert hurriedly moving into an alcove to avoid being seen.

Several things are worth emphasizing here. First, a clear, if fairly schematic, pattern is built across these three scenes. It's not just that the camera moves parallel to the girls in these incidents; Lang gives meaning to directions, associating a rightward movement—Elsie, the first part of the last example—with danger and a leftward movement—the father and child going to school, the last movement with the mother—with safety. I don't think there's a larger significance beyond the way Lang builds associations across the film. It's something that lets the final encounter with the child—when Beckert himself will be marked—stand out from the others. That encounter is shot largely in static frames, but the first camera movement there is an astonishing circular track from the girl picking up the fallen knife around Beckert's back to see the chalk "M" imprinted there. The uniqueness of the shot marks this encounter as qualitatively different than his "usual" activities. Second, Lang is once again working with the aesthetic and dramatic possibilities of point of view. While a general sense of menace is associated with shots from the street, the final example heightens the tension through the whistling: the combination of sound and image makes us feel that we (along with the camera) inhabit the position of the murderer, so it comes as something of a surprise to see Beckert duck into the alcove as the child and her mother go by. But we can also see here a shift in Lang's treatment of point of view from *Dr. Mabuse* and *Metropolis*. While he is still interested in playing with the conventions of point of view, he now uses *sound* to help orient us, a tendency most visible when the beggar holds his hands up to his ears to cover the music—at which point we, too, can no longer hear it—but also evident in the way images are frequently driven by, or act in concert with, words being spoken.

The third point about camera movement has to do with stylistic tendencies. Take the scene when Beckert enters a café right after his foiled attempt to kill the girl. The camera tracks in toward a hedge that forms a barrier between us and him, and we watch him order two cognacs and try to keep the mad whistling out of his head; when he gets up to leave, the camera pulls back toward the framing with which the shot began. Gunning rightly notes that this shot "emphasizes both the surreptitious nature of the camera . . . its spy-like nature, and Beckert's furtive nature, his hide-and-seek game with the camera."[30] But what's also important is Lang's use of camera movement to do this, his willingness to change the position of the camera so as to create a dynamic interaction with Beckert's state of mind. The prevalence of camera movement is a new feature of his style, part of the gulf that separates *M* from his silent films.

This shift in Lang's career is unique, and I know of no other director whose camera is so clearly liberated by the coming of sound. It's no longer controversial to point out that, after a brief hiccup, many filmmakers retained the extravagant use of movement across the historical divide marked by the emergence of synchronized sound recording. But no one else sees the coming of sound as an occasion to unchain the camera.[31] Despite the cumbersome sound equipment, and despite the general stylistic trends of the period, Lang's cinema becomes strikingly mobile, more open in its use of camera movements—and more open to different kinds of movement as well. The first sequence of *Das Testament des Dr. Mabuse* dramatizes this. Starting with a black screen, Lang introduces the pounding sound of machinery; he then cuts to a machine shop, the camera moving fluidly through the space. The camera passes by tools, lamps, and spare parts before moving toward a wall and tilting down to reveal Hoffmeister hiding behind a crate, seeking to avoid discovery. What stands out here is not just the sense of being in the midst of drama but also the way that the moving camera is given equal

weight to the sound: both are treated as means for exploring and revealing space and action.[32]

I describe this kind of camera movement as "open" to designate both
the formal inventiveness of Lang's camera movements *and* the way they
complicate (at least once we start paying attention to them) underlying
assumptions about his style. In the latter case, this has to do with what
Leo Braudy termed Lang's "closed" style, in which "the frame of the
screen totally defines the world inside as a picture frame does. . . . The
closed film's definition of its inner space is therefore geometrical and
architectural."[33] What I am marking as Lang's "open" use of camera
movements, as in the opening of *Testament* but more thoroughly present in *M*, creates a tension with this system of geometrical frames. It
introduces a lived perspective—and a more open sense of space—that
shifts the dramatic and existential tension of the films.

We can see both "open" and "closed" styles in the most famous camera movement in *M*, the stunning shot that moves through the beggars'
hall. The shot begins with a close-up of hands counting out the stub ends
of cigars and cigarettes, then begins to track across the space to show
various activities: a man wondering whether to smoke part of a cigar;
other men counting out pieces of sausage and cheese; still others playing
cards or drinking. The camera continues onward, moving through a gap
in curtains toward a bar area where a proprietor is eating sausage and
tabulating the cost of various foods on a board that resembles prices in
the stock market (as in *Dr. Mabuse der Spieler*). The camera moves up to
a wall, where it briefly pauses to execute a hidden cut (the blank surface
obscures it), then continues upward to show a window with various
people lined up inside. It briefly pulls back to reframe, then tracks in
toward the glass, a pane of which (almost) imperceptibly slides open
to allow the camera to "magically" pass into the room and continue to
move around—showing the beggars getting their orders from Schrenker.

By flaunting his virtuosity with the moving camera, Lang seems to
be doing two things. First, he is explicitly trying to beat Murnau at his
own game, to outdo two famous shots from the beginning of *Der letzte
Mann*.[34] One is when the camera moves down with an elevator, goes
through the hotel lobby, and eventually exits the revolving doors to
show the doorman at work on the street. The other is when the doorman
is being demoted, and the camera lingers outside the glass doors of the
office to observe the dejection registered by his back before slowly moving toward the door, executing a dissolve and arriving inside the room
to be witness to the scene. Lang may not have responded to Murnau's

film (and the technical challenge it laid out) at the time, but here, after the other filmmaker's death, he can one-up him once and for all.

Second, Lang is articulating a complex spatial arrangement by using the camera to create a fluid, organic social space comprising a wide range of activities. The geometrical patterns that define so much of Lang's aesthetic are still here, represented by the arrangement of objects in organized series—as well as the narrative content of the scene itself, the organization of the beggars to systematically survey the city—but this principle does not define the informal space of the beggars' hall. Indeed, a tension between schematically organized and humanly inhabited spaces is found throughout much of the film. It is part of what makes M more than an optical survey or study of surveillance, more than a study of the costs of built environments and the urban metropolis, creating a drama between modern transformations and the contingencies of human experience within them.

If we want, we could even divide the film according to the two kinds of spaces. On the one hand, there are the abstract, geometrical spaces: the maps that Schränker and the police use to organize the city, the raid on the office building (and the subsequent photographic record), and so on. On the other, there are the more intimate lived spaces that stand outside such patterns, such as the apartments or the cluttered attic in the building where Beckert hides. In *Metropolis*, Lang also established different kinds of spaces, marking them thematically and visually, but Heaven (the palace of the sons) and Hell (the workers' city) never came together; it's only in a third space, Earth (the city), that they can interact. M, by contrast, repeatedly shows the two kinds of spaces within the same place, so we get a curious dynamic in which the force of the geometrical comes about precisely because it stands against the lived environments, while the poignancy of those spaces emerges in contrast to the omnipresent anonymity that surrounds them. It's no coincidence, I think, that the film culminates in a location that combines both kinds of space, the disrepair of the factory intersecting with the ornamental pattern of the criminals massed in the background—a tension reflected in the intensely personal plea by Beckert counterposed to the impersonal hand of the law that "rescues" him.[35]

Lang often uses camera movements to create these complex spatial articulations, as in the famous opening of the film, which begins by connecting the murderer's actions to the anonymity of urban space. We hear, and only then see, children playing a "ring-around-the-rosie" game, with one girl marked out by the "man in black" and kicked out of the circle. The neutral grey space in which they're playing the game reflects the randomness with which the girl is chosen: nothing about her, no personal features, cause her to be selected, just as nothing about the space tells us anything about its particular history as a place. The scene is filmed from above, emphasizing the spatial arrangement between the children. But as they start the song over again, the camera begins to track forward and to the left, moving across the assembled children and revealing more of the courtyard: a couple of boxes stand against a wall; otherwise the space is empty. The camera (apparently on a crane) now starts to level out, positioning itself at an angle to the wall and tilting upward to bring a balcony into view; a low railing is visible, as well as several clotheslines on which laundry has been left to dry.[36] A woman walks by carrying a basket of clothes; she pauses, walks over to the railing, and yells at the children to stop singing. They do so, and she walks into the building—then, after a moment's pause, the song begins again.

This shot has been extensively discussed for its treatment of sound and urban space, but without noting how the movement of the camera radically transforms a sense of place; the focus has been more, and appropriately, on the function of the frame as a demarcation of space.[37] Initially, the shot is at a static position observing the children—an overhead perspective that will later be occupied by various technologies of surveillance—and appears to keep them contained within the boundaries of the frame and the confines of the courtyard. The camera's movement, however, changes the tenor of the shot. Not only does it open up the space of the scene, providing a new perspective, but it brings into view the pieces of laundry that suggest a more inhabited world. Later in the scene, hanging laundry will acquire a very different valence, as Frau Beckmann's cries of "Elsie!" ring out through empty spaces of the apartment building. But here the pieces of clothing suggest that the space of the courtyard is not as impersonal and anonymous as we initially supposed, that signs of human actions and habituations are present. Or rather, that while the building may be impersonal and anonymous, the actions of the tenants alleviate this, providing what might be described as a sense of home.

The next two shots continue this dynamic. After the children begin singing again, Lang cuts to a shot of a staircase inside the building. No person can initially be seen, although we hear the sound of labored breath; the woman from the previous shot soon struggles into view, climbing the staircase with a full basket of clothes. When she reaches the landing, the camera begins to move, tracking briefly in to a closer view and panning slightly to the right to follow her over to the door. This movement creates a new geometrical composition, with the landing in the center framed by staircases on either side of the frame (going down on the left, up on the right). Frau Beckmann opens the door, and the camera moves quickly toward them and begins reframing to follow their conversation; the balustrade forms a barrier between the women and the camera (and so between the women and us, too), but the angle is no longer exact. Frau Beckmann takes the laundry from the woman, and Lang cuts 180 degrees to the inside of the apartment; she says that the sound of singing is proof that the children are still alive and walks into her own space. As she does so, the camera pans right to follow her movement (we see the other woman shutting the door in the background) and begins to track back, an elegant movement that swiftly puts it into a position at the far end of the apartment. The camera then pans back to the left as she puts down the laundry and goes back to her washing. The room, we see, is not elegantly furnished, but it contains a great deal of stuff: chairs scattered to make work easier, crockery hung on the walls, pots on the stove, even a bottle of wine on the windowsill. There is no anonymous space here, no geometrical symmetry. There is clutter, deep signs marking intimacy and familial habituation.

It might be tempting to speak of Lang as approaching an overtly "open" style here, of the sort that Braudy associates with Jean Renoir, as he moves the camera in ways that actively respond to the lived environment in which people reside—and to their own sense of their world. Throughout the opening sequence of *M*, the camera moves to counterbalance the predominant motif of impersonal spatial organization, emphasizing the sense of a human, bodily presence within the spatial world. But Lang isn't Renoir. And so the sound of the cuckoo clock, a wonderful piece of anachronism within this cluttered space, is immediately followed by a cut to Elsie's school, where we hear the sound of a different clock striking midday. The abstract sense of time, the world organized according to impersonal criteria, intrudes once again and shatters—this time forever—the home of Frau Beckmann's apartment.[38]

Lang is not really an explorer of lived space, and much of the power of his films comes in their architectural designs and motifs of destiny, whether mechanical or supernatural. What I've been trying to show, though, is that the films are not based on these impersonal principles alone. Lang's films have dramatic and psychological power precisely because they stage a conflict between different kinds of spaces, hence different ways of inhabiting the world. If the films tend to resolve them-

FIGURE 9. *M* (Fritz Lang, 1931). Different expressions of space.

selves in favor of the geometrical and architectural (a pattern that, outside *Die Nibelungen*, is figured as urban and modern), they do so against a more fluid spatial construction. Rotwang's house in the middle of the city, Frau Beckmann's apartment in the middle of the courtyard: these are older, cluttered spaces that reside with the growth of modernity around them, and whose contingency—the ease with which their sanctity can be, or has been, destroyed—forms part of their poignancy.

A final example. In the stunning sequence in which Beckert is being tracked by the beggars, he finds himself caught up in the relay of whistles and trapped by a web of pursuers. Fleeing them, he winds up on an empty street in front of an office building, which Lang shows from overhead in an extreme long shot; he further brings out the schematic pattern of the space by letting the shot remain empty of human presence for a brief moment at its outset. Beckert enters, hurrying along the sidewalk. Noticing a man following him, he rushes across the street— only to see two other men enter at the top of the frame, blocking off that route of escape. The trio position themselves in a triangle around Beckert, who stands, isolated and alone, looking back and forth (see figure 9). This is Lang in his full geometrical glory, the empty urban setting containing precise human movements, the frame closing off the space around the characters. But then Lang does something extraordinary, cutting to a ground-level shot in front of Beckert that eliminates our sight of the pursuers and shows a courtyard behind him. We are now, suddenly, fully attuned with Beckert. As he whirls around to run toward the open space, the camera itself begins to hurry after him in a handheld shot, eventually framing him as he hides behind a pillar. It implicates us, precisely by identifying the camera with his pursuers; we can no longer observe from outside the action but are thoroughly enmeshed within it.

It's hard to imagine two adjacent shots that depict space, and the way we inhabit it, more differently, and I think Lang juxtaposes them with this intent. The spaces are not resolved in one direction so much as allowed to stand next to one another, letting their full contrasts interact: the peculiarly cluttered attic in the midst of the rationally organized building. This principle, I've tried to show, holds true for M as a whole, and for Lang's German films more generally. Thus, for all the shots that detail an urban modernity, trapping characters through their spatial grids, there are also shots like this handheld movement towards Beckert as he runs for safety, the physical presence of the camera conveyed through its instability. The shot expresses not only the aggression of his pursuers but also Beckert's fear and his sense of the collapse of a world that, however dangerous, was organized in such a way that he could remain anonymous; it has now become fully embodied and terrifyingly human.[39] The final part of the film is Lang's great attempt to reckon with this tension and our own place within the changing social world.

4.

I said at the outset of this chapter that the pair of filmmakers I bring together here—Fritz Lang and Guru Dutt—have little historical grounding to connect them. There is more than that. The type of film Dutt made, a familiar Hindi form that mixes melodrama with song sequences, was unknown to Lang—whose musical sequences are confined to You and Me (1938) and whose own engagement with India during the time of Dutt's career is represented by the orientalist fantasies of Tiger of Eschnapur (1959) and The Indian Tomb (1959).[40] Yet we find in Dutt's work the same formal device I isolated in Lang's films: the camera positioned at one character's optical point of view but expressing another character's state of mind, an interplay that creates a complex and dynamic sense of the psychological forces at work in a given scene. Dutt, of course, has his own uses for this technique, largely seeing in it a way to create a connection between individual and collective (or social) points of view that enables a fluctuation of identification on the part of the film audience. It is a formal project that serves as the grounds for a way of articulating a dissatisfaction or frustration with the Nehruvian state, the responsibilities of the people (the masses), and the burdens of the artist.

The film I focus on here—*Pyaasa* (Thirst, 1957)—articulates a tension between a condition of anomie within the postcolonial state and the poet's desire for a revolutionary romanticism that would transform the world.[41] It does so through an emphasis on the intersection of the individual and the family, and the relation of love and money—all of which is familiar to the history of melodrama, and to Dutt as well. As Darius Cooper remarks, "In his capable hands, melodrama became a revealing and critical genre through which the contradictions and deceptions of the middle-class or proletarian Indian aspiring towards bourgeois stability could be depicted, explored, commented upon, and critiqued."[42] What's unusual, however, is the way *Pyaasa* achieves its broader aims through the combination of point of view and the moving camera, a connection situated at the intersection of aesthetics and politics.

In analyzing the intersection of formal technique and political ambition in Dutt's film, I focus primarily on the song sequences.[43] There is a long-standing question in studying musical films, whether Indian or American: Should the emphasis be on the plot, the structure that frames the musical sequences, or rather on the musical numbers themselves? Richard Dyer's famous argument about the utopian potential of the genre, for example, focuses on the way the song numbers create a *feeling* of utopia—not a picture of the actual world but "what utopia would feel like rather than how it would be organized."[44] The emphasis on feeling displaces politics from narrative, moving instead toward the experience of the audience watching the film. Building off Dyer's argument, and discussing Indian cinema of the 1950s, Rochona Majumdar argues that Hindi films often used song sequences to explicitly create the image of a nation. She notes the autonomy of the "song text" from the rest of the film—an autonomy that persists into more contemporary Bollywood cinema—and shows how political allegories are constructed within them.[45] Existing in a different temporal register than the rest of the film, the 1950s Hindi film created fantasmatic accounts of what it was to be Indian. Discussing one of the archetypal song sequences from the period, "*mera joota hai japani*" (my shoes are Japanese) from *Shree 420* (*Mr. 420*; Raj Kapoor, 1955), Majumdar writes that it shows that

> the quality of being Indian is an agglomeration—sometimes absurd and comic in its self presentation—of varied elements, none complete in and of themselves, but adding up to something that constitutes a fulsome or plenitudinous present. They echo the spirit of India's first prime-minister Jawaharlal Nehru when he wrote "It was India's way in the past ... to welcome and absorb other cultures."[46]

This is a historically situated utopia, a fantasy of a national identity not founded on essential national characteristics but on a cosmopolitan ideal.

It's against this background of (cinematic) debates over nation and national identity that *Pyaasa* takes shape, a moment in which historical trauma is still apparent, and the hope for a new nation is fraught and fragile.[47] I argue that much of Dutt's work to unsettle the ambitions of the Nehruvian state takes place in the song sequences, in which the moving camera plays a complex game with how audience engages with the film's world.

Despite the importance of the song numbers, it's worth spending time on narrative; the plot is intricate, but it furnishes the ground against which the formal technique gains force. *Pyaasa* begins with Vijay—played by Dutt himself—an impoverished poet who is estranged (somewhat voluntarily) from his family, hoping to publish his poetry but finding his efforts rejected and his poems sold for scrap paper. Sleeping on a bench one night, he hears a prostitute named Gulab singing a song of seduction that is in fact one of his discarded poems. Following her, he discovers that she has his collection of poems, but she—incensed that he is not a paying customer—throws him out.

Soon thereafter, he catches sight of his college love, Meena, and an extended flashback shows us their relationship in hyperbolically romanticized terms. Dutt then fills out the present, especially through a key scene of comic relief from the masseur, Sattar, who, like Gulab, uses Vijay's poetry as a means to attract customers. Meanwhile, Vijay is convinced to attend a college reunion, where he recites a melancholy poem about difficult times and induces an emotional response from Meena. He is noticed by Mr. Ghosh, a publisher, who invites him to his office. But rather than publishing his poems, Ghosh puts Vijay to work, where he again meets Meena and has another flashback, this time to the moment of their separation (a memory that itself includes a dream sequence).

Ghosh asks Vijay to help with a party at his house, and there Vijay discovers that Meena is married to Ghosh. During the party, poets discuss the question of whether poetry must serve the cause of the nation or be an autonomous art devoted to love and other fine things. Vijay recites his own poem, producing another response in Meena—this time noticed by Ghosh. When Meena subsequently accuses Vijay of awakening her desire for him, he displays indifference, saying that she has always been selfish; Ghosh overhears her declaration of love—"Wonderful! My wife is no better than a streetwalker!"—sends Vijay out, and strikes

Meena. Meanwhile, Gulab remains smitten by Vijay, gazing after him but unable to approach.

The turning point in the plot comes when Vijay catches sight of his brothers performing mourning rituals. He learns from them that his mother has died, and they disavow him. Despondent, Vijay drinks with friends that evening and accompanies them to an erotic dance. Vijay notices that the dancer's baby is crying, but his friends refuse to let the dancer stop to tend to her child. Shaken, he stumbles into the street, where he sings about the corruption of the modern Indian state and the politicians who turn a blind eye to the prostitution of young women: "Where are those who claim to be proud of this land?" Drunk and in despair, he runs into Gulab, who takes him in and gives him a bed. Vijay wakes up while she sleeps and leaves; he gives his coat to a beggar, then walks through a rail yard looking at the oncoming trains. The beggar, following him, catches his foot in the tracks and, despite Vijay's efforts, is run over by a train.

Because the beggar was wearing Vijay's clothes, which contained a piece of his writing, everyone assumes that the mutilated body is Vijay's, and that he committed suicide. Distraught, Gulab goes to Ghosh's office to get Vijay's poetry published, where she meets Meena and refuses payment for the manuscript. Vijay's poems are a hit, selling out and earning a fortune for Ghosh. Vijay's friends and relations, having previously scorned him, show up to claim the profits.

Vijay, of course, is alive, but he is in shock at the death he witnessed and unable to speak or respond to the world. He comes out of it when he hears a nurse reciting his poetry, but the doctors believe him to be an impersonator, and he is sent to an asylum. Visiting him there, Ghosh and Vijay's friend deny his identity so that they can continue to profit from his death. Sattar, the masseur, eventually helps him escape, and Vijay attends a celebration marking the anniversary of his death. Bursting in, he sings his rejection of worldly affairs and the corruptness of a society that refuses the living only to venerate the dead. Now the people who denied him wish to embrace him. Vijay refuses fame—"The Vijay you wish to welcome, the Vijay for whom you shout slogans. . . . I am not that Vijay"—and flees. He goes to Gulab's house, where he asks her to accompany him to a place far from this world. They walk away from the camera into an amorphous distance.

Critics have taken several different tacks in approaching the film. It has been described as a national allegory of the Nehruvian state; a social melodrama and a form of critique (focused especially on prostitution); an allegory of Dutt's own life; and, most frequently, a drama of renunciation and refusal, the stance of the poet who rejects the corrupt world in which he lives.[48] None of these readings are entirely mistaken or incompatible, but *Pyaasa* is hard to pin down, as it is built out of a series of misleading generic structures. We might be inclined, for example, to classify the film under the rubric of the maternal melodrama and the logic of sacrifice. But if the elements are there—not least in the mother's death—*Pyaasa* does not follow through: at the beginning of the film Vijay has already left home; his mother does not sacrifice anything more for him. And we are missing the "maternal voice" that Lucy Fischer has argued is a structuring presence of the genre.[49] Other patterns emerge and fade away. It seems that the narrative is driven by Vijay pining after his lost love, and the repeated flashbacks suggest this—but he also repeatedly rejects Meena in the present and seems fairly indifferent to her presence (except for the memories she evokes). The narrative might be the story of a prostitute with a heart of gold, in which we wait for Vijay to realize Gulab's virtues and to fall in love, yet he remains sexually uninterested even to the end of the film. Perhaps more than anything, the film seems to be a social melodrama, concerned with the plight of the downtrodden, and moody in a way that resembles French poetic realism or Sadao Yamanaka's *Kōchiyama Sōshun* (*Priest of Darkness*, 1936), using a focus on prostitution to indict a system and to incite a desire for reform. But Vijay, having duly done both things, simply leaves, judging the world to be unredeemable. He resides in the mode of renunciation, giving up family, society, and worldly fame—everything— on the grounds that they do not live up to his vision of what the world ought to be.

Even at the end, it's hard to determine the terms on which Vijay's renunciation is made. Most readings of the film rely on narrative and dialogue—Nasreen Kabir, for example, notes that "the film's lyrics . . . are the essence of *Pyaasa*"—and as a result they miss the aspects that give the film its power.[50] These are the peculiarities and care that Dutt takes with form, especially the strange things he does with point of view.[51]

The centrality of point of view to *Pyaasa* is established in its first shots. Following a pan across a pond, we see Vijay asleep under a tree. A flower falls and wakes him up; he begins to sing about the world around him. This sequence is edited simply, according to a basic template of point-of-view construction: we see Vijay look, and then see what he sees. What we hear are his thoughts on, or response to, these sights. So after the flower falls on him, he sings, "These smiling flowers, this fragrant garden."[52] There is then a series of shots alternating between Vijay and nature—trees, clouds, and birds—"This world dipped in color and light." And then, finally, a series of close-ups of flowers, some of which have bees in them: "Drinking the nectar of the flowers, the bees sway." The mood here is languorous, even subdued, the drowsiness of the poet allowing for an almost Romantic appreciation of the natural world around him, inspired by its beauties. But all is not simply pastoral: as a bee flies off, landing in the grass, a man's shoe comes down and crushes it. "What can I give to you, O splendid Nature"—Vijay gets up and walks away—"All that I have is a few tears, a few sighs."

Although this abrupt ending invokes a familiar allegory of beauty being crushed by the indifferent modern world, we begin to gain a sense of how Vijay's poetry works. Rather than reciting mythical or canonical stories, he responds to the world that surrounds him with extemporaneous compositions. Yet the sequence as a whole has a more subtle and far-reaching effect. It works to establish and solidify our attachment to Vijay's point of view: we see what he sees, and our view of the world is matched by his lyrics. The result is a confluence of visual and aural perspectives that promises to orient us as we move through the film's world.[53]

Again, we have an assumption that the apparatus of the cinema—the relation of camera to world, of audience to screen—is organized around characters looking: Vijay looks at the world, and we see what he looks at. It's a construction that recurs throughout the opening scenes of *Pyaasa*. When Vijay first sees Gulab, for example, Dutt intercuts between his movement to get a better view and her own seductive attempts to get him to follow. (Later in the film, Gulab will be given her own point of view when she trails Vijay through the streets to find him on the roof of a building.) The achievements of *Pyaasa* are based on the initial establishment of this underlying model, as the film will work to unsettle the system it invokes.

In the film's movement away from straightforward models of identification, Dutt implicitly joins an alternate tradition of talking about point of view, one that restricts the strong form of character-based focalization. Kracauer, for example, describes a process of polymorphous identification that takes place at the cinema, where we turn into everything we see: "How could [we] resist these metamorphoses?" We are everywhere; we are nowhere—a life, as Kracauer puts it, "that belongs to no one."[54] Indeed, it is the work of the film to express these positions and to allow us to inhabit them while being presented the scene by the

FIGURE 10. *Pyaasa* (Guru Dutt, 1957). The camera's attunement to Vijay.

camera. As I argued in chapter 3, we are able to occupy other kinds of positions, other modes of orientation within and toward the world. Dutt will situate our viewing position at the intersection between two ways of negotiating point of view: a highly individualized, psychologically based mode of identification and a way of inhabiting the world of the film that resists such specification.[55]

The revision of point-of-view structures in *Pyaasa* is developed through an extensive motif of forward and backward moving tracking shots. An early example occurs during the reunion scene, when the destitute Vijay is called upon to sing for the wealthy assembled guests. As he is being pulled to the microphone, he looks out at the crowd and is visibly startled: his gaze becomes fixed, and the camera tracks in to him, moving from a medium shot to a close-up. Without pause, there is an almost 180-degree cut to show Meena, who lowers her program to look back as the camera also tracks in on her (though at a slower pace). A set of static shots secures the connection, ensuring that we grasp that they are looking at one another. A different rhythm begins as Vijay starts to recite: "I am weary of this troubled life, weary of this troubled existence." His words seem to push the camera back from its proximity to his face, slowly drawing back and, as it were, out into the world (see figure 10). As he continues, "The weariness of my heart may spurn the world," there is a cut to a shot of Meena, taken from a new angle—hence not the shot/reverse-shot pattern that was built up—in which the camera tracks slowly toward her. This is the literalization of a metaphor: his words strike her.

Alternations continue across the scene. An audience member challenges Vijay, asking how he can sing such a sad song on a happy occasion, and Vijay, as if responding directly to him, sings: "How can I sing of joy if I live in pain?"; the camera tracks in to him: "I can return to this life only what it has given to me." Dutt is building up a pattern: the camera moves in to Vijay when he sings about himself and his condition and outward from him when he sings about his past love (for Meena). The pattern changes, though, when Vijay announces his rejection of his desire: "Today I break all belief in the illusion of hope." As he sings these words, the camera rushes back from his face and then cuts exactly 180 degrees to a correspondingly swift track in to Meena, who is visibly struggling to control her own emotions. Another 180-degree cut moves back to Vijay, and the camera tracks in to his face as he vows "never shall I voice a complaint again" for the misery in which he currently finds himself.

Dutt is using the moving camera here to situate the viewer within the world of the film. Because of the relays of looks, moreover, we become attuned to the interior states of the characters—the use of close-ups secures that sense—and we are able to read the camera movement, the movement toward a character, as expressive of their subjectivity and point of view. In the first movement toward Meena, for example, the introduction of a musical phrase on a harmonica, a motif the film associates with the memory of her time with Vijay, cues us to the content of her thoughts.[56] What's crucial, though, is that the camera movements do not read as subjective shots, even when they are each ostensibly from the point of view of Vijay or Meena. As with the examples from Lang's *Dr. Mabuse*, these shots express the psychological state of the person they show. *Pyaasa* will continue to deploy this structure in key scenes of poetic expression.

The full expression of Dutt's use of point-of-view and axial tracking shots to convey psychological interiority and interpersonal relations comes in the song sequence after Vijay has been asked by Ghosh to serve guests at a party. The dinner conversation involves a debate over whether poetry should be political, whether it must be directed at the project of nation building. In the midst of this, Vijay moves away from the group and begins to sing, providing Dutt's answer to that debate:

Who are those fortunate to love and be loved in return?
When I asked for flowers, I was given a garland of thorns.
Who are those fortunate to love and be loved in return?

When I search for happiness
A forlorn, dusty path lay before me.
When I sought songs of desire, I heard frozen sighs.
Those who consoled me redoubled my heart's burdens.
When I asked for flowers, I was given a garland of thorns.
Who are those fortunate to love and be loved in return? [. . .]

If this is called living, then I'll live somehow.
I'll not complain, seal my lips and swallow my tears.
Why let sorrow worry me, familiar as it is?
When I asked for flowers, I was given a garland of thorns.
Who are those fortunate to love and be loved in return?

Vijay is proposing a fusion of the perspectives in the debate, creating a love song that has a social meaning as well: only those who are fortunate, who have means and social status, are able to enjoy love. Vijay cuts through the condescension of the older poets—one of whom remarks to Ghosh, "Even your servants are poets . . . go on, young man"—to silence the assembled audience with the power of his words.

Beyond the lyricism of Vijay's poetry, it is the camera that responds to and creates the emotional dynamics of the scene. It begins close to Vijay, who stands fixed in the corner of the room with his outstretched arms resting on the bookcases to each side—the first of what will become a series of Christ-like poses in the film.[57] As he begins to sing, the camera moves backward, again enacting the power of Vijay's words as they move out into the world, literalizing their public effect. The next shot flips 180 degrees around, and the camera begins to track through the room of people turned to look at Vijay, moving toward Meena, a pairing of shots that implies not only that the two are looking at one another but that Vijay's words are, in effect, hitting their target. (Throughout the song, Meena is increasingly overcome by emotion, eventually removing herself from the room.) Then Dutt provides a third term to complement this pairing of gazes: a shot of Ghosh turning to look at Meena. This shot also employs a forward track, but without the sense that the camera is at the position of someone looking at him. That is, as we move toward Ghosh, the effect is solely to express his increasing focus and attention and his dawning realization about the effect Vijay has on Meena. Ghosh is the unnoticed observer and provides us with a viewing position outside the dyad.

Dutt is drawing on the pattern he established in the reunion scene, using the three types of shots to articulate relations between the characters. Sometimes the camera moves out from Vijay; sometimes it moves in toward him. Sometimes Dutt pulls back to use a horizontal tracking shot to display the social dynamics of the room, with everyone remaining caught by Vijay's words. At some points, the pattern shifts, and a shot moving away from Meena is followed by one moving in toward Vijay, as if her desire were being thrown out to him. But each time the song returns to Vijay's claim of rejected love—"When I asked for flowers, I was given a garland of thorns / Who are those fortunate to love and be loved in return?"—the camera returns to the initial pattern that shows the effects of his words on Meena. Charged with leaving him because of his lack of money, she sinks down into a chair to absorb the impact of the words and her own emotions. She eventually leaves, leaving the chair rocking behind her; Ghosh's suspicions are thoroughly roused. The song ends.

With the party scene, the love plot of *Pyaasa* essentially concludes. There are still some minor things to work out, but we get no further sequence of comparable formal intensity between Meena and Vijay. What starts to matter instead is Vijay's increasing social awareness, and this takes the form of a new use of point of view. In the party scene, the moving camera positions us so that we are always looking at the world *as if* we were seeing it from the point of view of a single person within it.[58] Even when Vijay is singing to the group of assembled poets, the fiction established by the linked axial tracking shots is that his words are for Meena alone—or, more precisely, that her response is the one that matters, the one to which we are attuned. In the last part of the film, however, Dutt begins to build alternate structures. This search for an alternative to the individuality of the position of the camera, especially of the moving camera, marks the film's cinematic achievement. It is also a shift that enables Dutt to fully transition to the political.

The major change happens after Vijay learns of his mother's death. Drunk, and recognizing that the friends he is with care more about their own erotic gratification than about a mother's need to care for her sick child, Vijay despairs. In the midst of this, Dutt gives us two shots that are explicitly of Vijay's optical point of view: the first of his drunken stupor, with spinning spirals and other effects, the second of tears that blur the camera's lens. He exits the space and begins to walk through the streets, looking at the scenes of desperation around him. Vijay then begins to sing perhaps the most celebrated song of the film:

> These lanes, these houses of auctioned pleasure
> These ravaged caravans of life.
> Where are the guardians of dignity?
> Where are they who claim to be proud of India?
> Where are they? Where are they? Where are they?
>
> These twisting lanes, this infamous market
> These anonymous men, this clinking of coins
> This trading of chastity, this insistent haggling.
> Where are they who claim to be proud of India?
> Where are they? Where are they? Where are they?

The politics expressed by the song are far from the utopian optimism of the immediate postindependence moment. Indeed, if we pair this song with the college scenes of Vijay with Meena, we get a nice account of how the film's moods are pegged to different historical and political moments.[59] We might also note that Dutt is fairly vague about what caused this despair—unlike, for example, the way Ritwik Ghatak's more overtly political *Meghe Dhaka Tara* (*The Cloud-Capped Star*, 1960) is explicit about the effects of Partition and the gendered politics of civil society—and therefore also ambiguous about what might help produce a better life.[60] This is the expression of what we might call Vijay's postcolonial anomie.[61] As the heroic struggles of independence end and the more mundane work of nation building begins, a recognition of the vast divergence between ideal and reality sets in (Hannah Arendt famously argued that such a process happens to all revolutions). This awareness, especially among intellectuals in the postcolonial state, leads to a sense of norms breaking down and a loss of order in the world. There is an uncertainty about what has happened, or how to fix it, and it results in a form of political paralysis.

Such a mode of anomie runs through much of *Pyaasa* and underlies Vijay's fairly aimless wanderings (another form in which neorealism enters this period of Indian cinema). Vijay is distraught over the world, but with little sense of how to act. Toward the end of this key song, though, something changes. Continuing the refrain—"Where are they who claim to be proud of India?"—he now directly addresses the camera. Three stanzas are sung in this mode, and in the final one Dutt moves the camera in toward Vijay as he sings. The effect is startling. We are familiar with the tracking shot along an axial line toward the character, but for the first time there is no one within the world of the film to whom he is singing: the audience is not Meena, not anybody on the streets—it is us. We are being asked to do something.

> Summon the leaders of this land
> Show them these alleys, these lanes, this sight.
> Summon those who claim to be proud of India.
> Where are they who claim to be proud of India?
> Where are they? Where are they? Where are they?

In this moment, Dutt moves the logic of point of view and camera movement, so carefully built up across the film, in a new direction. The point of view is no longer that of the single individual: it is the collective "we" who are looking at Vijay, being addressed by him, and through the interplay of word and image being reaffirmed precisely as a "we."[62]

Here Dutt is working through one of the deep problems of political cinema: how to use the terms of film grammar, so deeply pegged to individual states of mind, to represent a general point of view. Sergei Eisenstein diagnosed this problem in his famous essay on Dickens and Griffith, noting how the solutions to American narratives relied on conceptions of the capacity of individual actions to alter political situations. His advice was to reject individualized point of view in favor of the creation of a film theory and practice that allowed for the expression of the point of view of the masses.[63] This involved a challenge to Hollywood models, and Eisenstein's success in articulating an alternative can be measured by Robert Warshow's criticism of his films as anti-humanist on the grounds that they deemphasize the perspective (and rights) of the individual.[64] We can also see the tension in the epilogue of *Battle of Algiers* (Gillo Pontecorvo, 1966), which uses a wall of sound—the undifferentiated amalgam of human voices—to represent the general will of the Algerian people. If the main body of the film is focused on the careful plotting by leaders of the FLN, Pontecorvo shows the new uprising as an expression of general will.[65] But it's no easy thing, and *Battle of Algiers* ends by picking out individuals from the crowd whose actions are made to stand in for the whole.

It's not a unique problem, even in mainstream cinema. Keating notes the difficulties that Hollywood filmmakers had "tell[ing] stories about the masses" during the Great Depression and argues that they sometimes used camera movement to frame the actions of characters against a wider economic frame.[66] But as Keating argues, this representation of the general happens by evacuating the personal, the domain of point of view, in favor of a depiction of numbers, a mode of abstract and overwhelming seriality. What Dutt achieves is, by contrast, a tension between Vijay's personal point of view and the point of view of the general—the collective, the multitude—in order to move the film into explicitly political topics.

Vijay comes back from the dead, positioned as even more Christ-like than before—he has, after all, also been denied by his friends—and interrupts a celebration of his poetry in which the people who rejected him now take his name in vain. As he hears Ghosh say, "If I could have saved Vijay, I would have given my fortune—and my life!" and then blame the assembled crowd for not buying his poetry, Vijay sinks down and begins to sing:

> This world of palaces, of thrones, of crowns
> This world of division, enemy of man
> This world of blind custom, hungry for wealth
> Would I care if such a world were mine?
>
> Bodies wounded, souls thirsting
> Confusion in eyes, despondency in hearts
> Is this a world or a place of bewilderment?
> Would I care if such a world were mine?

We quickly see the effect his words have on the audience, how they turn away from the stage to observe and listen to his song. But again, beneath the words is Dutt's favored formal pattern of camera movement, as the camera alternates shots between those tracking away from Vijay and those tracking toward other characters, conveying the force of his words and the responses they elicit: terror, desire, adoration, hope, and so on. Viewers are thus made to inhabit multiple *individual* positions, able to test out different ways of responding to Vijay's reappearance.

Dutt now ratchets up the intensity. After Vijay catalogs the commercial decadence of the world, recounting its ills and evils and calling for it to be fixed, Ghosh's collaborators grab him and try to push him out of the auditorium. The song then shifts, and Vijay sings:

> Burn this world, blow it asunder.
> Burn it; burn it.
> Burn this world, blow it asunder.
> Take this world away from my sight.
> Take charge of this world, it's yours.
> What would I care if such a world were mine?

As he sings, the camera performs an extraordinary gesture, rising up and away so that we can see Vijay struggling with an undifferentiated mass of humanity that swarms around him (see figure 11).

Dutt is putting us in a strange position. Even in the midst of Vijay's despair over prostitution, his excoriation of the world for letting this go on without caring, we were still able to evade blame. After all, Vijay is indicting those who only profess to love India—in other words, the politicians but not us. But now we're in a theater, a space that is fairly clearly an allegory for the cinema, for where we are. And the movement of the camera makes no distinctions between types of people. Vijay rejects the world and *everyone* in it. It does not live up to his criteria; he wants no part of it. No one escapes his condemnation; no one lives up to his demands.

FIGURE 11. *Pyaasa* (Guru Dutt, 1957). The camera moves from individual to crowd.

Dutt wants to be sure that we comprehend the difficulties of the position into which we are being put. So *Pyaasa* will return to the theater one more time, when Vijay is asked to affirm his identity as the author of his poetry and (presumably) gain influence over the mass of people. As his family and friends who previously denounced him line up to affirm his identity as "the great poet Vijay," we hear the song of denunciation from the previous theater scene softly playing as nondiegetic music. But Vijay refuses to play the game: "The Vijay you wish to welcome so warmly, the Vijay for whom you shout slogans. . . . I am not that Vijay. I am not Vijay." The audience reacts with anger, furious at having been (apparently) deceived; they riot, storming the stage with chairs in hand, looking to harm Vijay and the people they blame for their disillusionment. As Sattar rushes to save him, the song rises up in volume: "Burn this world, blow it asunder. Burn it! Burn it!" Sattar rescues Vijay from being attacked by the masses, and as we see Meena pressed back by the crowd, we hear again the lyrics of renunciation: "Take this world away from my sight; / The world belongs to you; / You keep it." The camera follows from behind as Sattar pushes Vijay out through swinging doors, but we are not able to go through; we are within the crowd, looking to get through.

The position we are placed in is disturbing. We may believe that we want to see Vijay succeed for noble motives, because we care for him—not because of his fame, or even his poetry, but because of our recognition of his person. We have, after all, cared for him over the past two hours. But Dutt keeps insisting, by way of the movement and position of the camera, that we are in—and no better than—the crowd trying to get at him. (When someone finally breaks through the doors, bringing us with them, it is Meena; this is not the person with whom we want to identify.) We are the mob, and the mob is us.[67]

Vijay's response is to follow through on his threat. Leaving Meena in the theater, he goes to Gulab's house, where she is recovering from serious injuries sustained in the first riot in the theater. He summons her to his side, and together they leave. They turn their backs on the audience, the world, and move into a vague and undefined distance, a sound stage suffused with fog. This is not, in any way, an ending that concerns politics. Vijay does not propose a five-point plan, much less a five-year plan. He does not call for concrete reforms, whether of living conditions, unemployment, or even the treatment of prostitutes. He does not think about using wealth that he might gain from the sale of his poems to transform the slums. (We know, cinematically, what such a transformation might look like; the end of Chaplin's *Easy Street* [1917] is an early example, in which the final shots show the slum dwellers transformed as if by magic into nascent bourgeoisie.) This kind of political uncertainty was apparently emphasized by Dutt; the screenwriter recalled, "I believed that Vijay should not leave and go away in the last scene of the film, but that he should stay and fight the system."[68] But Dutt has Vijay choose to leave—and so to leave everyone to their fate.

Vijay's motives are unclear. It's not his separation from his family that drives him to reject the world; that separation seems (more or less) voluntary. It's not his lack of employment; that's how the film starts, and it never leads him to radical gestures. Nor is it a problem of love; he no longer loves Meena—his poems are dedicated only to his *memory* of her—and never seems sexually attracted to Gulab, so that even their departure together is based not on reciprocal desire but on its renunciation.[69] It's not his recognition of the existence of absolute poverty and exploitation; he's depressed by that, but intends to keep going all the same. It's not even the commercialization of his poetry; we know that he composed advertising jingles for Sattar, and he believes his poems should have real monetary value.[70] What really gets him, it seems, is that his poems are successful *but in the wrong way*, and that people appreciate him *but in the wrong way*. If we are part of the crowd, part of those rejoicing in the success of his poems—simply because of their success—that is why we are left behind as well. This is the romanticism of his revolutionary gesture: the world must accord with his desires or be refused entirely.

Yet even within this narcissistic framework, the film gives us reason to be more charitable to Vijay's gesture of refusal. When he is locked in the asylum, he is visited by Ghosh and Shyam, an old friend. Vijay is immediately roused from despondency, calling out Shyam's name; the camera, following its usual pattern, tracks away from Vijay as if to mark the effect of his words, to bring them into the world and gain recognition from his friend. But Shyam and Ghosh are there to deny his identity, condemning Vijay to stay in the asylum—as far as he knows, for the rest of his life. Again, Dutt uses forward tracking shots to express the inner state of a character. When Vijay's identity is denied, the camera closes in on him—and effectively slams him behind the cell-like doors. This is the first time in the film that Vijay's words have not served his aims. And what the camera records is the failure of the fantasy his words enact: the idea of the face-to-face encounter and of the transformation

that can be affected in that mode. With that self/other connection elimi-
nated, Vijay is firmly thrown onto the relation between individual and
general, and when that fails, there is nothing else to which he can turn.
Absent a world that can accord with or sustain his desires, there is little
for him to salvage in this new land, this still-new country in which he
finds himself.

CHAPTER 5

Max Ophuls and the Limits of Virtuosity

Although never really a prominent motif in the history of film theory, the connection between camera movement and ethics surfaces at various moments. I argued in chapter 2 that the link was especially strong during the *nouvelle vague* period in France, when the intersection of the moving camera and the spectator's (ethical) relation to the world caused anxiety over our capacity to judge what was happening without being fully trapped by it. In this chapter, I take up a different way of attending to the curious but persistent intuition that camera movements are in some way deeply, perhaps inextricably, interwoven with concerns of ethics—that, as Jean-Luc Godard put it, "tracking shots are matters of morality."[1] In particular, I argue that the extended, virtuosic camera movements in the films of Max Ophuls present a way to work through how issues that camera movements raise about point of view might bear on matters of ethics.

Ophuls may seem like a curious choice to address this topic. He has long been considered one of the great filmmakers: Andrew Sarris placed him in the critical "pantheon" of directors; Robin Wood labeled him one of the cinema's premier stylists; Godard saw him as a luminary in the history of cinema, on a par with D. W. Griffith. And yet despite this praise—and often contained within it—a suspicion of formalism has attended Ophuls's career, a sense that he was *too* absorbed in the sweeping camera movements that permeate his films.[2] His camera movements have often seemed—to audiences, to studio executives, to critics—to be "mere virtuosity," a judgment that is then frequently extended to the films themselves. As Stephen Heath pithily (and rhetorically) asked in 1978, "Is an interest in 'the work of Max Ophuls' today anything more than academic?"[3]

When critics have argued that Ophuls's films do take up ethical concerns, this has generally involved discussions of themes associated with desire and its frustration, in particular the organization of gender roles in a stratified social world. Alternately, attention has been paid to the models of exchange and circulation that run through his work, the intimations of an economic system that underlies the movement and actions of characters.[4] Both approaches, however, struggle to incorporate the virtuosic camera movements, at most seeing them as bearing the excess of emotion that the characters are unable to express—considerations familiar to melodrama. In other words, critics have found it hard to bring aesthetic and ethical considerations together when talking about Ophuls's use of camera movements.[5]

To a certain extent, this difficulty is connected to long-standing debates about the relation between aesthetic form and ethics, debates that have taken place across various media (especially literature).[6] But film presents its own difficulties in this area, and these bear on the challenges Ophuls's films pose. Part of the challenge has to do with film's unique formal features—camera movements are certainly among them—but it also involves two critical traditions within film studies. On the one hand, there is a tendency to focus on characters as the source of ethical value, seeing in them exemplary models of action (both positive and negative). Criticism then involves the application of familiar modes of reasoning, analysis, and judgment to characters.[7] This problem is by no means unique to film, but it is exacerbated there: not only do audiences see persons on-screen as fully embodied individuals—they are *there*—but the formal devices employed by classical Hollywood cinema (in particular) are oriented by attention to and attunement with characters. Form makes itself invisible so as to better draw us into story and characters. On the other hand, where formal devices are more explicitly in view, they are often treated as having a built-in and absolute ethical significance. This has ranged from Sergei Eisenstein's argument that parallel editing in Griffith necessarily expresses a capitalist morality, to André Bazin's discussions of the moral agency attending the long take, to Jean-Louis Baudry's claim that the very apparatus of cinema imposes the terms of a bourgeois ideology on spectators.[8] I think both traditions, seemingly opposed to one another, reflect a shared problem: they isolate one side of the equation as the primary bearer of ethical content. Something is being missed, and Ophuls's use of camera movements helps us see what that might be.

Ophuls's camera movements, I argue, bring aesthetics and ethics together in a compelling, if unusual, way, as he uses them to create a complex—and morally complicated—engagement with the worlds of his films. Two features of his films are central to my argument. The prominence of camera movements is one; the second involves what we might describe as the conditions for autonomy and the way they are shown to be absent or lost. This feature requires more effort to discern, but once recognized, it follows contours that are relatively familiar to ethical thought. The power of Ophuls's films lies in the way the two features work off and with one another.

The particular kind of relation this entails, which takes shape between camera movements and the world of a film, is bound up with the nature of the ethical concerns that structure Ophuls's films. Rather than focusing on the role of action or the vagaries of moral psychology, Ophuls creates worlds in which the very possibility for moral action is limited, constrained, even absent; he shows worlds defined by forms of ethical failure. My argument is that the ethical work of the films is done through—their ethical content is expressed by—a specific kind of camera movement, one that responds to *both* the states of mind of characters *and* the social world they inhabit. (It does not, that is, create a straightforward identification with characters.) I call this structure "dual attunement," and it enables Ophuls's camera to articulate the nature of the moral claims and demands that characters make but that are missed or denied by the world they inhabit.[9] In the case of *Madame de . . . (The Earrings of Madame de . . .*, 1953), the film I focus on in this chapter, the camera movements provide a moral perspective on the film's world that the characters themselves are unable to take.

All of this is, to be sure, both abstract and programmatic. To get beyond it, to show that Ophuls's films confirm the intuition that camera movements can involve matters of ethics, we need to engage the details of the films themselves. It takes patient, fine-grained, and descriptive analysis—a kind of attention that, surprisingly, is rarely given to Ophuls—to see how the camera movements do the work I am claiming for them. In the process, I court some rather obvious form/content problems, but I argue at the end that we shouldn't be too worried about that.

2.

Just about everyone who comes to watch Ophuls's films notices that they are filled with extravagant and extended tracking shots. They are almost impossible to avoid: his stylistic signature, so to speak. Lutz Bacher has meticulously detailed the fights Ophuls had with studio executives in Hollywood over them, the terms of which are captured in a short poem (or perhaps doggerel) written by James Mason on the set of *Caught* (1949):

> I think I know the reason why
> Producers tend to make him cry.
> Inevitably they demand
> Some stationary set-ups, and
> A shot that does not call for tracks
> Is agony for poor dear Max
> Who, separated from his dolly,
> Is wrapped in deepest melancholy.
> Once, when they took away his crane,
> I thought he'd never smile again.[10]

But if it's obvious that camera movements are important for Ophuls, it is surprisingly difficult to grasp *how* they work.

In narrative cinema, camera movements tend to show new things, revealing aspects of a scene that have hitherto remained hidden. They can also follow a character's movement. Or they can take a character's point of view and so indicate their perspective or subjective state. These three uses can of course go together.

Many of the camera movements in Ophuls's films operate in one of these ways, but there is a class of camera movement that does something different—and it's these camera movements that present difficulties. A shot from late in *Letter from an Unknown Woman* (1948) can serve as an initial example. At this point in the film, Lisa Berndle (Joan Fontaine) is married to a military officer (Marcel Journet) but has a child fathered years ago by Stefan Brand (Louis Jordan), a womanizing pianist she has loved since childhood but who is unaware of his parenthood. The shot opens a momentous scene at the opera, when Lisa will reencounter Stefan and find that her carefully constructed life starts to crumble around her.

Ophuls has emphasized the stability of the life Lisa has created in the previous scene, when she instructs her son to call her husband "father" rather than "sir." There is a dissolve from the child's bedroom to a shot of a poster for *Die Zauberflöte* (*The Magic Flute*) on a pillar in the middle of a foyer in the opera house, and we hear the sounds of an orchestra warming up. The camera begins to track to the right, picking up a middle-aged couple as they walk out from behind the pillar and move across the foyer. The camera follows them until they disappear behind a group of people, then latches onto two women and an elderly man in military uniform walking to the left (the opposite direction). As the camera comes to a position behind them, two younger officers begin to walk to the right, and it reverses direction again to follow them back across the foyer, where they begin to ascend one of the two main staircases. As they do so, two women descend that staircase, moving to the left, and the camera shifts its position, rising up slightly to create a downward angle on them.

Throughout these fluid movements, starting when the camera leaves its position behind the pillar, Lisa has been speaking in voice-over. She says, "The course of our lives can be changed by such little things. So many passing by, each intent on his own problems. So many faces, that one might easily have been lost. I know now: Nothing happens by chance. Every moment is measured; every step is counted." As she says, "I know now," the camera circles behind and tracks with the two women as they walk down the staircase, across the foyer, and up the *other* staircase.[11] As they leave the shot, Lisa's voice-over stops and the sound of the orchestra rises in volume. The camera comes to a brief pause for the first time, waiting in place to frame Lisa and her husband as they walk into view from behind the staircase and begin to ascend it.

The camera now rises up and to the right to stay level with them, moving parallel to the rising banister. As Lisa and her husband near the top, caught up in their own (inaudible) conversation, we hear the voice of a woman offscreen: "Look, isn't that Stefan Brand?" The camera reaches the level of the second floor and begins to move backward, panning slightly to the right as it does so to reveal a cluster of people looking over a railing into the foyer below (a hallway is in the background, leading presumably to the seats). Lisa passes behind them, her head turning as she apparently hears the comment; slowly, she walks over and looks down. Ophuls now introduces a cut for the first time since the sequence began over a minute earlier, and a brief shot/reverse-shot pattern shows Lisa looking at Stefan, who is greeting two women on the staircase below. Ophuls inserts three shots (of Stefan, of Lisa, and of Stefan again) to give us a sense of the effect of her recognition of Stefan and her dismay as she hears the people around her discuss the dissipation of his musical talent into romantic pursuits. Ophuls then returns to the original shot, picking up where it left off, with the camera still moving slightly back and to the right. As the group around Lisa disperses, the empty space they clear out reveals her husband looking at her from a middle distance in the hallway behind her. He says, "Lisa!" and holds out his hand, and they walk back toward their seats. A man's voice says, "Second act! Curtain going up!," confirming that a dramatic shift has just taken place in the film. The camera ends the scene by tracking slowly to the right, passing behind an ornate candelabra, and then moving slightly upward to show the couple walking into the background; Lisa turns back once, then they disappear, and the opera begins again.[12]

It's an extraordinary, virtuosic shot—but it's not at all evident how we should understand the various movements of the camera. A first pass would simply be to say that the extended tracking shot emphasizes the drama of Stefan's reentrance into Lisa's life, the combination of the movement of couples and the movement of the camera creating a rhythmic structure that adds to the intensity. Taking the interpretation a step further, we might note that the camera seems to mirror Lisa's voice-over description of a metaphysics of fate. As we hear her words, the camera "performs" them: it moves back and forth across the foyer of the opera house, picking out random couples and fragments of conversations ("so many faces"), before settling on Lisa and her husband as they begin to ascend the staircase. The camera appears bound to the terms of Lisa's enunciative authority.

Several aspects of the shot, however, suggest a different account. The first is that we see more than Lisa's point of view, more than the things she notices. After she recognizes Stefan and we *feel* her absorption in his presence, the camera moves back to show her husband looking on with some consternation. This brief movement of the camera steps away from Lisa's perspective to emphasize the world in which it is embedded, to remind the viewer of the social obligations she has (the family we saw in the previous scene). The second aspect involves the voice over. Ophuls has a tendency—I return to this later on—to have a character ascribe encounters to fate or destiny even as he shows them to be the result of normal social interactions.[13] Is it so unlikely that Lisa would see Stefan again, given that they live in the same city and attend concerts? (Zweig's novella is explicit that she has seen him at several concerts in the intervening years.) Third, and most importantly, it's not at all clear that the camera's movements actually do reflect the terms of Lisa's statement. We could easily say that the camera demonstrates not fate but the chance by which someone is picked out of a crowd, the contingency of discovery.[14] Yet that goes too far; in a sense, the camera knows where to find Lisa, already knows where she's going to appear. If it's not an example of a metaphysics of fate, neither is it the revelation of chance. The camera may be buffeted and swept along by the tumult of society, but it acts and moves based on privileged knowledge about Lisa and her husband.[15]

My point is not that the camera fails to identify with Lisa's point of view but that such a reading is, on its own, incomplete. If the camera suggests the contours of her state of mind—how she understands the situation—it also stands outside her subjective position, incorporating it into a larger perspective. This is the formal structure I'm calling "dual attunement," a camera movement that takes account of the subjective states of characters while at the same time revealing their place within a social world—something they seem unable to see or acknowledge.[16]

Along with camera movement, I want to call attention to the second feature I described as important to Ophuls's films. Again and again, Ophuls shows characters who lose autonomy, which we can think of here in a fairly minimal sense as the ability to decide their own actions and to will their own ends. It might be tempting to rephrase this in weaker terms as having to do more simply with agency and so avoid the stronger claims about the nature of action, will, and desire that the idea of autonomy brings with it. But which account we give matters less than recognizing the diagnosis Ophuls provides, the way he shows the loss of autonomy (or agency) to be the result of supraindividual constraints.[17]

This feature appears in various guises across Ophuls's films. It's in *Caught* (1949), where Leonora's desires are shaped and defined from the outset by images of consumer culture; in *La signora di tutti* (1934), where Gaby is imprisoned within the social apparatus that produces her as a desirable star; in *The Reckless Moment* (1949), where Lucia is trapped by the ideology and material clutter of domesticity; in *Letter from an Unknown Woman*, where Lisa is locked within her own memory and self-deception; in *La ronde* (1950), where the prostitute in the opening sequence is hauntingly caught up in the logic of circulation (represented by the carousel); and, most shockingly, in *Lola Montès* (1955), which ends with Lola literally caged by the weight of her past— or rather, by the public perception of that past. We can also discern this feature behind the changes Ophuls makes to the novels and stories he adapts. In three adaptations set in the fin-de-siècle era, he repeat- edly takes characters who are civilians in the original text and makes them into military officers.[18] In *Liebelei* (1933), Fritz and Theo are changed from students into cavalry lieutenants, while the "Gentleman" of the Schnitzler novella becomes a baron; in *Letter from an Unknown Woman*, the second part is altered to transform Lisa from a successful courtesan into the wife of a military officer; and in *Madame de . . .*, the husband is no longer a businessman but a general.[19] In each case, the modification moves the action of the film into a sphere of society that functions according to rigid and regimented conventions. Much of the tragedy that occurs in these films results from the constraints society imposes on action.

This feature of Ophuls's work is important to keep in sight. There is a temptation to think of his films as following a familiar form of melodrama in which a female character is oppressed, mistreated, or manipulated by a male character (usually her husband). George Cukor's *Gaslight* (1944) is a characteristic example of this, and Ophuls's penchant for showing the harm done by male figures of authority in their domestic relationships might be evidence for such a reading. Yet there is a key and telling difference: in Ophuls's films, it is rarely the case that individuals have an explicitly malignant presence or bear sole responsibility for the harm done to others. Even though male characters in his films cause harm to others, and frequently do so in explicitly gendered ways, they are often shown to be themselves caught up in a web of unhappy outcomes, doomed to actions they neither desire nor will; they are part of, and shaped by, the larger structures that create the problems in the first place.

This distinction reveals an important aspect of the nature of autonomy and its absence in Ophuls's films. The threat to individuals, and to their autonomy, originates with sources that are supraindividual in nature: society, culture, and politics. The characters are caught up in a set of rules and practices that explicitly prescribe their possible modes of behavior, deliberation, or action. It is the rules and practices themselves that are dangerous. In Ophuls's films, individuals, especially women, repeatedly desire to break out of the structures that enclose them, yet prove unable to do so. The reasons for this failure lie in the rigid social order above and beyond the characters, but they also have to do with the way characters have internalized its norms. The failures Ophuls shows involve a world that does not equip individuals with the resources that would allow them to incorporate and work with new facts and values, to successfully negotiate the challenges they face. These resources would be emotional, deliberative, creative . . . an open-ended list of practical capacities that the films show in action—or, more frequently, not in action—at various points in their narratives.

The two general features of Ophuls's films that I've been describing are bound up with one another; the camera movements that exhibit a "dual attunement" structure take on ethical significance—in a sense, they gain ethical content—in relation to the problem of autonomy. They work by providing a moral perspective on the world the film shows, a perspective the characters are themselves unable to achieve or even to recognize as a possibility. These camera movements, the central "aesthetic form" of the films, give a sense of the shape of the ethical demands raised by the characters, demands we would want a world to meet—but such a responsive world may not be possible.

To get at the way this dynamic functions, I'm going to work through several scenes from Ophuls's penultimate film, *Madame de. . . .* My goal is to show how Ophuls uses camera movements to negotiate a problem that emerges from within the world of the film, to provide a perspective that characters within it lack. Doing this, I think, will not only tell us something important about the stakes of Ophuls's style but also provide a way to productively think about the relation between aesthetics and ethics in film—and the work of camera movement in bringing them together.

3.

The plot of *Madame de . . .* has few participants but is fairly convoluted in its entanglements. The film begins when Louise—the last name of the family is never provided—sells a pair of heart-shaped diamond earrings in order to pay a debt, earrings that originally were a wedding present from her husband, André. In order to disguise what she has done, Louise pretends to lose the earrings during a trip to the opera. When the loss is made public, the jeweler she sold them to rushes to see André, tells him what happened, and sells the earrings back to him. André subsequently gives them to Lola, his mistress, whom he is sending away to Constantinople, where she loses them in a flurry of gambling.

A new series of events begins when Baron Fabrizio Donati, an Italian diplomat, buys the earrings while on his way to Paris. There he meets Louise and, while André is away on military activities, they fall in love as dancing partners over the course of a series of balls. André, on his return, suggests that Louise leave Paris to hide her increasingly noticeable passion; right before her departure, Donati unexpectedly visits and

presents her with the earrings as a gift. On Louise's return from a pro-
longed absence, she and Donati admit their love, the sign of which is her
decision to wear the earrings in public. To disguise the fact of the gift,
she tells André that she found them in a pair of old gloves, something
which he of course knows to be untrue (though she does not know this).

A crisis occurs when André confronts Donati, informing him about
the history of the earrings and instructing him—as a way of warding off
scandal and embarrassment—to sell them to the jeweler. Donati rejects
Louise, apparently for having lied to him about this history, and she
falls ill from despair. In the meantime, André again buys the earrings
back from the jeweler and orders Louise to present them as a gift to
his niece. The niece also sells them to the jeweler, but this time André
refuses to buy them back; Louise, in turn, sells all her possessions in
order to get the earrings for herself. Out of a combination of anger and
helplessness, André challenges Donati to a duel. Louise, unable to prevent André from killing Donati, collapses and dies.[20] The film ends with
a shot of the earrings, now resting as a memorial in a church.

The overall structure of the plot may be familiar—it follows a template
already established in *La Princesse de Clèves*—but the film is an exquisite catalog of the intricate forms of lies, love, deception, and anguish.
My concern, however, is with the specific work done by Ophuls's camera, and this already takes shape in the opening moments of the film.

Madame de ... begins in a peculiar manner, with two title cards
announcing that there almost was no story to be told, hence no film to
be made. Louise, the first card tells us, "was a very elegant, brilliant, and
celebrated woman. She seemed destined to a life without *histoire*"—the
word means both "story" and "history"—and that, according to the
second card, "probably" nothing would have happened to disturb that
state, to create a narrative, were it not for "this jewel."[21] The deictic
"this" gestures toward the image that is to follow, the first shot of the
film; it signals that the objects we're about to see are central to the very
possibility of narrative.[22]

A fade from the title cards brings us to a close-up of a jewel box. A
gloved hand enters from the rear and left of the frame, pulling open a
drawer to reveal a pair of beautiful earrings. The hand reaches for them,
hesitates, then drops down: a woman's voice says, "If only they weren't
the ones he gave me the morning after our wedding [*le lendemain
de notre marriage*]." The camera follows the hand as it moves across
various objects while the woman asks, almost absent-mindedly, "What
should I do?" She begins to hum along with the tune being played in the

film, which until then had seemed explicitly nondiegetic. As the camera begins to pan and track to the right with her movements, passing by several closets and cupboards, we finally get a sense—first as a shadow, then as a profile, then as a reflection in a mirror—of the person engaged in this activity. For much of the next two minutes, the camera remains over her right shoulder as she reaches into the frame to examine one object, then another.

In a certain sense, the action in the shot is simple. We see an unidentified character—we assume she is "Madame de . . ."—looking to sell some of her possessions in order to pay off a debt of twenty thousand francs.[23] But she's having trouble deciding what to sell; having already turned away from the earrings, she looks to her dresses, then to her furs. She accidentally knocks over a Bible on the top shelf, gasps, and says, "I've never needed it so much," but this is not exactly a religious epiphany, as she immediately wonders which hat will best suit her for the task she has to accomplish. Still humming along with the (nondiegetic) music, she walks back to the table and sits down, at which point we see her face for the first time, reflected in a mirror on the table. She puts a hat on and pulls down its veil, and the camera draws back to show a full profile of her in medium shot as she considers other jewelry—a necklace, a cross—before deciding, with a sigh, to sell the earrings. "I like these the least," she says, and then reasons: "After all, they're mine; I can do with them as I please." She holds them up to her ears to examine herself in the mirror, gives a brief exclamation of satisfaction, and then packs them into a handbag. The camera follows her as she gets up, closes the doors to a closet, gathers up several items, and goes out the door.

Ophuls's camera achieves a complex position within the scene. In *Caught*, Leonora's perusing of images of goods begins over the credits with a point-of-view shot of images from fashion magazines; this is followed by an over-the-shoulder shot of her and her roommate looking through them. In neither shot do we see the women's faces, yet we are still moved into their perspective. *Madame de . . .* clearly follows a similar pattern, but aims at a different result.[24] While the camera doesn't create a strict identification with Louise's point of view, it is carefully linked to her movements, following her across the room to track her activities and deliberations. More generally, it is for the most part responsive to her state of mind and attention, an affinity emphasized by Ophuls's wonderful use of music: Louise hums along with the apparently nondiegetic melody that's playing, filling in the gaps it leaves, and the music in turn starts to respond to her. It's as if she were attuned to the formal logic of the film itself. Yet Ophuls is careful to keep a degree of distance and separation, always remaining slightly apart; he never actually creates a genuine point-of-view shot. The camera is thus introduced as an agent that is neither wholly bound up with characters in the film nor exactly indifferent to their perspective. It is, from the start, dually attuned, responsive to social situations as well as to the states of mind of characters.[25]

Ophuls is here following, yet also departing from, a standard type of shot that engages the perspective of a character. As Gilberto Perez observes, it is by no means unusual to have a camera movement pay attention simultaneously to a character and to their surroundings.[26] Yet Ophuls is insistent that the environment that surrounds Louise, that shapes the form of her action, is not just physical but social and moral as well, and the camera is used to give specificity to those aspects of the world.

The shot tells us two main things about Louise and her world. The first is that she is wealthy, or at least is in a position of wealth. This wealth does not make money irrelevant to her (or to the film), but it tells us that the way money matters here is not shaped by real necessity.[27] The hesitation she experiences is thus not one of cost—she clearly has many items that would cover the debt—but of *value*: the different kinds of value invested in her possessions and the difficulty of weighing them against one another. Three kinds of value seem involved. The first is monetary, the simple question of what her various possessions will sell for. The second is social, the relation of the objects to socially defined needs: the value of the furs as a form of conspicuous consumption, or of the earrings as a marriage gift from her husband. The third is a little trickier, because less frequently discussed in these contexts; it might be called "sentimental" value, arising out of an individual's particular desire (whether based on aesthetic or personal grounds) for the object. "I'd rather die than do without it," Louise says of her necklace.[28]

Internal to this account is the idea that final value is neither absolute nor inherent in the object, but rather the result of a specific, individual judgment (or valuation). Even where extrapersonal factors are involved, the extent to which they matter is a function of Louise's appraisal of their respective merits. In her situation, the monetary value is obviously the first consideration; the dresses, with which she would gladly part, will not do because their sale will not bring in enough money. And so she is left to decide between the value of the other objects she has, eventually concluding that the social value of the wedding present—more specifically, a present given the morning after, as if for the consummation of their marriage—is less than the sentimental value of the necklace and cross. It's a judgment.

The second thing we learn from the opening shot has to do with Louise's deliberations. Ophuls gives us an externalization of her process of valuation, a monologue of sorts that allows us to understand *how* she judges the value of her possessions. We get, in this, a sense of her position within a broader social world, of the conventions that delineate, but do not strictly define, the terms of her deliberation, and of the forms of "subjective justification" she uses in deciding how and why she should act. We also see where justification slides into rationalization; when she says, "After all, they're mine. I can do with them as I please," it feels disingenuous. Ophuls thus presents a general picture of Louise's "deliberative field": the range of factors, both moral and nonmoral, that go into the process of deciding a course of action.[29]

In conjunction with the opening title cards, these lessons lead into the two main interpretations of the film. The first emphasizes the circulation of the earrings, the way that Louise's actions—and ultimately, her unhappy fate—seem to be a by-product of their movement. Throughout the film, characters make use of the earrings for what they believe will be a singular act, a sale or a gift. Each time, however, the earrings become caught up in a system of transfers that returns them to circulation, to new acts of giving and exchange. From this perspective, the film offers a critique of the possibility of human agency, showing a world in which human actions are subordinate to the larger patterns of social, economic, and even erotic exchange.[30]

The second interpretation follows a more humanist line. It emphasizes the way that Louise looks at the earrings in the opening scene primarily in terms of their economic value, downplaying their significance as a gift, which carries with it obligations. The narrative of the film then tells a familiar kind of story. When Louise meets Donati and falls in love with him, she apparently experiences romantic love for the first time. She becomes a better person. She gains, that is, a more genuine or authentic character, and this change is expressed by an ability to properly see and value the earrings as a gift from a lover. The film, in short, is the story of her "spiritual odyssey."[31]

While I do not think either interpretation is right, what interests me is an assumption they share: that Louise makes a *mistake* when she decides to sell the earrings. Either she is ignorant of the nature of the economic system and the vagaries of exchange, or she improperly judges the value of the earrings. In both cases, she fails to see that the earrings in some way embody her marriage (a category mistake of sorts), and that selling them is therefore akin to dissolving that arrangement.[32]

It's not hard to see why this assumption is made. If Louise never sold the earrings in the first place, Donati would not have been able to give them to her, and perhaps their affair would not have reached the end it did. But if it is true that the sale eventually leads to tragedy, it does not thereby follow that Louise was mistaken in her decision. (Hegel observes that, because we cannot foresee all the effects of our actions, consequences cannot be the basis for moral responsibility.[33]) It's crucial for my understanding of *Madame de . . .*, and of Ophuls's ambitions more generally, that we understand Louise's decision differently. I think we can.

It is, first of all, simply incorrect to say that Louise fails to see the earrings as symbolic of her commitment to André. When she says, in the film's opening lines, "If only he hadn't give them to me," the implication is that, were it otherwise, she would have been perfectly free to sell them, because only then would they have had solely monetary or sentimental value. She hesitates to sell the earrings precisely because she is aware of their social value, despite the fact that she isn't terribly fond of them. Indeed, it is her initial recognition of the earrings as a gift—something that carries with it certain obligations—that prompts her to see if a better option can be found. Nor is it the case, as it is also tempting to think, that her sale of the earrings amounts to a rejection of her marriage. As Louise explains to her maid, and later to the jeweler, if she can manufacture a reasonably convincing account of their absence the marriage will not be harmed. She winds up telling André that they must have fallen off on the way to the opera.

· And her judgment proves correct. The key here is André, since he does in fact discover the real reason for the sudden "loss" of the earrings. If initially put out, he seems to recognize what Louise has done and why she has done it, and even manages to extract an indirect apology. This comes in an amusing scene in which she pretends to ask forgiveness for having lost the earrings but is in fact asking forgiveness for having sold them, and he pretends to accept her apology for having lost the earrings but in fact is forgiving her for having sold them. By this time, André has not only bought back the jewels himself but has sent them to Constantinople with his (ex-)mistress.[34] And so he gets some pleasure out of Louise's apology by feigning to be hard of hearing and asking her to repeat herself. But there is no indication that he thinks (that she thinks) their marriage has been invalidated, and Ophuls takes some care to indicate that things in their lives go on as before.[35]

I cannot stress this point enough. It means that, rather than making a mistaken judgment of the situation, Louise exhibits a deep skill—a literacy—at working within her social world; she is virtuosic in her ability to manipulate its conventions to resolve various crises, to satisfy her needs. (In fact, both she and André are virtuosic in this regard; his abilities become clear in conversations with various men at the opera, especially in his deflection of a question about his own possible impropriety.) If we recognize this fact about her, it changes how we understand the film. *Madame de . . .* is not a story of Louise's failure to live within a rigidly stratified society; far from it. As long as the challenges she faces arise within the normal functioning of that world, she will be fine. Indeed, she is able to use her virtuosity within this sphere—her knowledge of what counts as acceptable forms of lying and deceit—to create some space outside the parameters of her own marriage: she can flirt, resolve situations without involving her husband, and so on. The problem that derails her, and that defines the film's tragic narrative, involves the introduction of a new fact—a new kind of value, in the form of a claim to happiness—that is outside familiar social conventions and renders inadequate, even dangerous, her virtuosity within them. Louise turns out to be ill-equipped to negotiate the new situations that arise and the demands they place on her.

4.

If we accept this reading of the first part of the film, then Ophuls leaves Louise and André in their enjoyable, if somewhat superficial, marriage, what the opening titles called *"une jolie vie sans histoire."*[36] In that case, the story actually begins when Donati arrives from Constantinople with the earrings in tow. We reencounter the jewels in a close-up inside a suitcase, the camera pulling back to reveal Donati attempting to convince a customs official to delay him so that he can attract the attention of a woman (Louise). Though this attempt fails, he meets her again when their carriages collide in the street. They flirt, but he fails to get her name. What they call "fate" works for them a second time when they are seated next to each other at a party; Donati learns that Louise is André's wife, that everyone thinks he and she were made for each other, that she "torture[s]" her suitors, and that he enjoys dancing with her. Over the course of a series of dances, they fall in love.

It's in this sequence—one of the greatest in any of Ophuls's films—
that we get the most extensive use of dually attuned camera movements
to articulate and express a set of ethical claims. On the one hand, the
sequence displays the social conventions that delimit the acceptable
modes of behavior, along with the forms of justification and action that
can take place within it. On the other, it contains a series of camera
movements that, I argue, suggest the ethical contours of an appropriate response to the new emotional and social situation that arises. The
beauty and power lie in the way they go together.

The sequence is divided into two sections, each of which takes up
one aspect of this dynamic. I work through both in detail here, beginning with the way Ophuls sets out the social world that will provide
the terms out of which the relationship between Louise and Donati will
emerge—and therefore also the terms against which the camera movements in the second section will define themselves.

The first section begins with the third meeting between Louise and
Donati. After the scene in which their carriages collide, there is a dissolve to two hands reaching for name cards laid out on a table; they
have been seated next to each other at a ball. As Donati reads Louise's
name on the card, Ophuls cuts to a shot from behind them, the camera swiveling around the table and pulling back to pick up André
approaching to greet Donati. ("My dear friend, I'm delighted to see
you. I thought you were still in Constantinople.") Ophuls then introduces an astonishing shot: the camera is positioned in front of Louise
and Donati, who sit behind an elegant table, and it remains motionless
for over a minute. Behind them is an extraordinarily large mirror (actually composed out of multiple mirrors), which shows a dance in front
of them, and so behind us; this is society, their world. André remarks,
"I see you've already met my wife; you'll get along very well," and then
walks away. Donati begins to explain to Louise how he knows her husband but is interrupted by a woman who speaks to him in Italian. She
leaves, and Donati explains that "the Marquise" is upset because she
had wanted to introduce them to each other and is planning to throw
a party for them "on Thursday"; he adds, "She says that we're made
for each other." As befits a scene played in front of a mirror, a military
officer now enters from the other side of the frame to speak with Louise in Polish. She tells Donati that "the Colonel" is upset because he
had wanted to introduce them to each other and is planning to throw
a party for them "on Friday"; she adds, "He says that we're made for
each other. Of course."

Much as Lisa and Stefan do in *Letter from an Unknown Woman*, both Louise and Donati attribute their meeting to something they call "fate" or "destiny." And again, we should be suspicious of this attribution. In part, they appear to regard the idea of destiny less seriously than Lisa did in the earlier film; when Louise, at the end of their meeting on the street, says that they should trust fate to bring them together again, Donati replies, running after her, "I'm not so sure." Moreover, the scene presents an even stronger reason to reject the explanation that fate guides their lives: their meeting is *massively* overdetermined by the social world they inhabit. Everyone introduces them to each other: the colonel, the marquise—even André wants them to meet. If they are "fated" to meet, this is only because everyone wants them to.[37]

The reason behind the general desire to bring them together is telling. People say that Louise and Donati are "made for each other," and we might think this means that they share some inner quality, whether it be moral integrity, aesthetic appreciation, or any of the standard virtues. They will, after all, have a "great affair." But that seems misleading; these are not, after all, particularly deep or virtuous characters. It would be more accurate to say that people have in mind the fact that both are incorrigible flirts: they enjoy the pleasures of the erotic encounter but are without depth, hence without the danger of actually falling in love. André himself admits as much when he remarks that Donati will be able to amuse Louise while he is away; Donati is not going to be one of the lovestruck suitors.

Ophuls provides an emblem for this social world in the dance reflected in the mirror behind the table. The dancers we see there are mobile, passing from one partner to another in an endless cycle; they are without history, without depth, without emotion. I take this to be a wonderful bit of play: the mirrors reflect the dance, which in turn reflects the underlying structure of the social world.[38] All is reflection, all is surface, all is play and movement. The dance embodies the socially prescribed form of circulation, the shifting patterns of social life. The fluidity of relations prevents fixity, prevents people from establishing and sealing off a relationship. The dance has its motions, and we soon learn that Louise can play with its patterns, manipulating hopes to provide herself with pleasure.

The growing flirtation between Louise and Donati is interrupted when one of her suitors comes up to ask her for a dance. She leaves, and Ophuls cuts to a shot on the dance floor, where the suitor tries to persuade her to allow him to visit "when the general leaves on maneuvers"—to initiate an affair. Louise responds, "I can't keep you from hoping," and there is a cut to a shot of André and Donati seated at the table; the framing is different, but we can still see the dance reflected in the mirror behind them. André tells Donati that Louise will find him "tremendously entertaining," but warns that "she's an incorrigible flirt." Donati recognizes the method of "torture through hope," says that he has experienced it before, and acknowledges that it's terribly painful. They laugh with some worldly pleasure.

At this moment, Ophuls breaks the formal pattern he has built up, cutting to a shot that shows a part of the room we have not yet seen, the camera panning right to follow a man who is hurrying past dancers and musicians. He rushes up to André and asks, somewhat incongruously, "Is it true what they say?" (He is a journalist.) André tries to brush him away with a "no," and then a "yes" to a following inquiry about whether they are talking about the same thing. During this exchange, Donati has been looking out at the dancers; he now gets up, despite André's request to stay, and the journalist sits down in his place to talk about "the peace conference."

It is a familiar kind of dance that Donati intends to join when he rises from the table. But it is not the dance he and Louise have. It's as if the shot of the man hurrying along the edge of the room—the intrusion that gives Donati the excuse to get up—breaks the rhythm of the scene and so enables a different kind of dancing to begin. It initiates a series of dances in which Louise and Donati will fall in love while dancing, even because they are dancing. Several formal shifts mark the change: the quick tempo of the music becomes a less rigid, more expressive melody; the style of dance shifts from back-and-forth movements to a slow, clockwise circling; and the camera itself begins a counterclockwise circling. These features work together to create a kind of figure/ground reversal within the frame: Louise and Donati remain still while the background moves around them. They are dancing a dance within a dance; there is no intimation that partners will be changed, or that the particular identity of the partner does not matter. The dancers are no longer fungible. Taken together, these features suggest that the dance effectively isolates Louise and Donati from their surroundings.

The film thus codes the process of falling in love as an increasing removal from the circulatory movement of society.[39] "They're always together," the admiral's wife says in the third dance; "they're always the last to leave," remarks one of the musicians in the final shot. Later in the film, after they have admitted their love for one another, Donati scrawls his name across all the dances on Louise's card: "All the dances . . . Donati!" It's a gesture that undoes the social mechanism that encourages circulation, replacing flirtation with love. And it's the fact that they thereby fall outside the sanctioned form of behavior and emotion that drives the complications of the rest of the plot, eventually resulting in their deaths at the end of the film.

It's in the relationship between Louise and Donati that the ethical stakes of the film become evident. Put succinctly, these stakes involve a claim to happiness. It's not that Louise wasn't happy before—Ophuls shows the pleasure she takes in life with André—but the film suggests that there is something different in her relationship with Donati. It offers a new and better form of happiness, or at least she feels that it does, and the ethical demand she implicitly makes is that this happiness ought to be allowed to exist. To be sure, the content of her understanding of and desire for happiness is not especially unique, mixed as it is with a fairly conventional idea of romantic love. It's an image of love familiar to nineteenth-century fiction: Emma Bovary, Anna Karenina—characters who are in love with being in love and with the idea of romantic love as a forbidden activity. Even so, Louise and Donati are genuinely captured by it. And it is partly the fact that this feeling seems new for each of them that gives the film its poignancy; if they experience a kind of passion that is almost adolescent in its intensity, they are no longer themselves young—or free to enjoy it.

One of the genuine difficulties—and pleasures—of *Madame de . . .* lies in tracking the complexity and fluctuations of the relationship between Louise and Donati: when it is socially accepted flirtation, when it crosses into still-familiar forms of transgression, and when it exceeds the conventional forms of affairs. At some point we have to take the emotion seriously—as involving a claim to genuine happiness—if we are going to be able to accept the drama in the latter half of the film. Louise's quasi-suicidal despair, Donati's despondency and resignation, André's increasingly desperate actions (his challenge of Donati to a duel, as several observers note, violates social rules): all these suggest that something more than convention is at stake.

Still, we might wonder: To what extent does it matter that this happiness is, to put it bluntly, based on adultery? We feel sympathy for Louise and Donati, but also for André (perhaps even more so at times). I think one could reasonably ask how we are to make sense of a world in which it's acceptable to break marriage vows (or similar obligations) when competing ambitions or desires arise. And so there is a question about whether the kinds of ethical demands at stake in *Madame de . . .* are compelling or worth considering to begin with. The answer, it seems to me, lies in the world the film shows, since it is one in which indulging temptations to break marriage vows is generally allowed: husbands can have mistresses, wives can flirt openly and destructively, and so on. The desire to transgress the terms of the obligations to a partner are allowed, even encouraged, to emerge and develop: "We have been playing with fire, you and I," André tells Louise late in the film. Indeed, one way to look at *Madame de . . .* is as showing that when the institution of marriage functions primarily as a contract of sorts, love becomes possible only as a fairly conventional form of adultery. The myth of romantic love—and Ophuls is consistent across his films in seeing it as a myth, an unsustainable fantasy that nevertheless guides the actions of characters—is bound up with the deadening of the institution of marriage.[40]

At this point, it might look like Louise's discovery of the importance of a kind of real happiness entails a reading of the film that best fits the idea of a "spiritual odyssey." From being merely concerned with the frivolous pleasures of aristocratic life, she comes to recognize the value of seriousness, of care and commitment. This would be an important discovery. There is a long tradition—from Aristotle to Kant, Mill to Cavell—of thinking that happiness is central to ethics, that it is bound up with the very possibility for moral action and development, for living a full life.[41] These values are certainly at stake in *Madame de. . . .* But if we think of them in terms of Louise or Donati's state of mind, the discussion is simply being pegged at the wrong level.

Madame de . . . does contain an intimation of what would enable Louise and Donati to go beyond their world's prescribed limits, of what their demands for happiness mean, and of what would allow them to realize these demands. As we'll see, it is articulated in and through the film's aesthetic form, through camera movements that are attuned both to the characters' needs and to the world around them: the world that subverts their claims to happiness, and which they are unable to get beyond. Ophuls provides this intimation despite their blindness to the possibility for more creative action, a blindness even to what their demands actually are. The crisis that emerges, and which eventually results in their deaths, is not just a result of the social order's refusal to allow the relationship to exist. Ophuls makes the failure more general, even symptomatic. Louise and Donati have the forms of their deliberation shaped by—are themselves wholly within—a world that does not contain resources that would enable a more successful negotiation of their new emotion, their sense of a new kind of happiness. It turns out that the virtuosic manipulation of stable conventions only goes so far; it is simply inadequate to certain moral problems, problems that require genuine creativity to negotiate.

Let's pick up where we left off in the sequence, since it's across the dances that the camera movements do the work I am claiming for them. I have already mentioned the formal shifts that occur as Louise and Donati begin to dance together. The slow pace of the dance, coupled with the corresponding movement of the camera, give the sequence a languorous, almost elegiac feel. The circular movements isolate them from the crowd, drawing their attention inward toward one another— and bringing our attention with them.

A cut within this first dance moves to a shot slightly farther away, and we see the pair briefly reflected in a mirror in the background. They spin off to the right, away from the mirror and the other couples, caught up in each other and yet reminded of the social world by the promise of future encounters: the Marquise says, "Until Thursday," and the Colonel, "Until Friday." These two initial shots exhibit a dynamic that runs through the sequence: along with Louise and Donati, we become absorbed in and caught up by the dance, only to be brought back into an awareness of the social world in which it takes place. The Marquise and the Colonel fulfill this function here, as does the mirror, which refers back to the reflected dance in the first section, suggesting that the specialness of *this* dance is still located within a social context. But when they move off on their own, we are able to forget that. If the promise of future dances brings with it the social world, it seems to be organizing itself around their desires: they will keep dancing.

An overlapping dissolve reveals Louise and Donati still dancing in a clockwise rotation, a military band continuing the music in an enclosure in the middle of the room (see figure 12). Donati notes that they have gone four days without seeing each other. "Are there no more dances in Paris?" he asks, and the two maintain polite banter. The camera tracks to the right, following them all the way around in an extended circle. Conventions and formalities are still in place—Donati asks, "Do you have news of your husband?"—but each is more interested in the other than in anything else.

A dissolve to the third dance, two days later, begins with a shot of a large painting of what looks like a military scene placed in the middle of a room. Suddenly, Louise and Donati come together in front of the

FIGURE 12. *Madame de . . .* (Max Ophuls, 1953).

camera, as if they are invoked by its presence. With fewer and fewer couples around them, they have begun to retreat away from the gaze of society; as Louise makes a mocking comment about the costume worn by "the Admiral's wife," they dance behind the painting. (Do they now have something to hide, a reason to be hidden?) There is a cut to the Admiral and his wife, tripping in from right to left, who remark on the couple's overt infatuation. They exit in that direction and, from behind a painting, Louise and Donati swirl out to the right, then go back again to the left in front of it (see figure 13). He asks if she has "any news," and she replies, "Of whom? Ah, yes. He's very well, thank you." They move behind another painting, and there is a dissolve to the fourth dance, a mere twenty-four hours of mutually acknowledged "torture" later. This dance shows a marked change in the relation between Louise and Donati. As they dance, moving to the left, a man dancing with another partner greets Louise, though he has to do so twice before eliciting a response from her. Donati is irked by this intrusion; he says he doesn't like that man, and Louise accuses him of beginning to hope—and thus to fall in love with her. Donati, smiling, answers in the affirmative, and they dance in silence for almost thirty seconds before Louise draws them back into the social world by repeating the familiar refrain, this time without the prompting questions: "I heard from my husband. He's very well, thank you." The hold of conventions is weakening.

The fifth and final dance begins differently, not with Louise and Donati but with an orchestra packing up to leave. The musicians note that this couple is "always the last to leave," a phrase that evokes the comments of the band in *Letter from an Unknown Woman*, who "prefer married people because they have somewhere to go." Louise and

FIGURE 13. *Madame de . . .* (Max Ophuls, 1953).

Donati, however, do not have Lisa and Stefan's excuse. They are not young and single; they are dancing but dressed to leave. These are signs of an attraction that has, and can have, no home.

A musician stands up—"Baron or no Baron, I'm going home"—and walks to the left, the camera panning and tracking to follow him across the room. He gets a light for his cigarette from a servant underneath a mirror, which shows a reflection of Louise and Donati: they are dancing alone on the other side of the room, pressed close up against one another. The camera continues to follow the musician, eventually leaving him as he passes the two dancers (see figure 14).[42] Only a harp is left playing the tune, a piano replacing it as the camera moves closer to the couple. Louise says, "Aren't you going to ask me about my husband?"; when Donati answers, "No," she continues: "You're right [*vous avez raison*]. He's coming back tomorrow." They fall silent, pressing their cheeks together as they circle in the same spot. All pretense of forward movement is gone, as if they were simply trying to be together in the realization that the time in which they could ignore the outside world is coming to an end.

A servant now passes in the background, and the camera leaves Louise and Donati to follow him while he slowly puts out the candles in the room. It's a gesture that seems designed to leave Louise and Donati to themselves, to permit them some final moments of privacy and intimacy before the social world returns. Yet even though they are out of sight, we can still hear their feet shuffling and see them reflected in the mirror when the servant passes it. The camera continues its movement across the room to the right, eventually closing in on the harp as a cover is thrown over it; as the cover fills the screen, the image fades to black.[43]

FIGURE 14. *Madame de . . .* (Max Ophuls, 1953).

The logic of the dance sequence is both simple and elegant. Ophuls marks the shift from flirtation to love through the differences in each dance: Donati's inquiry (or lack thereof) into André's well-being, their interest (or lack thereof) in the social world around them, and even the very tempo of their movement.

But more is going on here than a graceful device for tracking the growth of their relationship. The form of the shots works to give us a feel for the emotional tenor of the dances: the circling camera takes an active role in creating the mood—the flirtation and enchantment, pain and love—that permeates the scene. Ophuls employs his camera to articulate the form of the experience sought by Louise and Donati, an aesthetic articulation of their desire to have a relationship outside social conventions.[44] Not only is it a demand that cannot be realized within the contours of their world; they cannot bring themselves to express or admit their need. In their silence, it is the camera that, as it repeatedly circles the pair, works to enclose them within the private space they implicitly desire. (It seals them off from the world in a way that makes them almost an object of aesthetic contemplation, perhaps even a work of art.) The camera movements thus give us an intimation of the shape of their experience, the claims for happiness being placed on the world. They effect something like an aesthetic reordering, even a reimagining, of the social world to which Louise and Donati belong.

Our sense of the content of their desire, however, results not only from the camera movements but also from the way the sequence disrupts a linear flow of time. It's not simply a matter of Ophuls showing the series of dances in a succession of unbroken takes, instances of continuous duration. The sequence as a whole is organized so that the length of time between each encounter continually divides in half: two weeks between the customs depot in Basel and the accident on the street, one week until the first party, four days until the next one, two days, then one. And yet as the number of days between encounters decreases, the encounters themselves get progressively longer, from thirty seconds in the opening dance to almost two minutes in the final shot. The work here is precise and choreographed. Coupled with the camera movements that circle the dancing couple, as if to shield them from the very passage of time they dread, the effect is to create a specific impression of time: it contracts to a point while at the same time opening onto infinity. The formal structure of the film, reinforced by the movements of the camera, creates a sense of time within the sequence that mirrors Louise and Donati's own experience of time as they dance.

This is not the only film in which Ophuls figures romantic happiness as an escape from historical time. In *Liebelei*, a film to which *Madame de* . . . frequently alludes, the two young lovers go for a sleigh ride. Fritz asks Christine how long she will love him, and she replies, "For eternity."[45] What this means is shown a moment later, when they drive by a graveyard covered in snow; the desire to love forever, Ophuls suggests, is really a wish for death, the only state in which that goal can be realized. *Liebelei*'s cruel irony lies in the lovers' failure to recognize this.[46]

Madame de . . . does something slightly different. Rather than the desire to be together for eternity, for all time, Ophuls shows the desire for there to be *no time*, since with the passing of time will come André's return—and the end of their dances. It's a wish, we might say, for presentness, a fantasy that to be always in the present is to have nothing to do with the flow of time. (Wittgenstein writes, "If by eternity is understood not endless temporal duration but timelessness, then he lives eternally who lives in the present."[47]) The transition to the last dance makes this explicit. Unlike the other transitions between encounters, we are not told how much time has passed since the previous dance but simply see the pair still dancing at the end of an evening. Not only has everyone else gone, but they have overcoats on; it's as if they can't stop dancing, can't accept the imminence of their separation. To wish to be in the present is to wish to be outside the flow of time altogether.

Yet they cannot stay in the self-enclosed world of the dance forever; with the recognition of André's imminent return comes a reminder of the passage of time. And if we are absorbed in a sense of presentness along with them—whether it's wonder at the beauty of the image, the repetitive intensity of the dances, or even straightforward identification with what we imagine their psychological states to be—we are likewise reminded of the existence of the world that prevents the full realization of their fantasy of insularity. There is a conflict between Louise and Donati's experience of time in the dances themselves and the onward movement of the world in which they have this experience.

This tension is brought out in the final dance, when it becomes evident that Louise and Donati have transgressed the boundaries of what they expected to be possible. There, Ophuls introduces two modifications to the pattern built up across the sequence. One is that, for the first time since the initial dance, before they began to fall in love, he places mirrors in the scene. This gesture evokes the image of social circulation with which the sequence began, at once registering the distinctness of this dance and reminding us of the world that surrounds the couple.

In short, it works against the impression of self-enclosure the sequence otherwise generates.

The second modification involves the musicians. While Ophuls shows a band at several points during this sequence, it is only in the last shot that they are individuated. Here he shows the people—the musicians and footmen—whose work makes possible Louise and Donati's chance at happiness; their sudden presence at the end undermines the autonomy and isolation of the dance.[48] It suggests that Louise and Donati are absorbed in each other to the extent that they are unable to see the world around them, are unable to recognize that they have stayed past their time. Ophuls's genius is that we feel neither anger with the musicians and footmen for disrupting the dance nor contempt at the couple for prolonging the evening.[49] Each group simply fails to recognize the other's desires and so cannot allow for their respective satisfaction. Only the camera takes it all in, responding to both desires through its sweeping movements; it not only articulates the contours of Louise and Donati's experience but shows how it plays out in a broader context. What we have in the sequence is a critique, in the full sense of the term, of Louise and Donati's desire for presentness, for being outside both time and society. The experience of presentness, despite its promises and pleasures, proves impossible to sustain.[50]

We might understand *Madame de . . .* , then, as operating by way of a competition between two kinds of virtuosity (or rather, following a remark by Ophuls, between virtuosity and artistry—or even, following Kant, between virtuosity and genius).[51] There is the skill Louise deploys as she manipulates the conventions and values of the social order to which she belongs; its value system is an instrument, and she plays it exceedingly well. But if her virtuosity is successful in its own sphere, within set parameters, it fails when it needs to adapt to new kinds of values and to the new demand for happiness that arises. Against this, there is Ophuls's camera, whose virtuosity is defined by the *creative* ability to respond to new situations and to acknowledge the demands of the characters: those they express, those they feel but are unable to articulate, even those they fail to recognize but that lurk in the background. The ethical content of the film, its moral imagination, is expressed in and through these dually attuned camera movements.

And yet there are limits. The camera's aesthetic reimagining of the social world is unable to materially change it; it is unable to alter events. Louise and Donati break apart; André kills Donati; Louise dies of grief. The camera can only do so much.

5.

I said at the outset of this chapter that my argument was going to risk a problem of form and content. Following the analysis of *Madame de . . .* , we can now see what that is. The problem involves an apparently fixed division of labor, with the camera movements taking shape against a stable, independent, and clearly defined content. The distinction I drew between the world shown by the film and the work done by its formal features seems to imply that Ophuls's camera movements have meaning defined independently of the film's content. And their meaning, moreover, appears to be the primary work done by the film as a whole.

This reading of Ophuls's camera movements might seem to be supported by a feature of his films: they are frequently set in the past, often represented by the fin-de-siècle moment in Europe (Vienna is his preferred city). The past is one of the more conspicuous tropes in Ophuls's work. In *La ronde*, the master of ceremonies (and directorial stand-in) makes it into a principle: "I adore the past. It's so much more peaceful than the present, and so much more certain than the future." The worry this raises is not exactly one of nostalgia, but rather that the particular intersection of aesthetics and ethics I've been describing may depend on the presence of the older world. After all, Ophuls seems to prefer the fin de siècle because its society is governed by strictly defined rules and conventions and thereby furnishes a stable background for the work of the film. It is no small matter that the social world to which Louise belongs, the world that shapes the contours of her deliberative field, is hostile to the intrusion of new kinds of morally salient facts, as well as to new forms of happiness. It's hostile enough, in fact, that it readily resorts to duels—socially sanctioned killings that follow a carefully delineated set of rules—to preserve its own sense of order and stability.[52] Against fixed social conventions, the fluid camera movements may all too easily be able to articulate the films' ethical alternative.

If this way of thinking about the dually attuned camera movements were right, it would make Ophuls's films more schematic and less interesting than I think they are. But there is a different way to treat the tension. We can begin to rethink the apparent problem of form and content by taking a closer look at what's at stake in the idea of the past. The past is important to Ophuls for a variety of reasons, and not just for the considerations mentioned here, but I think it matters especially as a way to make explicit and vivid something about film itself. It functions, that is, as a complex meta-cinematic trope, revealing something about the kind of world a film has, even the kind of thing a film is. This idea may not be immediately intuitive, but it is important for thinking about how Ophuls uses camera movements.

The basic idea, certainly not unique to Ophuls, is that the world of a film is self-sufficient, sealed off from both its maker and its audience. There is a limit to what we can discover about or do with such a world; at most, we are able to take up positions toward it, appreciating its beauty while acknowledging its flaws and impossibilities. What happens in Ophuls's work is that the setting of the action in the past becomes an exemplary figure for this way of thinking, as it places the films in a world shielded from us by the passage of time. The story has already run its course; it is not something that can be intervened with or whose outcome can be changed. (Ophuls is not a director of the counterfactual.) The principle articulated by the master of ceremonies in *La ronde* makes this explicit, as he describes the past as something fixed and therefore permanently (ontologically) sealed off from the present. Indeed, one way to think about Ophuls's line of thought here is as following the form of Stanley Cavell's intuitions about the ontology of a photograph: "The reality in a photograph is present to me while I am not present to it; and a world I know, and see, but to which I am nevertheless not present (through no fault of my subjectivity), is a world past."[53] Yet Ophuls reverses the direction of Cavell's chain of reasoning. He uses the sense of a world past, the repeated setting of films in earlier historical periods, to evoke the conditions of film as a medium.

Two other features of Ophuls's films support such an interpretation. The first has to do with narrative structure, with his penchant for telling stories through flashbacks. Several major films—*La signora di tutti, Letter from an Unknown Woman, Lola Montès*—start at the end, constructing a narrative whose outcome is foretold: "By the time you read this letter, I may be dead," begins *Letter from an Unknown Woman*. The second involves Ophuls's interest in literary adaptations. By one count, twenty of the twenty-five films he made were direct adaptations of literary works; whatever else is involved in this decision, one consequence is that the stories being told are already known.[54]

In the combination of these features, Ophuls manifests an ontological honesty toward the worlds he creates by refusing to interfere with their resolution. He simply allows the stories to run their course, and if the situation does not produce an ideal outcome, the issue is not forced.[55] This is worth noting. The use of dramatic narrative shifts to bring about a better ending is a well-known narrative principle, not least in Hollywood cinema. It's also in Douglas Sirk's ironic use of impossibly happy endings to suggest the very unreality of any possible happy outcome and in Bertolt Brecht's avoiding of the tragic ending by the miraculous arrival of the king's messenger bearing pardons for all.[56] Whatever we may think of the narratives that result, both Sirk and Brecht allow themselves to interfere with the narrative worlds they create. Ophuls, however, constructs a situation in which he can do nothing. The worlds of his films stand on their own.

If we expand the analysis of Ophuls's camera movements out from *Madame de . . .* to look at the way the dual attunement structure functions in other films—even ones set in the present—we can see the force of this interpretation. One example is Ophuls's lone Italian film, *La signora di tutti*, a film organized around the constraints and demands of what it is to be a star, to be "everybody's woman." We are first introduced to the heroine, Gaby Doriot, in the context of negotiations over her contract—the terms are debated in her absence—and are repeatedly shown ways in which her life is defined by the economic and social apparatus of stardom. The film's narrative is an extensive flashback as she lies dying from a suicide attempt, remembering the missed possibilities for happiness during her rise from poverty to stardom. Early in this story, she falls in love with Roberto, the son of a wealthy banker, a relationship that will prove disastrous. The scene in which this happens takes place at a ball being thrown by his father, and Ophuls again uses extended tracking shots to trace their developing interest in one another.

The sequence begins as Roberto, standing on a balcony overlooking the ballroom, spots Gaby sitting by herself. As Roberto walks down a set of stairs, Ophuls cuts to a tracking shot that follows him while he greets various people, moves over to Gaby, and asks her to dance; she accepts, rises somewhat awkwardly, and as they begin to dance, closes her eyes partially as if in a dream. The camera follows the pair through the crowd, moving past other dancing couples and eventually framing them within an open space at the center of the dance; as in *Madame de . . .*, the couple is caught up in their own activity, indifferent to the world around them. (Again, dancing is figured as a socially sanctioned mode of intimacy, a way of being together without violating codes of propriety. It also leads to deeper emotions, or even produces them itself.) Roberto whirls Gaby through a series of beads and curtains, and Ophuls cuts 180 degrees to a shot from inside another room, perhaps a library, as they enter through curtains, still dancing. Gaby, now wide-eyed and smiling blissfully, thanks Roberto for the invitation to dance, for taking her away from her loneliness. They circle the room, the camera following them; Gaby says, "I would like always to dance," breaks away from Roberto, and whirls around in a combination of relief and joy, before tripping over a chair and stumbling to the floor.

At this point, Ophuls does something startling with the camera. Gaby says that her "head is spinning"; taking up the cue, the camera executes a 360-degree pan around the room. We might take the pan to constitute an identification with Gaby's point of view, a moment that shows her disorientation.[57] But this way of reading the shot ignores the larger economy of the scene, in which the camera's movements have already given it agency of its own. In this larger context, the pan is less an expression of what Gaby sees than a response to how she feels, an instance of the dual attunement structure. The camera accepts her unmet need to have her desire for happiness acknowledged; if people won't respond to her half-expressed wishes, the camera will.

The 360-degree pan is coupled with a second gesture a moment later, a strange wipe that goes right to left, pivoting diagonally from the bottom center of the screen very much like a car's windshield wiper. If we follow cinematic convention, the wipe elides a moment when something happens that cannot be shown: a convention parodied in *La ronde* when Ophuls cuts from a romantic encounter to the master of ceremonies "censoring" the film by cutting a large section out of it. Gaby herself seems to suggest something like this, saying in wonder: "What did you do there?" But what is elided is not something sexually illicit so much as the feeling of a desire impossible to achieve: the moment of falling in love, of recognizing new claims to happiness. It is a moment that can't be shown, and it is a desire that both Gaby and Roberto will disavow at crucial moments in the film. As with *Madame de . . .* , Ophuls is clear that the impulse the camera acts upon cannot materially change the world it shows—we know from the outset that Gaby will commit suicide in the end—but we are nonetheless given a sense of the form of an appropriate response, and even more a sense of the content it should respond to.[58]

A second example is from *Caught*, one of Ophuls's American films. When I mentioned the film earlier, I noted that Leonora Ames defines herself by the images in fashion magazines in the first shots of the film, that is, by her status as a consumer. "I want that," she says, looking through their images. She gets it by marrying a millionaire, Smith Ohlrig, all the while convincing herself that she does so for love, thus following the fantasies set up by the magazines even more closely. Ohlrig is, unsurprisingly, something of a brute, and she leaves him to work in the office of two doctors, where she falls in love with one of them, Larry Quinada—and he with her, eventually asking her to marry him. The dilemma is that Leonora is not only still married but pregnant with Ohlrig's child, which Quinada does not know.

In the midst of these events, Ophuls inserts a curious scene: the two doctors lean against their respective doorjambs across the central room of their office suite, discussing the events of the day. As they do so, Quinada remarks that Leonora has been absent from work and has in fact moved out to Long Island; she had described her previous occupation there as "a paid companion to somebody rich." The discussion turns to Quinada's relationship with Leonora, and Hoffman—the other doctor—seems to be trying to figure out its extent, namely whether Quinada could be the father of Leonora's child. The scene ends with Hoffman suggesting that Quinada go out to Long Island to get Leonora, and to see what is going on there.

What stands out in this fairly banal conversation are two camera movements that bookend the scene, the camera twisting around the object between the two men: Leonora's unoccupied desk. The scene begins with an overhead shot of the desk, as the camera moves down slightly while tilting upward to come horizontal to the ground, then tracks and pans to the left to bring Hoffman into view.[59] The camera briefly moves forward past the desk toward Hoffman, and then, while still going forward, begins to pivot back around to the right, eventually coming to frame Quinada over the top of Leonora's empty desk. From there, the scene plays out in a familiar shot/reverse-shot pattern until the final shot, which begins with the exact framing from the end of the first shot. As Quinada humorously imagines introducing himself to Leonora's rich companion, the camera tracks forward toward him, then pivots back around to the left to bring Hoffman into the frame (it does so while continuing to move toward Quinada, though it's now traveling backward). The camera pauses for a few seconds, then lifts upward and tilts down to bring Leonora's desk back into the center of the frame from an overhead angle; Ophuls holds the shot before dissolving to the next scene.

At a basic level, the two camera movements remind the viewer of Leonora in spite of, or perhaps because of, her absence, confirming at the level of form that she is the subject of conversation, the point around which everything turns. It's a curiously structured scene. The camera movements mirror each other in both order and direction. In the first, the camera tilts up and moves down before pivoting to the right to show Quinada offscreen. In the second, the camera pivots to the left to show Hoffman offscreen before moving up and tilting down. They create a perfect enclosure around the scene, a sealed world of sorts. Ophuls's trademark grace may be here, but the confined space the camera has to operate in puts pressure on it. We feel Leonora's sense of confinement, her difficulty in being trapped between the reality of her situation and a hope for a new life—and her inability to model a way to escape. In this, Ophuls's camera is able to provide the perspective on the world of the film that is missing within it.[60]

From these discussions, we can see why a standard model of form and content is inadequate to Ophuls's films, and therefore why we shouldn't be worried about problems that tend to arise from it. Ophuls in fact uses camera movements in a dynamic interplay with the *world* of the film, an interplay that generates the films' ethical content. The critical difficulty is that the terms of this engagement are defined by an ontological condition—one posited by the films themselves—that resembles a form/content divide but is in fact structured quite differently. Ophuls's interest has to do with the narrative integrity, or independence, of the film's world, and the way that world is essentially sealed off from the camera.[61] The structural tension that enables and determines the dually attuned camera movements is organized in relation to, and in the space allowed by, this ontological condition that defines the worlds of Ophuls's films.

The force and distinctiveness of this commitment become striking in contrast with filmmakers who use virtuosic camera movements to intervene in the worlds of their films. Orson Welles, for example, makes the camera an active agent that reveals things to the audience that are, or are suggested to be, of narrative importance; the revelation of the sled at the end of *Citizen Kane* is something that only we, the audience of the film, can ever or will ever know (its destruction confirms this). Jean Renoir uses the camera to reframe action, showing the alignment of various characters in ways that foretell narrative events, as when new spaces are repeatedly revealed by the camera in the "danse maca-bre" sequence in *La règle du jeu*. And Alfred Hitchcock has a penchant for using the camera to mark characters with guilt, to intrude into the world he creates—even to alter it—so as to impose a clear moral and narrative order.[62] The tracking shot at the end of *Young and Innocent* (1937) goes over the heads of the dancing crowd to move in on the drummer of the band, the guilty man the main characters are looking for; the track in to a close-up reveals the twitch in his eye that confirms his identity as the murderer. For these directors, the moving camera discovers things that the characters in the film ought to see but cannot or will not see; it operates within the world of the film, changing the very mode by which narrative information is presented. The revelation of the drummer, or of the sled, is not just some new fact to be seen but a shift in our underlying epistemic relation to the film's world.

Ophuls, by contrast, accepts the independence of the worlds he creates and brings to the screen. He can work with them, but not on them; it is as if they are self-standing, wholly autonomous from his authority—as if he had never created them in the first place. There are (ontological) constraints to what his camera movements can do, a point at which their creative virtuosity can do no more; they cannot enter or change the world of the film.

By this point, we have returned to lines of thought in which it might easily seem that camera movements are unrelated to matters of ethics, even if they're not just ornamental or "merely virtuosic." In Ophuls's films, however, the ontological, epistemic, even metaphysical concerns that camera movements raise and negotiate are inseparable from the ethical work they do. In each of the films I have discussed, the camera movements pick up the need for a world that makes room for the varying (and variable) demands for happiness by its inhabitants and then show the precise contours of these demands. Ophuls's camera, in other words, provides a moral perspective on the world, a perspective those inside it are often incapable of taking. What I've been calling its "dual attunement" is the condition for the expression of the films' ethical content. If the camera cannot, on its own, effect the changes (implicitly) demanded by characters in the films, it nonetheless functions as a fine-tuned way to process the moral status of the world through aesthetic means. Ophuls uses the camera movements to express an aesthetic articulation of a moral attitude for the audience.

Ophuls's films work with and reveal the limits of virtuosity, the places where the skilled manipulation of conventions isn't sufficient to negotiate the demands of new values, whether moral or not. This happens in various guises and forms; we may even recognize ourselves there. These are places where an approach to ethics and film that focuses primarily on character psychology, or on the dynamics of identification, comes to feel inadequate. In the face of such challenges, Ophuls's films suggest that what matters may be the movements of the camera itself.

CHAPTER 6

The Curious Ironist

Terrence Malick and the Drama
of Perspective

I.

One of the most common criticisms of Terrence Malick's films is that they are marked by stylistic excess, to the detriment of narrative pleasure or even, at times, comprehensibility. Central to this complaint is the charge of overuse of and indulgence in the moving camera. A particularly strident criticism is made by Robert Koehler:

> The Steadicam and handheld camera strategy that Malick has been using with his preferred cinematographer Emmanuel Lubezki have brought out all his worst instincts. Tools with few limitations, handheld cameras can be lilted, swung, or rotated in any possible direction and axis. Lubezki and Malick's work appears unmoored, lacking in a governing idea for the their uses of the camera. . . . So, because the cameras can be swung around willy-nilly, they are. If they can be made with a nearly unvarying use of ultra wide-angle lenses, as short as 14mm, to simulate the human eye's close-up perception when the body and head shift or move quickly or suddenly, they are, but without the crucial element of thought behind the movement. Malick, once an artist with a disciplined sensibility for scale and sensation, has gone goofy with the devices.[1]

The camera movements are too abundant, and there is no rationale for them within the world of the film or the logic of a judiciously balanced style.

It's not hard to see what Koehler is thinking of. Take a sequence from *The Thin Red Line*, Malick's film about the Battle of Guadalcanal. An

American battalion has overrun a Japanese position, and the soldiers are sprinting through an encampment, firing at everyone they see. The sequence is not filmed in the manner of classical Hollywood; we have no clear sense of the overall spatial arrangement of the encampment that would orient us in the battle, nor do we follow an individual soldier through it. Instead, Malick's camera remains mobile and flexible, always moving through space along with the characters but shifting between positions rapidly and without explanation. We are following an American soldier running through a building, firing at Japanese soldiers who appear in his line of sight, and then all of a sudden we are in a trench as Japanese soldiers fire at the Americans running by (and are shot in return). We see soldiers sometimes from the front, sometimes from the back. Sometimes the camera seems to glide around as if a detached spirit; sometimes it appears to exist within the world—whether because it tangibly brushes aside the leaves of a tree or because a soldier suddenly looks at it, as if it were the incarnation of his enemy.

This sequence is emblematic of the way the entire film is constructed, and also—as I argue here—of Malick's style in the years following his "return" to filmmaking with *The Thin Red Line*. The style is difficult to account for, much less to describe. It may be tempting to see Malick as part of a widespread stylistic shift starting in the late 1990s toward a "post-classical" or "post-continuity" cinema, in which the stable organization of space and action is broken down. In films like *The Bourne Identity* (Doug Liman, 2002) or *The Hurt Locker*, a combination of rapid camera movements and disorienting editing patterns defines a style that is held together not by clarity of vision but by a tight focus on the movement of bodies and their trajectories.[2] Indeed, several commentators have placed Malick's cinema within this context.[3] But to do so misses much of what's distinctive in these films; as Tom Gunning observes, "Malick has fashioned his own alternative to continuity editing."[4] Central to this difference is the rapidity with which Malick shifts positions within a scene, taking up different points of view—and different ways of moving—thus making it hard to ever gain a clear sense of what we're seeing and how we're seeing it. We are even precluded from having our perception of events routed through specific individuals.

To be sure, such ambiguity is part of the point of *The Thin Red Line*: to immerse the viewer in the chaos of the battlefield and the way that soldiers act without awareness of anything beyond what's right in front of them. It conveys the simultaneous adrenaline and fear, the manic exhilaration of killing and the suddenness of being killed. All this is part and parcel of the way that Malick negotiates the terms of the genre of the war film and the broader existential questions it entails.

But this kind of reading, powerful though it is, can obscure what is at stake in Malick's cinema. One of the striking features of his films in these years—*The Thin Red Line*, *The New World*, and *The Tree of Life*—is the way they take shape against large-scale events of history and politics. They show transformations whose arcs are outside the control of people within the films and that may not, in a sense, be in the control of any individual at all. *The Thin Red Line* is set within the Pacific theater of World War II, in which the events shown are only a stepping-stone in a larger campaign to retake islands from the Japanese forces. *The New World* focuses on the colonial project of settlement of Jamestown and the initial meeting between the English settlers and Native Americans, yet it also treats these events as part of the global capitalist market emerging out of London. This feature is even more explicit in *The Tree of Life*, which is comprised of supraindividual processes, from the sequence imagining the origins of the cosmos, to the judgment of God, to the legal and economic forces haunting the father, to a child's incomprehension of the world of adults, to Jack's childhood shock at his own physical and mental developments (which are happening, as it were, outside his understanding and control).

In the face of these seemingly anonymous or unauthored events and processes, characters reach out for explanation; they ask about meaning. We find this repeatedly in the opening voice-overs of the films. *The Thin Red Line* begins: "What's this war at the heart of nature? Why does nature vie with itself—the land contend with the sea? Is there an avenging power in nature? Not one power but two?" *The New World* begins: "Come, Spirit. Help us sing the story of our land. You are our mother, we your field of corn. We rise from out of the soul of you." *The Tree of Life* begins with two voice-overs. First is a man's voice, "Brother, mother: it was they who led me to your door," followed quickly by a woman's: "The nuns taught us that there are two ways through life, the way of nature and the way of grace. You have to choose which one you'll follow." Even with *Song to Song* (2017), we get into deep waters quickly: "I went through a period where sex had to be violent. I was desperate to feel something real. Nothing felt real. Every kiss felt half as real as it should be. You're just reaching for air." These openings suggest that the characters are thinking about their situation with the utmost seriousness, that they take the stakes of understanding their world to be high and involving questions of nature, technology, grace, evil, desire, and so on. This interplay between the supraindividual forces, individuals' questions about meaning, and especially, formal innovation, is the engine that drives Malick's films.

Yet the presence of metaphysical questions has warranted a kind of interpretive practice that misses this tense dynamic. Malick has become something of a poster child for film-philosophy. There are by now multiple books as well as articles treating Malick's films as a form of philosophy, analyzing what Thomas Deane Tucker calls a "uniquely metaphysical cinema."[5] Buttressing these interpretations is Malick's biography, as his engagement with Martin Heidegger—both as a student and as the translator of The Essence of Reasons—becomes a warrant for treating his films as engagements with or examples of Heideggerian ideas and methods.[6]

There are two deep problems with this approach. The first has to do with its repeated appeal to biography. There is no question that aspects of Malick's films, from the natural imagery associated with the four basic elements to meditations over the nature of "world," resonate with themes prominent in Heidegger's work. But this fact can be misleading. Matthew Evertson has argued that such themes and imagery are also found in a tradition of midcentury American literature, citing in particular the novels of Wright Morris. Written in the 1950s and 1960s and set on the American plains, Morris's novels are closely related to Badlands (1973) and Days of Heaven (1978) but also resonate across Malick's later career.[7] Or there is Witt's evocation of "one big soul" in The Thin Red Line, a speech that seems to be Malick's own cri de coeur, a religiously tinted evocation of our human connectedness that proposes the unity of the world and the embeddedness of the individual within the whole. Yet it is also a verbatim quotation—not from a philosophical text but from John Steinbeck's Grapes of Wrath (1939), when the itinerant preacher Jim Casy tells Tom Joad: "Maybe all men got one big soul ever'body's a part of," a line Tom himself repeats at the end of the novel when he tells Ma Joad that he'll "be there" when injustices take place.[8] It's even plausible to read Witt's speech as emerging from the cultural imagination of the time, an allusion toward which a vaguely southern soldier might have reached in order to make sense of a confusing and overwhelming situation.

That doesn't mean that it's Morris or Steinbeck instead of Heidegger who should be identified as the source of Malick's preoccupations, imagery, and concerns. Nor does it mean that Malick needs to be read within a strictly American intellectual context. Rather, we should remember that an appeal to "context" is always tricky, and that it's fairly useless to isolate any individual source or sources as the "key" to Malick's work. After all, a general preoccupation with existentialism, and with ways of being in the world, ran through Western intellectual circles from the 1930s at least through the 1960s.[9] Malick has a set of concerns common to and shared by a large number of intellectual figures of his generation, so to get at what's going on in his films requires giving the films themselves the authority to speak on their own terms—within a general set of preoccupations rather than a specific doctrine.

The second problem with the film-philosophical approach has to do with a model of interpretive sincerity, a belief that the films offer direct articulations of philosophical positions. This kind of claim is often presented as Malick's rejection of irony—an irony that is assumed to characterize much of contemporary popular culture. In this vein, Lloyd Michaels writes (in 2009): "Perhaps the most consistent quality among Malick's four features to date has been their resistance to the irony, fragmentation, and lack of conviction that characterizes postmodernism as well as much of modern cinema"—which is, he clarifies later, "the postmodernist glibness of Quentin Tarantino and the Coen Brothers."[10] While Malick's first films are sometimes recognized as possessing a kind of irony, especially in their use of deadpan narrators who do not wholly understand their situation, his films from the late 1990s have come to be seen as works by a fundamentally serious, or at least earnest, filmmaker. Jaimey Fisher, for example, contrasts the "sardonic irony" of the novel *The Thin Red Line* with the contemplative nature of the film.[11] The danger is that this mood is taken to warrant a mode of reading. Voice-overs that suggest philosophical positions, or redolent shots of natural beauty, can simply be taken at face value, an assumption that allows the critics to provide a straightforward and uncomplicated articulation of the views of the film.

I take a different approach in this chapter, arguing that the formal strategy that underlies *The Thin Red Line*, *The New World*, and *The Tree of Life* is fundamentally based on a particular use of camera movement to articulate the film's world. Rather than unmotivated excess or an exemplification of philosophical positions, I argue that the camera movements are part of an aesthetic system that is best described as as "antiperspectival." Put succinctly, on this view Malick uses the moving camera to revise and undo fundamental assumptions about how space (and time) can be organized and about how we inhabit positions—epistemic as well as perceptual—within the world of the film. We can see this already taking shape in the sequence from *The Thin Red Line* that I discussed. The camera has no stable given; it doesn't stay outside the events to look at the whole, nor does it follow any particular individual. With any given cut to a new shot, we do not know how we will be looking or from whose perspective: it may be an American; it may be a Japanese; it may be a group; it may be dirt and mud and sticks.

If Malick repeatedly invokes supraindividual narratives, sweeping arcs of history that shape the context within which his characters act, the counterpart is not simply a turn to the individual, whether this is form (post-continuity) or politics (liberalism). Malick rarely pits individuals against systems, even as he shows the consequences of people trying to make sense of the world around them.[12] Instead he uses the moving camera to create multiple paths through the world—multiple and varied positions that the viewer is able to occupy—that provide a way to negotiate the varying pressures placed on the way characters respond to the world around them. This could be described as a phenomenological project, though it lacks the stability of a given subject position and instead reaches for a fantasy of experience before the imposition of perspective. This is how Maurice Merleau-Ponty describes it:

> Before, my glance, running freely over depth, height, and width, was not subject to any point of view, because it adopted them and rejected them in turn. Now I renounce that ubiquity and agree to let only that which could be seen from a certain reference point by an immobile eye fixed on a certain "vanishing point" of a certain "vanishing line" figure in my drawing.[13]

The aim of Malick's antiperspectival project, I argue, is to *animate* the eye and the positions from which it can see. What the moving camera does is to ensure that there is no settled orientation, no distinct view or position we can firmly identify as exemplary. The power of his films is built out of this unique formal flexibility.

2.

The idea of perspectivalism in cinema is a vexed one. The ur-text remains André Bazin's 1945 essay, "The Ontology of the Photographic Image," published in a volume on cinema and painting. There, Bazin placed the visual arts "under psychoanalysis" in order to understand their fundamental principle, namely a concern with depicting and preserving the real. Moving forward in time from Egyptian mummies, Bazin saw two competing poles of artistic aspiration: one was aesthetic, seeking spiritual truths in "the symbolism of form"; the other was psychological, the desire "to replace the outside world with its double." The history of painting, as he saw it, involved a movement from the former toward the latter, toward the demands for a kind of illusionism. This illusionism is the domain of the visual arts, and it's here that perspective enters.

Yet if perspective was the highest move toward the reproduction of the world, Bazin nonetheless thought that it imposed something between artist and world. Perspective involved a grid of knowledge, a sense of how an image *ought* to look. This claim is at the heart of one of his most perplexing statements: "Perspective was the original sin of Western Painting. Niépce and Lumière were the redeemers."[14] It's important, I think, to hear Bazin as playfully—if also seriously—toying with the Christian theology he knew so well. The original sin is of course the eating of the apple from the tree of good and evil—that is to say, of knowledge. And so perspective is the original sin of painting because it removes the immediacy of image to world that structured earlier—and more theological—pictorial traditions. Photography is then figured as Christ, "redeeming" painting by incorporating sin—that is, perspective—into its very being. For Bazin, photographic media thus become centrally about realistic depiction, while painting is freed to pass into the realm of abstraction.

From here it was an easy step for Bazin to conclude that cinema is based on the terms of Renaissance perspective, a visual arrangement that is built into the very technology of camera lenses. This view is by no means unique to Bazin. It's present in an early essay by Hubert Damisch on the phenomenology of photography; it appears at the beginning of an essay on point of view by Jacques Aumont; and it would, as Anne Friedberg notes, shape many of the debates in French film theory over the ensuing decades.[15] We can see the sheer familiarity of the association in the way Richard de Cordova mentions it almost as an aside in a discussion of early films that contain, he says, "the perspectival system that had been dominant since the sixteenth century in painting (the system upon which photography itself had been modeled)."[16]

Two core assumptions run through this line of thought. The first is a reliance on a specific model of perspective, one that is taken to stand in for the broader enterprise of perspectival construction. The model is the single-point perspective that emerged in the Italian Renaissance, whose mathematical theorization is usually traced back to Alberti. The second assumption involves what seems to be an almost irresistible desire to see in perspective a key to a broader way of thinking: about subject to world, about ideology, and about the meaning of space.[17] The move from technical construction to social meaning is part of what makes perspective such an important, if misused, topic.

The sense of perspective as a way of ordering the world that echoes outward across theories of self, society, and general ideology gains additional charge from Erwin Panofsky's seminal *Perspective as Symbolic Form*. Each era, he argued, had its own system of perspective, one that was correlated to a broader way of seeing the world. Panofsky started from an early model predicated on what he characterized as "experiential" or "psychophysiological" space, constructed around the aggregation of views from different binocular positions.[18] This mode in turn corresponds to a particular worldview based on a kind of immanence to the world. By contrast, Panofsky argued, Renaissance perspective is grounded in the mathematical organization of spatial relations in the world, an abstract system that allows bodies to be plotted in space. No longer based on the logic of physically inhabited space, in which the viewer is part of the picture, it places all objects in relation to a single, static position. Structuring this technical system is the idea that the position of the viewer is outside the image (the feature that led a number of theorists in the 1970s to label this position—stripping it of historical specificity—the "transcendental subject"). Panofsky drew a larger lesson, taking the isolated individual standing outside the world and looking at it within a frame to symbolize the modern condition, one of being withdrawn from the world. Perspective, he noted, is "a construction that is itself comprehensible only for a quite specific, indeed specifically modern, sense of space, or if you will, sense of the world."[19]

When films and filmmakers engage the idea of perspective, then, it's not just visual form that's at stake. There are meanings associated with the form, views and positions that make up a worldview; perspective is the technical apparatus associated with visual modernity. As Damisch notes, Panofsky (and others) took for granted the idea that "spatial relations are simultaneously the conditions and the expression of relations between individuals acting in history, whether real or imagined."[20] To act on one is to act on the other.

Debates over perspective—even for the technical arts whose apparatuses are described as constructed according to its principles—are thus never simply about visual form. If an antiperspectival tendency runs across the history of cinema, it is in no small part because the terrain of perspective invariably leads beyond pictorial organization.[21] This holds for those who seek an altogether different grounding, whether that's

German Expressionist cinema of the 1920s, Sergei Eisenstein's interest in Piranesi and El Greco, Jean-Luc Godard's use of horizontal tracking shots against flat backgrounds, or Sergei Parajanov's reliance on the inverted perspective of medieval painting and Persian miniatures. The antiperspectival tendency is also present when Jacques Rivette, writing on Kenji Mizoguchi, speaks of "the serene joy of one who has conquered the illusory phenomena of perspectives."[22] And it's there in a long-standing history of animation practices that play with perspective, from the use of multiple planes of space in anime to Caroline Leaf's all-over animation style, in which the film world itself continually transforms, to the spatial games of *The Thief and the Cobbler* (Richard Williams, 1993/2013).[23]

This is the loose tradition in which I want to situate Malick, seeing in his films an engagement with antiperspectivalism that does not entail a rejection of perspective—as in Stan Brakhage's call to "imagine an eye unruled by man-made laws of perspective"—but rather a sustained revision and reworking of its terms.[24] Some of this is narrational, as in Malick's eschewal of single narrators in favor of multiple voices—a dialogue between ways of inhabiting the film's world. Some of this is temporal, as in his increasing movement outside, or away from, models of historical and linear time. But nowhere is a revision of a perspectivalist approach more present than in his treatment of the moving camera, as he simultaneously draws on and subverts the implicit assumption of a connection between viewer and camera to create an uncertain and fluctuating position for the spectator. Out of this construction a broader polyvocality of film style emerges, a logic that refuses familiar forms of identification and order.

Before turning in detail to the camera movements, I want to dwell on the idea of multiple voices, multiple ways of describing or inhabiting the films' worlds. I'm describing this this aspect of Malick's films as an antiperspectival aesthetic; it's also, importantly, a mode of *irony*. I do not mean the mode of irony prominent in popular culture, which is marked by a fundamental detachment from what is being said, a refusal to accept responsibility for words and actions. A more conventional use of the term, that is what Jedediah Purdy employs in his diagnosis of the culture of the 1990s:

> [Jerry Seinfeld] is irony incarnate. Autonomous by virtue of his detachment, disloyal in a manner too vague to be mistaken for treachery, he is matchless in discerning the surfaces whose creature he is. The point of irony is a quiet refusal to believe in the depths of relationships, the sincerity of motivation, or the truth of speech—especially earnest speech.[25]

In suggesting that Malick is an ironic filmmaker, I mean a different sense of irony, one that emerges from a long-standing philosophical (and literary) position that rests on the dispersal of authority within a text.[26] This tradition treats the use of authorial surrogates not as stand-ins for the views of the author but as alternative perspectives within the text. Søren Kierkegaard found it in Plato's use of Socrates, for example, which he took as a lesson for himself: one could use surrogates to set out positions that are distinct from, yet in dialogue with, one another. The lesson is not to endorse one of the views set out by a surrogate, but to allow the positions to play off each other and to give the reader a different way of making sense of arguments. What's at stake in this mode is both a formal principle and a type of content: a way of using one voice to challenge the views of another, from the ethical position being taken to the very words being endorsed.[27]

Within this tradition, irony is not opposed to models of seriousness. Søren Kierkegaard, writing under the pseudonym Johannes Climacus, makes this explicit: "From the fact that irony is present, it does not follow that earnestness is excluded."[28] Many, if not all, of the elements of Malick's style suggest a full endorsement of what is being said. Yet they are placed in the film not as exemplars of its position, stand-ins for the position of the film itself, but rather as discrete, individual voices that articulate different—and often competing—ways of moving through and understanding the films' worlds. The dispersal of speaking authority is highlighted by Malick's penchant for having characters speak in quotations. The use of Steinbeck in *The Thin Red Line* is one example; in *The New World*, Pocahontas speaks lines by Sappho to describe John Smith; and in *The Tree of Life*, a priest's sermon on Job is comprised of Kierkegaard's words. These are not quite gestures of Brechtian distanciation—the quotations are not (always) recognized by character or viewer—but they serve a general tendency of depsychologization by alienating speakers from their words.[29] If the creation of multiple perspectives is a core feature of Malick's antiperspectival strategy, the model of irony, I think, is its corollary, an orientation that allows more radical elements of his work to emerge. As with the tradition of antiperspectivalism, Malick's use of irony has a number of different modes, depending, not least, on the project of the film.

An example is the "All things shining" that concludes the final voiceover of *The Thin Red Line*. It seems to be a view of the world, of the soldiers in it, and of nature all around them. If the film starts with a "war within the heart of nature," which we presume to be World War II, then it is against this background of fighting and killing, of comradeship and betrayal, that the voice seems to celebrate an achievement:

> Where is it that we were together? Who were you that I lived with, walked with? The brother. The friend. Darkness, light. Strife and love. Are they the workings of one mind? The features of the same face? Oh, my soul. Let me be in you now. Look out through my eyes. Look out at the things you made. All things shining.

Pippin has aptly described such speeches as "vernacular metaphysics," a fusion of the terms of the war genre—the evocation of the "band of brothers"—with more poetic meditations. He takes this fusion to emblematize Malick's distinctive approach, a welding of genre forms with philosophically inclined sentiment.[30]

Yet we should pause before taking these words to be a summation of the film's worldview, exemplifying its point and message.[31] After all, *The Thin Red Line* does not in fact conclude with them. The voice-over is delivered over a series of shots that show the squad being taken away from Guadalcanal, ending with Private Doll standing at the stern of the boat, looking out over the receding wake and the islands in the distance. It's a melancholy shot, filled with memories of the loss of friends and a recognition that he remains alive—and the complexities of that awareness. But three shots then follow: a tracking shot down a river and toward two boats paddled by several Melanesians; a shot of two brightly colored parrots sitting on the branch of a tree; and the film's final image, a coconut alone on a beach, filmed from ground level to show the ocean behind it, a green shoot starting to grow upward from its husk. This is nature, counterposed to the social world; images, counterposed to language. And the power of these images of the natural world provides reason to doubt that any words spoken could account for them.

Two deep aspects of Malick's cinematic style run through this ending, both of which deal centrally with matters of perspective and point of view. The first has to do with voice-overs, the presence of which is inescapable across his career. Pippin notes that, starting with *The Thin Red Line*, the voice-overs are what "have most divided audiences and critics."[32] It is not just their overtly philosophical and metaphysical language that causes anxiety; in *The Thin Red Line*, the problem is a more basic one of comprehension:

> We often do not know with any certainty who is speaking the voice-overs, so it is hard to place a monologue in the plot. . . . Unless one has an *extremely*

sensitive ear, it is almost impossible to realize that the voice we hear at the very beginning . . . and which will voice the last reflection we hear ("All things shining")—belongs not to Witt, an almost inescapable attribution on first hearing, but to a character we have barely caught a glimpse of: one Private Edward B. Train.[33]

This is a problem that runs throughout the film. It's not only that the actors have similar accents; under their helmets, they often look similar, and at times voice-overs that belong to one character appear over a shot of another character.

More broadly, Malick's use of voice-over follows the tendency within an ironic tradition to have surrogates for the author's views creating distance from what is being said. Plato's Socrates is the most famous example; Marcel Proust's Marcel is another—they do not speak for the author so much as articulate a view from within the world of a text.[34] The principle is also behind Kierkegaard's use of pseudonyms and the complex array of positionings within and across his texts. A result is that no character, no voice has sole narrative authority. For Malick's cinema, as Gunning writes, this means that the use of "voice-over diffuses; rather than presenting a single character's account of events, it selectively 'tunes in' to the interior monologues of a number of characters."[35] No character—whether Witt, Bell, or Welsh, or more minor characters like Train or Doll—speaks *for* the film. They all speak from within it, articulating a certain experience, a way of seeing and understanding the world around them, one that the film itself is then able to take up a position toward, whether that means (implicitly) criticizing it or treating it as a partial view of a more expansive whole. "All things shining": this is not Malick uttering a final statement, a summation of his work, but a character within the film's diegetic world attempting to make sense of it. The lines are inherently partial, part of a refusal of what Lee Carruthers describes as Malick's target: "a monolithic understanding" of a person, event, or state of being.[36] If we miss this fact, we miss the film.

While *The New World* contains multiple voice-overs, Malick really returns to them in *The Tree of Life*. There, the power of certain voices—in particular Jack's and Mrs. O'Brien's—seems to be such that they *ought* to express the view of the film as a whole. After all, we might think, if the film is not about them, whom is it about? The mother's voice in particular seems to function as the film's moral compass—certainly it seems that way to Jack—and triggers the theological inquiry about the place of evil in the world that motivates the beginning of the film. (Depending on how we read the film, it may be his imagining of her thoughts.) And it's from within Jack's reflections that we get the central narrative, the story of his childhood in Waco. There are, however, reasons to be suspicious of the connection between voice and film. In the most explicit thematic statement, one that most critics have assumed structures the film, Mrs. O'Brien talks about "two ways through life: the way of nature and the way of grace." This leads quickly to a larger opposition: nature is aggressive, demanding, self-serving, a way of trying to get ahead in the world; grace is about presence, acceptance, regarding the needs of others. And yet the entire speech is framed with the phrase, "the nuns taught us . . . ," a rhetorical gesture of distancing. Indeed, the opposition between nature and grace is something that the death of Mrs. O'Brien's son in the film's opening scenes will cause her to doubt. If the nuns said that only good things happen to people who follow the path of grace, and she has done that, how could such awful things have happened to her? We can also ask, more importantly: Does it make sense to think of *Malick* as opposing nature and grace? Would that mean that we had to think about all the glorious images of nature in his films as somehow *opposed* to grace? Do the glorious final images of *The New World*, for example, images full of natural beauty, fall on the side of the self-serving?

Malick's reliance on such ambiguities makes for interpretive difficulties. Mrs. O'Brien, whirling a young Jack around and pointing to the sky, says breathlessly: "That's where God lives!" It seems a gesture toward the heavens above, toward boundless space that's divided from the earth. A few shots earlier, Mr. O'Brien was teaching Jack a lesson about property: "You see this line [drawn between his property and their neighbors' yard]? Let's not cross it. . . . Stay out of there." There is a rhyme between the moments, based on a clear distinction between here and there, but what should we make of it? Is Heaven as forbidden a place as the neighbors' yard? Or should we see them as opposites, two different ways of being separate, one that forbids (father) and one that welcomes (mother)?

The second key issue raised by the final sequence of *The Thin Red Line* has to do with the natural world. Images of nature are at the heart of Malick's cinema. There are numerous shots of oceans, trees, grass blowing in the wind, clouds, birds, rivers, rocks . . . the list goes on. It's no coincidence that the openings and endings of Malick's films are often comprised of such images. *The Thin Red Line* starts with a shot of a crocodile submerging itself in an algae-covered pond and ends with the coconut on the beach. *The New World* begins with underwater shots, showing fish, and soon we see Native Americans—called, significantly, "naturals" by the colonists—diving into the water; it ends with images of nature in America. In *The Tree of Life*, many of the framing images of the film are of natural phenomena: the origins of the cosmos, certainly, but also the extraordinarily vivid field of sunflowers shown toward the end of the film. If the beauty of the natural world runs through these films, along with it comes a sense of its immanence, so it's natural that critics have described the ambition of the films as giving us unmediated access to nature and all it means.[37]

Yet despite the prominence of nature in his films, Malick is not exactly interested in nature as such. He does not provide a study of its transformations (as Alexander Dovzhenko does in *Earth* [1930]), nor does he explore natural phenomena (as Werner Herzog does in *Encounters at the End of the World* [2009]). His concern, rather, is with vision and perception, with how we see the (natural) world. The films point toward the fantasy of an unmediated encounter—the power of the images of nature gives a sense of directness to our view of them—yet they are filled with and by forms of mediated looking. This is one of the constitutive tensions in Malick's work.

Here we need to keep in mind the range of media and technologies of vision that run across his films. In *Badlands*, Holly looks at photos in her father's stereopticon. Initially they provide a sense of travel, images from around the world; later, they seem to comment more directly on her musings: about her family, about Kit, about the murders, about her future. She uses the images to project her own fantasies, the dream that she "would fall asleep and be taken off to some magical land," the technologies of vision that substitute for her gaze being unable to actually transport her. There are the photographs at the beginning of *Days of Heaven*, images used to elicit not just the historical moment but a sense of it as a *historical* moment. The credits of *The New World* contain a map whose features are progressively drawn in order to evoke the creation of the film's own world. Richard Neer writes: "A blank map of Virginia fills in magically, as bits of clip art seem to float before it; we also see seventeenth-century prints of ships crossing the sea, and colonists battling Indians. . . . [I]t combines an archaic form of mechanical reproduction—prints—with a futuristic one—CGI."[38] *The Tree of Life* features images taken from Thomas Wilfred's *Lumia* machines, a technology designed to produce abstract patterns of light; there are also extraordinary shots taken from or based on scientific images. *To the Wonder* (2012) features, among many visual displays, images of Skype video calls. And then there is cinema. A screening of Charlie Chaplin's *The Immigrant* (1917) is featured in *Days of Heaven*: "What Malick emphasizes is not Chaplin's narrative ... but rather a fleeting series of images impressed upon his young narrator."[39] *Song to Song* contains a cinematic entr'acte of sorts, which combines apparently documentary footage of the moon—and other images of space exploration—with the shocking ax murder that opens Dimitri Kirsanoff's *Ménilmontant* (1926).

Other forms of technologically mediated imagery are less explicit but no less important. One version of this is the dinosaur sequence in *The Tree of Life*. The CGI dinosaurs seem real, vivid; we respond to them as if we were actually looking at them—they are there. And yet, more than anything else in the film, we know they are not in any sense "there"— dinosaurs are, after all, extinct; they *cannot* be filmed. What we see must be generated by technology, a fact that Malick implicitly recognizes in his presentation of them—not least through his evocation of other dinosaur imagery, from *Fantasia* (Disney, 1940) to *Jurassic Park* (Steven Spielberg, 1993). Or we might think of another emblematic image, of sunlight streaming through the leaves of trees. If we take this to be an image of the natural world, it is equally true that what we see cannot exist without camera technology, that the lens flares are an artifact of the apparatus and not in the world itself.

Perhaps no cinematic technology is more evident in Malick's films than the Steadicam that dominates his style since *The Thin Red Line*. Every commentator seems to notice that Malick employs, as Landreville puts it, "an extensive use of Steadicam to free both camera operators and actors to indulge in caprices and in-the-moment choices."[40] Indeed, it is probably right to think of Malick's films as a duet or dialogue with his cinematographer, especially in the films he makes with Lubezki. Call it, perhaps, a displacement of the authorial function, even a practical enactment of the ironic mode of presentation. As a camera technology, the movement of the Steadicam is unique and uniquely palpable—a technology that an early practitioner called a "floating camera system."[41] With a set of stabilizer systems anchoring the camera apparatus to the body of the operator, the Steadicam provides an experience of movement that both is and is not like that of human motility. While it can move fluidly through space, and without the constraints of traditional tracking shots, the very smoothness of the camera's movement—its apparent detachment from the terrain—means that it feels divorced from the operator's body. The camera seems to become a kind of character, one that is within the world of the film yet also not quite of it (this is the case, for example, with the shots from *The Shining* I discussed in chapter 3).

All of these are technologically mediated forms of vision, ways in which media shape characters'—as well as viewers'—perceptions and experiences of the world. The specific feeling of mediation is a matter of technique and of how Malick uses the camera. We see this already in the first shot of *The Thin Red Line*, in which an alligator descends from the banks of a river and swims out into the algae-covered water before submerging within its depths. There is an allegorical reading to the scene, about the death, destructiveness, and danger that lie beneath the placid surface of the natural world; it cuts against any reading that treats nature as something that stands for a set of values opposed to the human war we will soon see. ("Nature is cruel," Tall will tell Staros in the process of removing him from command.) And yet as important as the allegory is the work of the camera, which tracks and pans with the alligator, reframing to keep its body in the center of the image. As the alligator begins to submerge, however, the camera starts to zoom in to the reptile's head, moving in so that we become attuned to the eyes as they close before dropping out of sight. The camera holds, and then there is a dissolve into a series of shots of trees framed against the sky as a voice wonders about the existence of "an avenging power in nature." Because of the movements of the camera, we do not just see the alligator moving through the water. We do not see the world, as it were, through a transparent window; it is *shown* to us by camera technology, with the track and the zoom creating a filtering of the world. We are being drawn in, held by the gaze of the alligator, before being released to the trees.

In saying this, I don't mean to return to the model I described and criticized in the first part of the book, in which we relate to the moving camera *as if* it were another character—a quasi-human entity—within the world of the film. Rather, following the alternate position I developed there, I'm arguing that Malick uses a sense of mediated and technological vision to *express* perspectives on the scene. Across the film, some perspectives—as they are articulated by the movement of the camera—are aligned to a character, some respond to a character, and some are descriptive of a general emotional situation (which can be glossed as "mood").

When I suggested that we can understand Malick as an ironist, it's this flexibility that I had in mind. There is no settled position within the film, no distinct viewpoint that we can accept as irrefutably Malick's own. Jeremy Millington puts it like this: "The broader point to be drawn is that [*The Thin Red Line*] encourages dramatically different readings with relative ease without ever fully endorsing one, presenting a range of ideas within the narrative, as well as in its broad and often conflicting allusions."[42] Rather than a doctrine, there are only different perspectives, multiple ways of approaching the world. What I focus on here, then, is not trying to derive a final position that Malick's films lead us to occupy, but analyzing the stylistic grammar or platform out of which the films' multiple perspectives are built. At the heart of this is the moving camera and how it becomes tied to multiple ways of inhabiting the worlds of the films.

3.

The contours of Malick's use of camera movement unfold over the course of *The Thin Red Line*, *The New World*, and *The Tree of Life*. Although there are rarely shots that could be construed as optical points of view, camera movements are often pegged to particular characters, expressing something about the way they view or inhabit the world around them. But they also, as we'll see, depart from individual focalizations to express a view not tied to any particular person. Scenes are then built as an agglomeration of perspectives rather than an intersection of space and action, which relies on a stable viewpoint on the world. While Malick's more recent films—what Robert Sinnerbrink calls the "weightless trilogy"—continue to deploy a heightened use of camera movement, they lack the structural dissonance that is present in those three earlier films.[43] I want to bring out the earlier idiosyncratic formal structure as the texture of an antiperspectival, ironic cinema.

An example of this mode occurs during the first battle sequence in *The Thin Red Line*. The film shows part of the Battle of Guadalcanal, focusing on a company assigned to take a hill as part of the initial assault on the island. Following the genre of the war film, Malick emphasizes a group of characters within the film—soldiers, such as Witt and Welsh, and officers, such as Staros and Tall—although many others are present as well. As the Americans attempt to destroy the bunker on top of the hill and are initially repelled in their assault, conflicts emerge. Tall urges Staros to make a frontal assault on the hill; Staros refuses, and eventually the assault is undertaken by a small group of soldiers, including Witt and Bell. The attack succeeds, and the company overruns the Japanese position; as a reward they are given leave. Afterward, on a patrol up a river, they encounter a Japanese group, and Witt sacrifices himself to allow the rest of the company to survive. The narrative is filled with other components—Witt going AWOL with Melanesians, Bell receiving a letter from his wife informing him that she is leaving him—and poetic reveries.

The sequence I discuss here begins after the Americans, having advanced some way into the island with little difficulty, suddenly encounter a strong defense from a hill. Machine gun and rifle fire pins them down and begins to decimate the unit. As soldiers seek cover in the tall grass and fire uphill, Malick tracks horizontally to the left behind them. The camera moves rapidly, and without change in direction. A sharp cut suddenly switches the angle of action ninety degrees; the camera is stationary, while soldiers run away from it into the open fields where shells are exploding. Another cut takes us to a mirror of the first shot, this time a quick horizontal movement to the left from in front of the soldiers, but rather than shooting, they are now being shot.

A shift in the sequence's tempo comes with the next shot. Initially tracking behind a soldier who is running into battle, it seems as though we are in the familiar model of following an individual through space. But he is quickly shot, falling out of the frame, and the camera continues to progress on its own terms, freed from the constraints of following another body. It seems to drift, floating over the terrain—an effect characteristic of Steadicam—before apparently following the sound of a voice to track in to a soldier who is looking back toward his own lines. The camera holds, a pause that effects a shift in the action. Another explosion happens in the middle distance; the soldier ducks down as others are killed (see figure 15). A cut brings us to a medium shot of a soldier cowering in the grass, breathing sharply in panic. Another cut takes us to two soldiers in medium close-up, one of whom—Staros—is chanting "calm down" to himself (and, presumably, to the world at large); he licks his lips and looks around nervously. Two quick shots now show soldiers pressed down into the grass, eyes wide open and looking around rapidly. This cluster of fairly static shots ends with a return to Staros, this time isolated within the frame and looking toward the front lines through binoculars; he turns back toward the camera and calls for stretcher-bearers.

These shots illustrate how Malick simultaneously evokes and subverts the formal conventions of classical Hollywood cinema. The shot of Staros looking through binoculars, according to classical film grammar, would retroactively confer point-of-view status on the two shots of soldiers cowering against the grass. Yet the shots remain isolated from one another. Partly this has to do with the angle of the shots of the soldiers, as the camera is close to ground level and not from the raised position of Staros. But it is also the way Malick builds the scene: each section is separate from one the others, a partial perspective on the action taking place. The shots never combine to produce a final perspective from which a clear meaning can be extracted.

The next part of the sequence is comprised of a single, extended shot, following the call for "stretcher-bearers." The camera begins as if to the side of the hill, off the ground and moving forward; the hill runs from the top of the left side of the frame toward the bottom right, creating a vacant space in the frame that the camera moves through. It picks up a line of soldiers with stretchers running through the paths in the grass to the left side of the frame; they dodge explosions, and then the camera floats up and behind them. We feel, given the combination of Staros's call and the focus of this shot, that they are the object of interest, and we suspect that once the camera gets behind them it will follow their path through the battle to pick up the wounded. But the camera does something else. Almost appearing indifferent to their actions, it crosses their path and continues in a horizontal movement to the left. New pieces of the battle come into view: wounded soldiers being carried off on the shoulders of others, more soldiers rising up out of the grass to charge forward, and the omnipresent explosions and bullets from the Japanese encampment. The sequence ends almost as it began, with a horizontal track to the left as soldiers charge forward and are killed by incoming fire. While the battle goes on, this formal rhyme marks a kind of closure.

This entire sequence lasts only about forty-five seconds, an extremely brief amount of time, and contains little narratively significant action. The complexity of the camera movement, and of the editing patterns, seems almost unnecessary; it's the kind of sequence that critics often gloss by simply acknowledging Malick's penchant for moving the camera, spatial ambiguity, and enigmatic narrative organization. What I am trying to pull out, however, is the presence of a more complex arrangement, one that the spectator experiences—and struggles to find a secure place in—as the camera moves through the world of the film. We are never at a point of view from outside (whether that is thought of as a "transcendental subject," an authorial perspective, or some other position); we never get a sense of perceptual or epistemic order or control. We are always immersed in events, and often—but not always—aligned with individual characters, their movements, and their actions. It is the

1

3

5

FIGURE 15. *The Thin Red Line* (Terrence Malick, 1998). The camera's path through the battle.

agglomeration of these partial perspectives that creates the fluctuating mood and tone of the sequences as a whole.

Such sequences show how Malick works with cinematic convention. It's certainly true that classical cinema uses the moving camera as a way to attune viewers to the perspective of a character or characters or to

2

4

create a general mood. But these moments often require point-of-view shots, as Stanley Cavell describes:

> It is sometimes said, and it is natural to suppose, that the camera is an extension of the eye. Then it ought to follow that if you place the camera at the physical point of view of a character, it will objectively reveal what the character is viewing. But the fact is, if we have been given the idea that the camera is placed so that what we see is what the character sees *as he sees it,* then what is shown to us is not just something seen but a specific *mood* in which it is seen. In *Paths of Glory,* we watch Kirk Douglas walking through the trenches lined with the men under his command, whom he, under orders, is about to order into what he knows is a doomed attack. When the camera then moves to a place behind his eyes, we do not gain but forgo an objective view of what he sees; we are given a vision constricted by his mood of numb and helpless rage.[44]

What Cavell gets right is the capacity of the camera to present more than sight: that the terms of its movements, in the context of a scene, can show how a character experiences the world. Malick takes this a step further, since nowhere in this battle scene does the camera correspond to the optical perspective of a character. The movement of the camera is sufficient, on its own, to do this work. In the horizontal tracking shots, for example, it can even seem indifferent to the fact that there are people in the frame—giving a sense of the rhythms of the battle, a generalized image, rather than any one person's perspective on it.

Within Malick's model of scene construction, the camera doesn't focus on any specific character's reaction, nor does it have a human-like presence in the film. The camera builds up an overall sense of the action through the ways it responds to what it's showing. (Its movements, that is, resemble the early shots of *The Shining* more than they do the walk through the trenches in *Paths of Glory*.) Thus, after the call for stretchers, the camera suddenly releases into speed, moving forward unfettered by the fighting going on around it; we could call this a fantasy of escape, a sense of relief (especially for the wounded) with the appearance of the medical corps. In contrast, the halting of the forward movement, the shift to the horizontal axis, changes the inclination of the shot, a forestalling of this earlier fantasy. Soldiers continue to march forward; shells continue to explode. The characters are caught up within the complex array of reactions and emotions; they are not constitutive of it.

Malick even extends this formal organization into long takes. The next morning the final assault on the hill begins, this time with a small group trying to sneak up to the bunker. The camera starts low to the ground, just at the top of the grass, following a soldier hurrying forward while crouched low; the hillside this time angles from the top right, but otherwise the composition is similar to the earlier shot. As the soldier reaches a small crest, the camera passes over him, moving onward to pick up the next few men in front. It slides out from the hill, losing the familiar moorings of terrestrial gravity but still gliding forward. Camera and soldiers continue onward, moving at a similar pace, and Malick begins a new phase of the shot: the camera drops down, moving toward the top of the rise, and becomes buried within the long strands of grass rising up from the hill. It's now in real proximity to the soldiers, hovering over their shoulders, and the feeling of speed is increased (it's not actually moving faster, just closer to the ground) as we hear the rough breathing of physical effort. The camera pushes through the grass for a few seconds before Malick cuts to a position in front of the group, watching them crawl up the sides of the hill. The restlessness of the camera precludes any focalizing point of view that we could use to ground our position in the scene. There are no givens; every position, every point of view—even the camera's own—is simply expressed by the movement of the camera.

I have consciously stayed away from questions of authorial intent throughout this chapter (and indeed the book as a whole). But there is an important way in which the terms that emerge in *The Thin Red Line*—about the way the camera articulates the world of the film and does so by establishing an interplay of points of view—resonate with Malick's early writing on the concept of "world" in Heidegger. Malick observes that what concerns Heidegger is not the world as "the totality of things" but rather "that in terms of which we understand them."[45] In this, Malick makes a subtle but important point about the "we" who strive to make sense of the world. Heidegger, he says, aims to provide the terms by which we *can* create a shared understanding or account of the world, precisely "because sometimes we *do not*, or do not seem to, share such notions." And it's at the moments when the shared sense of a world falls apart, when we no longer seamlessly move through the world, Malick argues, that the idea of "point of view" comes to be felt. Point of view, he suggests, is not a matter of a visual position—how I see the world—but rather an interpretive one—how I make sense of the world. It is something we come to be preoccupied with only when the coherence of the world, our reliance on the stability of the shared life we lead—"our schemes"—starts to disintegrate.[46]

While these topics form the underlying structure of *The Thin Red Line*, they become the overt content of *The New World*, in which a concern with point of view—as an epistemic rather than psychological problem—shapes its formal strategy. *The New World* is a version of the Pocahontas story, starting with the arrival of the English to create the settlement of Jamestown in what is now Virginia. There, they encounter the Powhatan, and John Smith is sent to establish contact with them. Captured, he is spared by the chief's daughter—referred to as "The Princess" within the film—and they fall in love. Smith returns to Jamestown, where he is placed in command, and the English are saved from starvation by the Powhatan. The English fail to leave the next spring, however, and the two sides engage in a battle, in which the English are victorious. Although the Princess is banished from her village and comes to live with Smith at the settlement, he decides to leave for new adventures, arranging for another settler to lie and say that he has died. She falls into despair, at which point the film pivots. A new settler, John Rolfe, becomes captivated by her; she has been newly baptized as Rebecca—the name she will use throughout the rest of the film—and begins working on his tobacco farm. Rolfe proposes marriage to her, and she accepts—although she tells him that, having learned that Smith is still alive, she is unable to love him. Nevertheless, they are happy together; they have a son, and they are chosen to go to England to meet the king and queen. There, Rebecca is enthralled by the commercial bustle of London and has a meeting with Smith, during which she refuses his appeal to return to their more innocent state. She embraces Rolfe and plays with her son. The film concludes with her death and the family returning to Virginia.

Malick's use of the moving camera intimately engages the shifting dynamics of the characters. This occurs in a marked way toward the end, when Smith comes to talk to Rebecca in England. Their encounter begins with two curious shots. The first one is of Smith, looking about him (somewhat broodingly) and inhabiting his usual mode of romantic behavior (he smooths out his hair); the other is also of Smith, this time framed through a doorway that Rebecca will soon enter. Both could be from her point of view, and they present Smith in an extremely theatricalized construction, in contrast to her own "natural" way of being in the world.

Broadly speaking, the scene involves her coming to recognize the limitations of the love they previously had: perhaps she has the sense that it is something that can no longer be captured, or recaptured; perhaps the problem is the seductiveness and fantasy of the very terms with which it began. The past remains the past. But Malick goes further, giving a visceral sense of their isolation from one another and then drawing a counterpoint by articulating an experience of profound and powerful pleasure in her engagement with Rolfe and, especially, her young son.

The scene begins with Rebecca and Smith walking down a tree-lined lane together, with her slightly in front. The shot is facing them, tracking backward and handheld; the trees recede from both sides of the frame to create a perspectival composition. The next shot flips 180 degrees: it moves forward, again handheld, toward a kind of gazebo in the background. No characters are in the shot; we might presume that it is from her point of view, but that isn't specified. A third shot moves somewhere else: not the end of the path that we had seen, but underneath a different structure by a pond overlooking the manor where the encounter is taking place. Rebecca is still in front of Smith, and as she comes to a halt he slowly moves up to be parallel to her, the camera following slowly behind.

Their somewhat enigmatic conversation begins. We get a shot of Smith, taken from below, as he looks slightly to the side of the camera. "You knew," he says, "I had promise, didn't you?" Malick cuts to

Rebecca, again from below, as she looks above and to the right of the camera and replies, "yes." Behind and above her we can see trees, and we realize that we're no longer under the enclosure; another dislocation has happened. (Is it temporal? Emotional?) After a pause, and a smile, Rebecca asks, "Did you find your Indies, John?" He furrows his brow and stares vacantly; she says, "You shall." Looks between them lead to a longer shot of Smith, who eventually says, "I may have sailed past them"—an implicit recognition of his failure to have recognized her value. She smiles, and the sequence ends.

What's remarkable in their exchange is the combination of a static frame and shot/reverse-shot editing. Although both are part of standard cinematic practice, they are rarely found in *The New World* and are almost entirely absent in Malick's late work. When he uses static shots, they carry dramatic weight, especially against—perhaps even as—the broader deployment of the moving camera. In this case, the stasis describes the end of the couple's relationship as the absence of movement or dynamism—or a future. (A moment early in the film foreshadows this. When Smith first wanders away from the settlement, Malick cuts away to the Princess and her brother in the grass. They are moving, playing, and the camera moves with them. Smith enters, and the camera basically freezes as the two stare at one another. The halt is dramatically motivated, of course, but it is also a formal articulation of their relationship and the way Smith's love will eliminate her capacity to move through and be happy in the world.)

Malick continues to use camera movements to elucidate the terms of a relationship. A shot from behind Smith shows Rebecca walking below him in a formal garden with well-groomed hedges behind her; the camera tracks slowly down and to the left as she walks, following her movements and leaving him out of the frame. Another set of shot/reverse-shot pairings then emerges. The first is a profile of Smith. "I thought it was a dream," he says, "what we know in the forest. It turns out it's the only truth." The second shot is of Rebecca, over his right shoulder, as she smiles. Malick repeats the pattern: "It seems as if I was speaking to you for the first time," followed by a closer view of her. A return shot to Smith is now from her perspective: he is shown frontally, looking directly at the camera. A return to the previous shot of Rebecca shows her no longer smiling; she turns and slowly walks away, and afterward we get the frontal shot of Smith following by the initial framing in profile. A cut to a shot of the manor, with rows of sculpted trees in front of it, reveals Smith walking slowly toward it.

Malick then inserts a curious shot of Rebecca standing in a tree, high on a branch, wearing her formal English dress. The shot is an echo of a moment earlier in the film when, at play and in love with Smith, she stood similarly—in harmony with nature, at one with her natural surroundings. The echo suggests the terms of Smith's offer to her: to find each other as they had been, not as they are now, an offer of nostalgic appeal, of a return to innocence. It is an appeal of melodrama, the fantasy of everlasting love that can—and should—become alive again. But she is no longer the same person; her new clothing marks her as being on the far side of experience.

Yet this is not an ending. Gunning writes, "Malick sees experience as not simply disillusionment but a reshaping of nature through an imagination that has been tested by loss and sustained by memory."[47] If Rebecca is no longer in love with Smith and recognizes their earlier love as limited, that knowledge allows her to proceed in new ways. And so the counterpart to Smith's appeal comes in the next part of the sequence. Malick cuts to a profile of Rolfe, kneeling by a window with his head bowed as if in prayer, a brief indication that he knows the stakes of the meeting between Rebecca and Smith. It is again a moment of hesitancy and, like the shot of Rebecca standing in the tree, of indeterminacy.

The sequence changes. We see Rolfe from behind as he walks down a stone path amid the gardens, yet now the camera is moving with him, no longer confined but again mobile, and as it moves Rebecca walks into the shot from behind it, moving swiftly forward. A 180-degree cut moves in front of them, then a close-up shows her hand slipping into the crook of his arm; she clutches his arm, and he pauses momentarily—the camera, though, keeps moving backward—and then they walk together. After a while, she stops their progress and moves in front to face him; the camera swirls up and around to the left, putting them both into profile and even moving a little behind him. It is the camera's first movement since the conversation with Smith began that is not strictly bound to the movement of a person. Rebecca asks, "Can we not go home?," looking up at him, and he breathes in response: "As soon as possible." Several shots go by: Rolfe smiling at her; Rebecca smiling at him. And then, with the camera behind her as she looks at him, she whispers, "My husband." They embrace, kiss, smile, and then start to walk away together. Malick then, and extraordinarily, cuts to the framing of the first shot that showed Rolfe walking—but now the pair are in the distance, and we are behind their son, who swings his arms happily from side to side. Several shots follow: Rolfe on a lawn throwing balls into the air for the boy to catch; Rebecca lying on the sunlit grass, apparently watching them; Rolfe looking back at her and smiling.

It's here that Malick's emphasis on stillness and stasis pays off, as he creates emotional release through the sudden freedom of the camera. The son runs along a hedge, then chases sheep; the camera, freed from characters, moves after him, reframing and angling to get new perspectives. Rebecca runs into the shot, moving with him, and they follow the sheep into the distance. There is a cut to a shot of Rolfe, looking at them and smiling, and then the sound of Richard Wagner's *Vorspiel* emerges, echoing the opening moments of the film and, as Neer puts it, "announcing that this is a new beginning, or rather a new iteration of an old beginning."[48]

What follows is an ecstatic sequence. A shot of Rebecca holding her son in her arms is followed by a shot of the two of them standing and whispering to each other. Then everything goes into motion. A shot shows Rebecca walking toward the camera from a tree in the middle distance, moving slightly stiltedly; it is as if the shot echoes the movements from her earlier conversation with Smith. But then the camera, moving with her to the left, suddenly goes behind a tree, and we see her son's arm on it. He ducks behind it and begins to run out to the right; as the camera follows him, moving swiftly, we see Rebecca crouch and then begin to run after him. This is play, a game of hide and seek, far from the formality of earlier conversation; it is an image of joy and love. The son reaches a hedge with Rebecca approaching, laughs, and then turns back to the left and runs along a hedge row into the distance at the top left of the screen. (See figure 16.) There is a cut to an almost identical image of a hedge, this time with Rebecca racing from the top left in a diagonal line toward the camera, exactly reversing his direction. She crosses the camera, and it moves to stay behind her shoulder as she runs along a hedge, then crouches behind it to hide. A new shot shows the son running, the camera following, and a quick cut to Rebecca moving to peer around a hedge; the camera goes ahead of her, and we see her son running away and going around a corner in the distance. A still shot of Rebecca pauses the action; she looks off to the right, the camera rotates around her, and she closes her eyes. We hear her voice-over: "Mother, now I know where you live," and a shot of her son still racing around hedges in their game, looking over his shoulder as if at the camera. There is a quick shot of Rebecca, close to the camera, hiding behind a hedge; her son is in the distance, looking for her. She darts off to the right, and he runs toward the camera, which swivels around the hedge to frame him—and then he turns and runs off into the distance, as if escaping from her (or from

1

3

FIGURE 16. *The New World* (Terrence Malick, 2004). Hide and seek.

the camera?). There is now a closer shot of him as he walks around a corner of the hedge, his arms tucked inside his shirt, looking around at the vacant spaces, and then a shot—as if from his point of view—initially moving toward the house and then turning swiftly to the right to see an empty expanse of garden.

The sequence is roughly comprised of two concurrent games of hide and seek, between Rebecca and her son and between the camera and the characters. Neer writes, "The camera is restless. Sometimes it accompanies mother and child, sometimes it holds still, sometimes it takes a POV, sometimes not; often it will seem to follow the figures, pursuing them after its own fashion. Such participation establishes an affinity between game and movie."[49] Yet what's curious in Neer's description is his treatment of the camera as if it were emotionally neutral, passing over the joy in the way the film sweeps us along, how the initial burst into movement as we catch sight of the son behind the tree is carried through the rhythms of their game, and the way the camera moves

to convey pleasure. This is why the formality of the conversation with Smith is so important: it establishes the negative valence of stillness, of formal and organized movements, and so sets the stage for the ecstatic release in play. (A mode, remarked Thoreau, of being "beside oneself in a sane sense."[50])

During the last pair of shots, a voice-over by Rolfe begins, reading a letter to his son that recounts Rebecca's death; this voice-over initiates the final movement of the sequence. Three shots mark her illness and death. The first is of her hand, with her wedding ring, clasped in Rolfe's; the second is of a circular mirror with a cloudy surface, in which Rolfe can be seen kneeling by her bed, her hand on his head; and the third is of his tear-stricken face looking up at her. All three shots are static, though with the slight movements of a handheld camera. There is then a shot of their son walking through a doorway made of branches, the camera low to the ground and following behind him. He is looking around, moving somewhat aimlessly. Rolfe's voice-over continues during this shot: "She

FIGURE 17. *The New World* (Terrence Malick, 2004).

gently reminded me that all must die. 'Tis enough, she said, that you, our child, shall live." This is followed by a new series of static shots: a stained glass window, high above; the empty sickbed; then two shots of a Native American, painted blue, first from in front as he sits in a chair and then from behind as he runs out of the house and into the garden. All this suggests the narrativized teleology around death: an abandoned child, an empty space, a seemingly spiritual figure leaving the place. Yet the sequence does not end here. A shot of the top of a tree follows, and the camera tilts down its length to reveal Rebecca walking around its trunk, her hand running over it. She walks off toward a pond behind her, and the camera begins to follow—before a cut takes us to a shot from behind her, now running and moving around trees, the camera rushing to catch up (see figure 17). Another shot continues this motion, as she turns a cartwheel, then a third stays slightly behind as she runs, then whirls, in the middle distance. A new shot shows her standing in the pond with rain pouring down; smiling, she reaches down to cup water in her hands, then pours it over herself in an evocation of rites shown at the beginning of the film. The camera moves in to frame her in a medium close-up. Another shot returns us to the bank beside the pond as she runs toward and past the camera, which turns to follow her movements; this shot apparently moves us back in time, as her dress is no longer wet from the rain and the pond. The sequence ends with a shot of a bird flying overhead, perhaps an allegory for both death and freedom, and then the film concludes with the departure of Rolfe and their son for America—and a set of images of nature that coincide with the swelling of the *Vorspiel*, before all goes quiet over the rushing water of a stream and the rustling leaves of a tree.

Neer reads the sequence in terms of Rebecca's death, seeing in it a reflection on the initial love-play between Smith and the Princess in the forest (and his subsequent abandonment of her). He writes, "The game begins with an embrace, not a withdrawal, and it ends with an abandonment of a different kind: the mother's abandonment of the child in death."[51] This is true, yet despite Rebecca's death and Rolfe's sadness in recounting it, the sense of pleasure, happiness, and freedom is not wholly undermined. The images of Rebecca in the final moments of the sequence are no less exhilarating than at the outset of the game, the camera is no less enraptured by her movement and sense of play, and the expressions of love for others and for the world are no less profound. The pleasure involved does not rely on a fantasy of escape, on getting away to find new adventures. That is Smith's model. Rather, it is based in an experience of now-ness, of being in the world in the present.

The scene in the garden constitutes an end not just of the story of the Princess/Rebecca but also of the film's large-scale narrative sweep. As many commenters have noted, the plot of *The New World* echoes the opening statement of Rousseau's *On the Social Contract*: "Man is born free, and everywhere he is in chains. . . . How has this change come about?"[52] The film seems to answer this question by framing it within a colonial standpoint: from the "state of nature" that is present in the beginning, and in which the Princess thrives, Smith's arrival with the English will literally place her in chains; she will become wholly alienated from her way of life and sense of self. Yet this is not just a story about her, but about the "world" in the film's title. And Malick takes care not to present a radical separation between Native Americans and English settlers. Neer describes this dynamic:

The Native peoples have their own ways of dividing up the world and representing it. The English turn trees into palisades, but the Indians turn them into dwellings; the trunks of the forest can structure a shot just as well as a ship's rigging; the English have mirrors and print technology, but the Indians make wood statues and perform mimetic dances; it is an Indian who sells Pocahontas for a kettle, and Rolfe who rescues her from isolation. Smith idealizes the Indians, and Newport refers to them contemptuously as "Naturals," but their all-too-human behavior belies such fantasies; Powhatan's people put a noose around Smith's neck just as Newport did, and their village has its share of shots framed in windows and doors, its share of stark architectural frames. Nature is not a given in this film and its denizens are not Noble Savages, Rousseau notwithstanding.[53]

There is another important parallel. When Rebecca travels to England with Rolfe, she experiences London with the same sense of wonder that Smith experienced when he arrived in Virginia.[54] Here it is precisely the emergent global capitalist marketplace that is—from her perspective— the new world: goods from around the world; spectacular sights and sounds and smells. Malick relativizes newness, using Rebecca's travel to give a sense that what matters in thinking about questions of discovery, exploration, and wonder is bound up with the variances of perspective.

This returns us to the structure of the film. It is crucial that *The New World* does not end with the Princess's alienation, her isolation and abandonment, that it does not simply tell a story of loss. She becomes Rebecca and is loved by Rolfe, whom she eventually comes to love in turn. The second half of the film, which lacks the John Smith narrative, reveals Malick's broader ambition: not to be constrained by a narrative of a fall from grace but to redeem itself in terms of a(nother) new world. This does not mean that Malick strays from the Rousseauist framework. *On the Social Contract* is itself no nostalgic paean to the state of nature but an attempt to figure out the conditions for freedom within a social order: "To find a form of association . . . by means of which each person, joining forces with all, nevertheless obeys only himself and remains free as before." This, Rousseau remarks, "is the fundamental problem to which the social contract furnishes the solution."[55] And so the final sequence of *The New World* gives us the terms on which the film believes it can answer that question, the sense of freedom that is required in order to form a new (just?) society.

This ambition finds an echo in Rebecca's "Mother, now I know where you live," which functions as an answer to a question she asks earlier in the film, when she is in love with Smith: "Mother, where do you live? In the sky? The clouds? The sea? Show me your face. Give me a sign. We rise, we rise." There she is searching for answers: to understand her love for this new man—"A god, he seems to me"—and to place him in alignment with her own world. By the end of the film, the anxiety is gone, resulting in, as Sinnerbrink observes, a declaration of "reconciliation," a sense in which the central terms in the film are solved, "however fleetingly."[56]

Such fleetingness is tied up with Malick's refusal to provide an image of what this new society will look like. We get nothing as detailed as the depictions of the world of the Native Americans (natural) or the settlers (alienated). There are intimations, a sense of feeling—evanescent forms that are made to carry a great deal of weight. Malick relies on an intuitive and familiar affinity between domestic organization and national forms, the linking of the terms of marriage to the terms of a social order. In this context, it is not trivial that what instigates the move into play, between the members of the family themselves and between them and the camera, is Rebecca saying the word "husband"—a declaration that is given no further verbal explication. It is the first time she has used this phrase in the film, and she is not so much describing their legal status as recommitting to him, refounding their relationship. She had told Rolfe in Virginia that as long as she knew that Smith lived—even though she knew he had abandoned her—she considered herself already married, hence that they could not be genuinely married. To return to Rolfe after the conversation with Smith, and to call him "husband," is to make a declaration of the central condition of their relationship. Even outside the legal context, her word is performative, the creation of a state of being—a particular relation—in naming it.

In the focus on the word "husband" and on the logic of recommitting, Malick's film echoes Cavell's notion of "remarriage comedy." The model of that genre, of getting a couple *back* together, is taken by Cavell to be the central dynamic of a series of comedies of the 1930s and 1940s. And it is precisely over the dynamic of remarriage that the play over the "new" in the "new world" of Malick's film takes shape. Rolfe and Rebecca are not innocent; this is not their first love. Having been apart, now they must find each other (again). Cavell will take the status of marriage in this genre to be a way of thinking through the very idea of America, a unity between different forces that together constitute a new beginning, a new sense of purpose: "so that American mankind can refind its object, its dedication to a more perfect union, toward the perfected human community, its right to the pursuit of happiness."[57]

I don't mean to make *The New World* into a comedy of remarriage—it isn't—but the resonance offers ways to open up the work of Malick's film. One is that Cavell repeatedly returns to the idea of "play" as a way to describe the relationship between the couple and what marks them as special. "Almost without exception these films allow the principal pair to express the wish to be children again, or perhaps to be children together. In part this is a wish to make room for playfulness within the gravity of adulthood, in part it is a wish to be cared for first, and unconditionally."[58] Malick treads carefully here. Smith offers to Rebecca the chance to be children again, to play outside a social world. Yet the play she chooses is within society, "to make room . . . within the gravity of adulthood": to play as a family, and to position their child—a figure noticeably absent in Cavell's model—at the center of the games. It is not about a return to wild, uncultivated spaces. Cavell observes that reconciliation tends to happen in a space separate from normal social interactions, a "green world . . . in which perspective and renewal are to be achieved."[59] Unlike the wholly natural spaces of Shakespearean romances, the Hollywood comedies typically mark this as a country estate—a place they often call, Cavell notes, "Connecticut." The formal gardens in *The New World* are precisely this kind of green world in which nature and culture interact: not London, the site of new capitalism, nor Virginia, the site of untouched nature, but a hybrid form. The capacity to enable a reimagining of a relationship is marked precisely by the family's capacity to play within the space.

Yet if Malick follows Cavell in seeing marriage as "emblem of the promise [of] human society," the single word "husband" seems far from the extended dialogues Cavell analyzes, in which positions and relations are being constantly reconfigured and realigned, as well as from the deliberative discussions that Rousseau pictures as constituting the terms of a general will.[60] But the utterance is deceptively simple. In the "extended cut" of *The New World*, Malick begins the film with an epigraph attributed to John Smith: "How much they err, that think that everyone that has been at Virginia understands or knows what Virginia is." The claim is about experience and about the difference between legalistic terms and a genuine knowledge; if we apply it to Rebecca's situation, we could say that not everyone who has been married is actually married. The inadequacy of language in fact structures the initial marriage proposal that Rolfe makes in Virginia. After he and Rebecca run through fields, as if chasing each other in play, he says to her (looking not at her but off into the distance): "Suppose I asked you to marry me. What would you say?" She replies, framed from behind, "Are you asking me?" He nods, says "yes," and only then turns to her; he continues to talk, which she evades, then finally asks, "Won't you say 'yes'?" to which she replies: "If you like." Rituals have gone askew. The marriage ceremony itself will be shown devoid of performatives; they do not speak, and the only part of the ceremony we hear implicitly alludes to Smith (about whether there are impediments to the marriage). It is not that they are not married; they are, and the film shows that something at least resembling love emerges, that they are happy together—and that her happiness, if qualified, is still real. But the marriage has not been a real marriage, or so the final scene suggests.

Here we return to the framework of irony and what Jonathan Lear has characterized as ironic experience: a feeling of being confronted with the real meaning of a term that forces us to realize that we have not lived up to it. It is the ironic questioning of a Socrates or a Kierkegaard—"In all of Christendom, is there a Christian?"—an ostensibly nonsensical statement that is meant to show that we fail to be genuine Christians in everything it means (i.e., the example of Christ himself). Lear writes, "Irony . . . is the activity of bringing this falling short in a way that is meant to grab us."[61] This is not a form of distancing or pithy denial of commitment. As Lear argues, it is precisely my investment in an activity that allows for an ironic disruption to happen: I must care about something in order for it to strike me that I have fallen short of my ideal. "I can no longer live with the available social understanding . . . ; if I am to return to them it must be in a different way."[62] Within *The New World*, Rebecca's whispered "husband" does not indicate that she *failed* in not loving him fully before; indeed, it is clear to them that their marriage was not based on mutual love. ("You will learn to love me, in time," he says when he proposes.) But in uttering this word, and with her kiss, Rebecca imposes the ideal onto her life. It is a performative in a mode of irony: it does nothing within a legal framework, but calls into being the range of transformations required by accepting the word's meaning.

What this means, how it should be realized, is not shown in the film. The reason for this is partly narrative, as Rebecca will soon die; hence she has no chance to put this promise into practice. Malick is not providing a blueprint so much as an experience, trying to convey what such a belief would be: the "experience of utopia" that Richard Dyer analyzed in the Hollywood musical, in which precise terms are bypassed in favor of an ephemeral experience of a better possibility.[63]

The mode of experience touches all parts of the film, from narrative to voice-over to style. As with antiperspectivalism, Malick's core principles run all the way down.[64] So what differentiates the space of the garden at the end is not just the term of the narrative but also the camera's ability to move us through the world along with the play of mother and child, thereby giving us an intimation of the joy they are experiencing, the pleasure and community on which a social ideal could be described. The movement of the camera unites old and new worlds as well as generations, creating a promise of happiness that carries the viewer along with it. If the camera is not really in that world, even as it moves through its spaces, it nonetheless gives us an experience of immersion, a fantasy of being in that world—and of being there *in a particular way*. We might call this, again following Lear, a development of the "capacity" for being struck by the ironic distance between practical activity and the ideal.[65] The camera provides an intimation of how happiness, or freedom, ought to feel, an intimation of a regulative ideal that could guide our actions.

Once Rebecca has called Rolfe "husband," in other words, movements of the camera are allowed to resonate with unexpected connections: between the reimagining of their marriage and the creation of a new world, and between the experience of play and the mode of social organization. Cavell remarks that marriage is "the central social image of human change."[66] Malick's project in *The New World* rests on the antiperspectival position that there is no single standpoint from which a coherent view of the world can be taken, no way to assume visual control of space from outside it; everything is immersed in the world and in the multiple ways in which it can be and is inhabited. We grow because we are not fixed on our course.

4.

The ending of *The New World* poses an interpretive problem. Rebecca continues to dance, along with the camera, and to express her joy—yet the film has already shown her death. It's a difficult ordering to make sense of, with Malick weaving different temporal moments into a seamless flow. Neer writes:

> We see her deathbed in a convex mirror. Now a series of cross-cuts renders the narrative sequence obscure: past and present interfuse, both within the diegesis and between the diegetic world and the present day. The child searches the garden for his mother (so was the deathbed scene proleptic? But it was cast as Rolfe's recollection); the deathbed reappears, empty (does it await Pocahontas or has she already died?). . . . Pocahontas runs and dances alone in the garden, presumably while her son looks for her but also, just possibly, after her death, as a spirit. She splashes water on her head, a

self-baptism. Her grave appears, not freshly dug but overgrown with centuries of weeds, as it might look today if its location were known; like the film itself, it is a memorial in the here-and-now.[67]

I have already noted how the style of the film stays the same on either side of Rebecca's death, the camera continuing its movements and its responsiveness to her play and joy. Yet something else is happening as well. In these final moments, it is as if standard chronological order, the linear temporality of historical progression, is no longer capable of encompassing the emotional force of the sequence. The interaction of personal narrative, family dynamics, and political order seems to require the resources of the past and the future to unite in the now.

This rejection of linear time more or less involves a movement beyond the terms of perspective, doing away with the idea that there is a fixed position that can ground an understanding of the world. If this forms the culmination of *The New World*, its highest emotional peak, a movement toward an outside of human experience is the structuring principle of *The Tree of Life* as a whole. The film begins, after all, with an epigram from the Book of Job:

> Where were you when I laid the foundations of the earth? . . .
> When the morning stars sang together, and all the sons of
> God shouted for joy?
> (Job 38:4, 7)

The lines are God's response to Job when he asks for the reasons behind his suffering, for a justification that would explain the wrongs for which he is being punished. If he has lived a good life, how can God justify causing such pain? Malick provides not Job's question but God's wild answer: you weren't there at the beginning, at the moment of utmost joy, so how can you understand anything about the present?

The exchange between Job and God can function as a debate on perspective. Job is asking how he can achieve a point of view from which the suffering with which he has been afflicted makes sense, from which he can understand the moral order of the universe as it is applied to him. His question revolves around the terms of a perspectival understanding, the apprehension of the world not in itself but from one's own point of view.[68] And it is one reason that Kierkegaard, in his many writings on Job, sees him as emblematic of the human condition.[69] Job wants to know how he could know. God's response is to reject the terms of the question, to present a vision that is entirely outside the possibilities of perspective altogether; the problem is not, say, epistemic but metaphysical in nature.

The Job problem runs throughout *The Tree of Life*. Characters repeatedly wonder how something can be justified and then face the impossibility of occupying a position from which their question could be answered. This emerges not least in Malick's insistence on a distinction between the world of the adult and the world of the child. Throughout the sequences set in Waco, we are presented with information about the world as if we were limited to what the children can see or understand, forcing the spectator to be without knowledge of what is happening. Take the moment in which a very young Jack sees a man having what might be an epileptic fit on the front lawn; rather than lingering on his suffering, as if the man were a Job figure, the camera moves away with Jack as his mother covers his eyes. And then the scene ends, with no explanation, a haunting image made all the more disturbing by the lack of context. Other examples proliferate. We see the brothers mocking people with limps, then unnerved by a crippled man; they look at a man in a police car, raging against the police, then at a prisoner being given water by Mrs. O'Brien. There is even a trip to an African American neighborhood, shown as if it were a strange phenomenon that could never be explained. The adult world makes no sense to the children; it lacks order and rhythm and reason. Malick places us in that position with respect to the film's own world.

But Malick also goes further. Part of the project of *The Tree of Life* is to gain access to a vision from outside the constraints of perspective, in a sense to take the response of God seriously, as both an ethical and an aesthetic principle. It is not a unique fantasy. Hegel, for example, describes "Spirit emptied out into Time," an "externalization" that results in "a slow-moving succession of Spirits, a gallery of images"—as if the reach of time had become graspable in a single view.[70] Or there is Ralph Waldo Emerson: "I become a transparent eyeball; I am nothing; I see all; the currents of the Universal Being circulate through me; I am part or parcel of God."[71] The audacity of *The Tree of Life* is to picture this vision, to attempt to grasp the divine mode of seeing through explicitly human technologies. A result of this ambition is the division of the film into two temporal orders, one that is focused on the human—the scenes set in the present and in Jack's childhood—and another that presents the divine—the origins of the cosmos, the scene of paradise. One is historical, one is not (at least not in any conventional sense of the term). Job against God.

The Tree of Life begins with the mother receiving news of her son's death, followed by a sequence of her and the father as they try to cope with this shock. The film then moves to the present day, as a middle-aged Jack commemorates his brother's death and goes to work at his architectural firm. He wonders about his parents, how they dealt with the loss of their son and how his mother's faith could be sustained despite this pain. It's here that Malick inserts the Job problem, with a twenty-minute sequence detailing the creation of the cosmos and the development of life on earth until Jack's birth. The film then spends its middle hour in 1950s Texas, as three brothers—Jack, R.L. (the brother who will die), and Steve—grow toward adolescence. The film ends with a sequence that not only comes back to the present day but also creates an image of paradise, a sandy shore where all the people from the family's history—those who are dead, past selves, and so on—come together and are reunited.

It's difficult to get a handle on the film's narrative and on its narrational mode. After the initial sequence about the mother's life and the death of R.L., we see a shot of Jack (in the present) waking up on the anniversary of his brother's death. Should we read what's just come before as a dream? As nighttime thoughts? Similarly, the turn to history, both cosmic and personal, is occasioned after Jack imagines himself seeing his parents cope with the news of their son's death—literally imagining himself in the room with them. "How did she bear it?" he asks. It's entirely plausible to see the film's long middle section as Jack's effort to answer that question. The family's departure from his childhood home occasions the move back to the present, the visual indicator being the candle in a blue glass he lit at the film's beginning. At the same time, it's also plausible to read these shifts in time as Malick's own intervention, the presentation of the history of the cosmos as Malick's response to Jack's questions. (Is Malick God with respect to the film?) Put differently, the weaving together of the cosmic and the personal, the adult and the child, means that we can never get outside the basic problem of comprehension—that is, the problem of perspectival organization.[72]

Yet despite the opposition between two principles—perspective versus omnipresence, the human versus the divine—Malick creates space for an alternate possibility. This is the formal logic he developed in his two previous films, the antiperspectival strategy that uses camera movements to present the viewpoint of characters, attuned to the emotional resonance of a scene from multiple perspectives within it. It also changes the way irony is present in *The Tree of Life*, less the relation to an ideal that defines the ending of *The New World* and more a shuttling back and forth, a wavering between positions.[73]

The film's version of an antiperspectival strategy emerges during the scenes of early childhood. One form involves Jack as an infant, where the camera is repeatedly placed at his low position, close behind as he runs through space. After a few shots of a rainstorm, we see Jack inside at the window—now the day is suddenly sunny—then he turns and runs awkwardly through the house. The camera, initially 90 degrees to him, quickly swings around to follow as he finds his mother hiding behind curtains. Several shots later, we see Jack climbing stairs in a static shot from the top; a reverse-shot brings a rare optical point of view, following his perspective as he climbs. There is a shot of his mother, outside, playing with a butterfly; the camera whirls to follow the butterfly's movements on and around her, as if to follow the rapidity of the child's gaze and interest. Although the shots are from a low angle, they lack the sense of confinement or entrapment that often accompanies such images (think, for example, of the way ceilings in *Citizen Kane* control and constrain space). Here we have openness and a sense of the world as a place that can be moved through and explored. The child's raptness at the world, the experience the camera conveys to us through its movement, recalls the words of God's argument to Job: "When the morning stars sang together, and all the sons of God shouted for joy." Without knowledge of how and why things are, his mode of orientation toward the world is that of wonder.

The contrast comes when the second child, R.L., is born. The camera expresses the way this changes Jack's mode of being, as its movements following Jack to the crib are slow and stately, organized by linear paths rather than fluid expressions. Things happen from outside, without his ability to understand. A new baby somehow enters this world, without explanation, and the universe shifts.

Another danger, another shift. *The Tree of Life* moves the boys from their intimate family to the broader social world. No longer focused on the intense dyad of infant and mother, Malick now tracks a form of sociality between the brothers. He begins this with an extended sequence of them running around the house, playing games and enjoying their physical strength. Refusing to be attached to any one individual, the camera takes the group itself into account. After they all go to sleep, and the lights are turned out, Malick cuts to a shot of a tree at dusk, the camera tilting up to frame its branches against the sky. Then he quickly cuts—after a brief shot of a sleeping child—to a shot of another tree, the three boys climbing up it as the camera rises behind them. Another shot brings us a close-up of a can on the street, taken from its level, which is immediately kicked; the camera then races with boys and a dog after it. Before they reach the can, another hurried cut takes us to Jack swinging his youngest brother, Steve, in circles; the camera does not mimic their movements but continues toward them as they tumble to the ground. An almost seamless cut shows Jack getting up, looking off right, and then an apparent reverse-shot puts us in a new setting: a field of tall grass, with a forest in the middle distance to the left. R.L. and Steve are playing, rolling and throwing rocks down a hill; the camera pivots and shows Jack and their dog at the bottom. The two brothers race downhill, the camera following swiftly behind, jerking with steps and movements. A sudden cut now shows Jack and Steve rolling down the hill, followed on the side by the camera, and then another cut to Steve holding an insect and teasingly asking the dog, "Do you want to eat a grasshopper?" The dog moves off, and the camera continues past Steve to show Jack picking up a large bone and yelling, "I found a dinosaur bone!" A cut shows R.L. holding a football and running up the hill toward the camera, which moves backward quickly; he passes the camera, which pivots to follow him, then falls into the grass. A new shot, taken from below, shows Steve reaching down to help someone up—but it's Jack, not R.L., and Steve puts the grasshopper down his back. They laugh, and the camera follows their jostling movements as Jack tries to extract the insect.

What's so striking about this sequence is that the camera refuses to isolate one boy as its focus. We don't see this through Jack's perspective, nor through R.L.'s, nor through Steve's. Malick's editing patterns make this clear, as several cuts prompt us to believe that we are seeing from one point of view only to discover—whether because the setting has surprisingly changed or because that character is in the ensuing shot—that we were mistaken. R.L. and Steve run down the hill, then a cut to two bodies moving in an identical direction shows Jack and Steve. We are, if not at sea, removed from clear focalization that rests on individual psychology; the speed of the sequence, which lasts just under a minute, emphasizes the dislocation. Eisenstein would say that such patterns contribute to a kind of intellectual montage, in which an agglomeration of individual shots leads toward a general concept. But Malick isn't intellectualizing so much as being attuned to the group dynamics, interested in feeling what it is like to be part of this miniature collective. We can never rest where we are; all is whirling play, and the camera is caught up in it as much as the kids. We get a sense of how the world changes, phase by phase, as the universe—the world they inhabit—is reborn in each person, and of how they create a world together.

The sense that what's at stake is a collective subject is emphasized in the next brief sequence. We see a ball being thrown onto the house's roof, and the camera follows its movement as it bounces down and is caught by Jack. A quick cut now goes to Jack throwing the ball up again, this time over the house, then it seems as if a cut elides time: Jack breaks to the right, and we see R.L. and Steve running around the corner of the house to the left of the frame. The camera lets Jack go and stays with the two other boys as they chase Jack around and eventually throw the ball at him—all while we see another group of kids running away in the background. Another game: the kids are running through the streets, the camera moving after them and picking out one, then another, then another as they play in the streets around their house, racing behind trees to hide from their mother, who is calling them in to dinner.

This is glorious exaltation, reveling in the pleasure of health and activity.[74] Again, the camera doesn't give us a concept, nor does it try to convey what's going on in any of their minds. Its movements, and its refusal to align itself with any one of the three, give us a sense of a collective activity, a collective game, a collective pleasure. And so it's worth noting that the camera and the mood immediately halt with a cut to a shot inside the house. Not because they stop playing—we can hear them outside still—but because Malick has given us a shot of their father, framed in a close-up profile on the left side of the screen and lit with sharp, low-key lighting. His empty expression and unmoving features shift the tone of the film itself; he is an individual—and not, on the film's quasi-Freudian terms, part of the band of brothers. When we return to the kids, still playfully being herded inside by their mother, it is with a different feel, and Jack stays outside briefly, lurking in the shadows, as if resentful about what lies within. The house remains the domain of paternal authority.

The parental dynamic continues in the way Malick films scenes inside the house, especially his use of doors. Malick uses the mobile camera to present doorways as marking not a view but rather an expression of two spaces and the characters who move through them. In the moments of pleasure, of joy and release, the camera swirls through the spaces of the house. When the father goes away on a business trip, this is announced to R.L. as he walks into the kitchen, the camera following behind him. He turns away with a silly grin, and before he can leave the frame there is a cut to a slightly closer shot of the mother, who hears his exultant

FIGURE 18. *The Tree of Life* (Terrence Malick, 2011). Free play, open spaces.

whoop from another room; she turns from the sink, and wiping her hands, walks out of the kitchen. An immediate cut goes to R.L. running through the house yelling, the camera whipping around to the right to try to keep him in the frame; the mother is in the background, and the camera whips back to the left. Another cut begins with a fast pan to the right, which turns into a pivot, matching the movement in the previous shot; Jack is pretending to slam the screen door, mocking his father's commands, and R.L. is jumping on a couch. Other shots continue in this vein, until we see Steve holding up a lizard to chase their mother. The family races through the rooms of the house, the camera rushing behind them, trying to catch up, until they dash through the screen door outside, where they continue to play in the fields (see figure 18). Throughout the sequence, we feel the freedom, and the ability to traverse space is exquisite. The pleasure the film takes in childhood is not least connected to the way the camera shows these moments, taking on, expressing, and manifesting their emotional tone.

This freedom, though, serves as a counterpoint to other ways of treating doors. Sometimes this involves the father and the way he slows down the movement through the spaces of the house. But it emerges most poignantly in Jack's discovery of sexuality, and with it the possibility of real Oedipal violence and eroticism. In one scene this is linked to his theft of the nightgown of the teenager next door, but it is centrally charged in his relation to his parents. After his mother caresses his brow, he says, "You know I can't talk to you . . . don't look at me," with a degree of sadness, a wall suddenly between them. A quasi-allegorical shot of the house under dark storm clouds is shown, then we see a shot out through the front door, the mother reclining on the front steps with a cat climbing up her body to nestle between her breasts—an image of natural and untroubled eroticism. Another shot is through a different doorway, this time of the parents' bedroom, as she dresses; the camera pans with her movement, always staying on the other side of a divider. The next shot reverses direction, going from right to left, but still with the mother dressing. Finally we see Jack, the camera in front of him and moving backward; bathed in shadow, he slowly walks through the house and looks around him. One of Malick's rare shot/reverse-shot structures is now employed, as we see the mother through a semi-open door, dressing, and then go back to Jack as he now walks away while looking back over his shoulder.

Jack's discovery of sexuality and his recognition of the distance it places between him and his mother—in explicit and stark contrast to the way they ran together outdoors—is expressed by this different way of moving through space. Not only are barriers emphasized, but there is a sense, almost literal, that a wall has come between Jack and the world he inhabited. ("How do I get back?" he wonders.) The speed of the camera's movement, too, helps to replace the sense of play with heavy portent.

The changed—and charged—movement of the camera is even more pronounced in the sequence in which Jack fantasizes about killing his father. It begins with the camera tracking toward the family's car, which is raised up on a jack while the father lies under it. After a moment, Jack enters the frame from the right, walking with the camera—a play with point of view of the type that I discussed in chapter 3. A quick jump cut puts him closer, still walking, as he comes to a stop at the rear bumper; the camera, however, continues to move in until Jack walks around the car to where his father is. The camera then moves to frame the father under the car, while Jack now walks again toward the rear, where the car is on the jack. He stops, and at this point the camera moves in to focus on the jack, pausing, and then slowly tracks up and to the right to show Jack looking at it. The meaning is clear and is reiterated in the next shot: the camera at Jack's height, moving in toward him as he looks around to see if anyone is watching. He leans back to look at his father, looks at the jack again . . . but then the tension is diffused. Jack walks away, the camera tracking backward in front of him. There is a false 180-degree shot: the camera is now moving forward, but it is now inside the house, tracking in to a green wall. "Please, God. Kill him," Jack whispers in voice-over. "Let him die."

FIGURE 19. *The Tree of Life* (Terrence Malick, 2011). Constrained space.

These moments are not exactly studies in psychology; they are not about psychological nuance or complexity. In their generic articulation, they mark a transition of sorts, an anticipation of the more linear movements and sense of distance that define the scenes in the present. It is the movement out of childhood, away from the "natural" innocence that allowed the camera to move through spaces so freely. We see the contrasting view not just in the scenes of Oedipal conflict and fantasy but also in the shots of Jack as an adult, in which almost all of the camera's movements are linear: straight lines, often crossing the direction in which someone moves. Sometimes they are apparently from Jack's point of view; sometimes they move against the direction of his movement; sometimes they follow the lines of architecture. In his home, for example, we see his wife dressed and leaving their bedroom, the camera moving directly at her (see figure 19); it stops just past her, looking downstairs through a window at Jack pacing, before pivoting 180 degrees as she walks on. The next shot is again in a straight line, this time moving horizontally to match the wife's movements as she enters the house from the garden; she turns and climbs a stair, and the camera moves straight to follow her, before turning again and moving on a line through the kitchen to observe Jack, who has lit the candle to remember his brother.

This kind of linear movement defines the scenes in the present and stands in stark contrast to the scenes set in the past. We are reminded of this in a brief flashback between home and office, in which Jack remembers "the child that he was," and for a minute we are back in the free-flowing play of the brothers. The present just doesn't move as fast: it lacks energy, lacks a human feel. Some of this is about the architecture. Jack and his wife live in an explicitly modern house, all sharp angles and glass walls; the furniture looks unused. The office is in a glass skyscraper, the panes of glass broken by the straight lines of the steel supports. Little curves or flows. Yet this is not really about architecture, a style that responds to spaces. It is about being an adult, being enmeshed in a world where play no longer seems possible.[75]

The adult world is haunted by moral questions. A colleague talks to Jack about his failing marriage, Jack apologizes to his father for his anger, and so on. These are familiar, everyday problems, with familiar ways of talking about and resolving them, whether through legal procedures or conversations. The memory of R.L.'s death serves to blast apart this everyday framework, to render irrelevant the moral and epistemic framework with which we approach the world. Malick uses the memory, to put it bluntly, as a way to reintroduce the Job problem into the world. If the Job problem is constitutive of childhood—Why, Jack wonders at the drowning of a friend, did he die? What did he do to deserve it? "Why didn't you save him?" he asks both God and his father—adulthood seems to bring acceptance. Things happen. But Malick shows that the essential question is never far away, that because it is unanswerable, it never goes away. Kierkegaard describes this wonderfully as Job "walking with" us:

> In happy days, in prosperous times, Job walks along at the generation's side and safeguards its happiness, grapples with the anxious dream that some sudden unspeakable horror will assail a person and have the power to murder his soul as its certain prey. Only a light-minded person could wish that Job were not along, that his revered name did not remind him of what he is trying to forget, that life also has terror and anxiety; only a selfish person could wish that Job did not exist so that the idea of his suffering would not disturb his flimsy happiness with its rigorous earnestness and scare him out of a sense of security drunk with callousness and damnation. In tempestuous times, when the foundation of existence is tottering, when the moment shivers in anxious expectancy of what may come, when every explanation falls silent at the spectacle of the wild tumult, when a person's innermost being groans in despair and "in bitterness of soul" cries to heaven, then Job still walks along at the generation's side and guarantees that there is a victory, guarantees that even if the single individual loses in the struggle, there is still a God who, just as he proportions every temptation humanly, even though a person did not withstand the temptation, will still make its way out such that we can bear it—yes, even more gloriously than any human expectancy. [. . .] Only a soft person could wish that Job did not exist, that he could instead leave off thinking, the sooner the better, could give up all

movement in the most disgusting powerlessness, could blot himself out in the most wretched and miserable forgetfulness.[76]

These are the terms of Malick's sermon, echoed in the sermon on Job within *The Tree of Life*, in which the priest tells his congregation that they can never escape suffering or misfortune. "Is this a flaw in God's plan?" the preacher asks, and he later answers himself by saying that it was Job's gift to recognize God's work even in the cause of his suffering. This is an echo of Kierkegaard, who says—through a pseudonym, of course—that suffering "places a person in a purely personal relationship of opposition to God, in a relationship such that he cannot allow himself to be satisfied with any explanation at second hand."[77] The lesson from Job is about the necessity of attempting to confront the might of the divine plan, in all of its movement away from the human, of attempting to step outside our human need to achieve perspective.

To lose Job is to lose our sense of surprise, of wonder, and even of despair. The Job problem is one that cannot be contained within the perspectival structure in which we live, the human orientation on the world. And so the final sequences of the film burst outside of time altogether, presenting us with images of paradise—either in the world or as part of Jack's imagination—that stand outside historical time. It is as if the reconciliation there—when parents and children refind one another, when emotions can be transparent and love can be expressed—is a miracle, akin to having seen the origins of the cosmos, that could never be part of our world, our sense of time.

5.

Paired with the quotation from the Book of Job, *The Tree of Life* contains a second opening announcement that takes the form of a slowly moving, abstract pattern of colored lights against a black background. It is one of the *Lumia* by Thomas Wilfred, a technology he developed in which a box mechanically generates light patterns, constantly shifting and rotating over time, which unsettles the idea of a stable point of view. Without representation, without even a sense of distance, there is no way to establish ourselves in relation to this image. Despite its own warnings, *The Tree of Life* is going to try to imagine, to picture, precisely that which God declares to be outside human experience. Yet this is not an attempt to gain direct access to that perspective. The quotation from the Book of Job, after all, suggests that where Milton famously tried to "justify the ways of God to man," Malick is already announcing the impossibility of doing so.

Malick may not subscribe to the Miltonic logic of explanation, but he does follow Milton in one important way, namely the use of a range of visual technologies and analogies to model our mode of access to the divine. Joanna Picciotto, for example, has drawn attention to the way that Milton draws on the metaphors of scientific technology—especially Galileo's telescope—to provide the reader with an indication of how to imagine the Edenic state.[78] Milton positions his poem as a kind of technological tool—one that is on a par with the latest in visual technologies—to aid the reader's apprehension of the divine order.[79] In a similar way, Malick is interested in using technologies to think through how his own viewers—or readers—are encountering the world being shown, including what seem to be its divine aspects, and he does this through technologies that are also marked as new. There are the CGI dinosaurs, of course, but also the images recognizable as being produced by the Hubble telescope, such as the Horsehead Nebulae, animated digitally so that the camera even moves, impossibly, in the cosmos. (These images are recognizable even when individual shots are entirely the artifact of effects work.[80]) The analogy between technology and art is not perfect, nor is it meant to be. *Paradise Lost* is not exactly like Galileo's telescope; *The Tree of Life* is not exactly like digital imaging technology. But these technologies do provide a way for viewers to understand the terms of access to the world being shown, so that nothing exists in the work of art that is not folded into our world.

The Tree of Life is not, then, about direct access to theological questions, much less answers, but about the way these questions emerge from our world—and about how cinema can go about showing them to us. This is one of Malick's basic structures, the "vernacular" element that Pippin identified as inflecting the films' metaphysical questions. *The Thin Red Line* uses the conventions of the war genre; *The New World* uses the rhetoric of exploration films; and *The Tree of Life* combines, in a sense, the coming-of-age film with the visual and thematic rhetoric of Disney's *Fantasia*. Malick is not training us to leave human and worldly matters behind, to build a ladder that we then kick away, or to retreat from the modern to the comforts of nostalgia (whether nature or memory or grace). The antiperspectival stance immerses us in the world while also—and this is its power—providing us with a way to imagine being outside.

This is a tenuous position, and I have tried to show that Malick develops it across three films. It has, in a sense, several key criteria: an antiperspectivalism that is connected to an ethical principle of irony; a refusal of the camera to identify with either the spectator or any character; and a use of cross-temporal montage, bringing different times—and different orders of time—into alignment with each other. Central to all of this is the moving camera. The moving camera feels no loyalty to any one mode of focalization; it can shift between characters in the middle of a shot, forgo the logic of individualized focalization, or even glide free of any human orientation whatsoever. By immersing the viewer in the world yet denying them a fixed and stable standpoint, Malick creates an unmoored structure of spectatorship. It is a cinema of adjustment, a cinema without a final position—perhaps only, as with the insistence on the Job problem in *The Tree of Life*, with questions. This ironic positioning is at once the films' deepest difficulty and their greatest power.

The logic of this structure begins to change after *The Tree of Life*. *To the Wonder* retains the expressive camera work but is largely oriented around the actions of characters; even when Marina spins through spaces, as Rebecca does at the end of *The New World*, the camera now simply follows, focusing our attention on her movements without altering the terms of our relation to her. The resonance between microcosm and macrocosm that *The New World* and *The Tree of Life* deploy, one in which the camera is often at an emotional angle to the characters, is missing. *Knight of Cups* (2015) continues this trend, especially around its focalization through a character. And even *Voyage of Time* (2016), which extrapolates from the cosmic sequence in *The Tree of Life*, is curiously linear.

None of these films are easy. But their use of a psychologically attuned camera and their turn toward a mode of linear temporality—a single kind of temporality—make the difficulties practical rather than conceptual. *Song to Song* makes this shift clear. It is, in a sense, a straightforward story, following the relationships and career paths of a set of central characters; the difficulty it presents to a viewer has to do with Malick's refusal to create causal transitions between scenes and to omit key information. Even the camera, which retains its virtuosity, is attuned to character dynamics: a wide-angle shot in the sequence in Mexico, where BV and Faye begin their relationship, rapidly whips back and forth between them as they stand below a stone arch. It's hard to see, but not to understand: with Faye's voice-over dominating the scene, the camera is presenting her point of view as she becomes excited by BV. Then it shifts, of course, moving to the point of view of someone else, but each time the camera is attuned to *someone*. We might say that this is the logic of the song, and the pop song in particular, in which the music is there to support a given theme. From song to song: the film moves in this manner, with its virtuosic yet fundamentally structured techniques serving to reflect the actions and relationships of the characters.

Song to Song follows Malick's tendency to use musical metaphors to model films. But the three films that I've been discussing differ significantly from the model of the song. *The Thin Red Line* draws on the logic of the chorale or symphony, in which the range of parts—and the different accents they take in relation to the whole—expands outward from the small group. It is not, say, a quartet, but a coalescence of a multitude of positions in order to express the whole: a model matched to the military unit. *The New World*, by contrast, declares its affinity with opera at the outset, not least that musical form's use of different voices to call a world into being. And *The Tree of Life* runs through different models depending on the scene, from Zbigniew Preisner's 2010 *Lacrimosa* to *Má Vlast: Vltava* by Bedřich Smetana (1875) to Bach's *Toccata and Fugue in D. Minor* (ca. 1703–1707).[81] The arrangement and number of instruments and the musical movements from which they are taken provide different models for understanding the perspectives being offered through image and sound. We are never allowed to settle, even into disorientation; the film forces our constant adjustment toward its, and our, world.

CHAPTER 7

Beyond the (Single) Camera

I.

One of the fascinating features attending the rise of digital cinema has been its hospitality to camera movement. It's not just the omnipresence of the moving camera that defines contemporary cinematic grammar, whether that style is described as "post-continuity," "chaos cinema," or "post-cinema." There is a deep affinity between models of cinema that eschew the constraints of a photographic ontology and the prominence of the moving camera. The photographic theory of cinema had served as a kind of ontological guarantee that what we saw on screen existed in the world in front of the camera. Now, it's as if the unburdening of the camera from its relation to the world suddenly enables it to swoop through spaces, move around as if it were a protagonist within the world of a film, and give a full sense of inhabiting or moving through space. This shift in turn corresponds to the emergence of phenomenology and theories of affect as a way of talking about film, models that move the location of significance away from the relation between world and image and onto the relation between image and spectator (especially the body of the spectator). It seems to be the role of the moving camera to link technological transformations to this new site of meaning.

While the history of animation, and special effects, is recognized as a background for the shift, digital technologies seem to introduce a new model of the moving camera. In this view, what we are seeing is not simply new technological possibilities for moving the camera—in the way, for example, technicians develop a new crab dolly or crane—but an entirely different kind of movement altogether. There is, for example, the signature shot in the first street race in *The Fast and the Furious* (Rob Cohen, 2001), when Brian releases nitrous into the car and the camera swiftly emerges from the cannister of nitrous and moves through the car's engine and into the exhaust, where it's released in a burst of fire. Or consider a shot in another racing film, *Talladega Nights: The Ballad of Ricky Bobby* (Adam McKay, 2006), in which the camera swoops down out of the sky, moves through the rear windshield of the car, passes by the driver—around whom it pivots—then moves up and through the front windshield. William Brown describes these shots as a new "non-human cinema," fully divorced from the limitations of the human body and perceptual apparatus. He writes:

> In *Panic Room* ([David Fincher,] 2002), the "camera" can pass between the legs of a bannister frame and through a keyhole. In *Fight Club* [(David Fincher, 1999)], the "camera" can move down through an office block, into a basement car park, towards a van, through a bullet hole in the rear window of the van, and into a close-up of a bomb. . . . On another occasion still, the "camera" drifts past an outsize Starbuck's coffee cup and various other bits of detritus before emerging from the inside of a water paper bin and into the narrator's office. Each of these is a further instance in which the "camera" performs an "impossible" and continuous shot, a shot that is made possible by its having been finally put together not with a camera at all, but with a computer.[1]

Impossible shots run throughout contemporary cinema. Mike Jones observes that the camera in the opening shot of *Angels in America* (Mike Nichols, 2004) "moves in one continuous take from a cloud bank high over the city of San Francisco, across the continental United States, over Chicago and St. Louis to New York, folding distance and time as it goes—as traditional montage editing would do—only it is a continuous and unbroken take."[2] Surveying a range of similar shots, Jones concludes that the new virtual camera is "not just a hybrid, evolutionary or progressive movement from the physical camera but rather one of a profound conceptual shift in what we see and how we see it."[3]

Yet accounts of camera movement have long had an ambivalent relationship to the camera. David Bordwell, for example, has only just isolated "spatial perception" as a problem to address in his 1977 essay on camera movement when he remarks that thinking about a physical camera is a trap. "Camera movement during filming," he writes, "is neither a necessary nor a sufficient condition for the perception of camera movement in the finished film."[4] Immobile cameras are used in process shots, or when a background is unrolled behind a scene; they are equally a part of the perception of camera movements in cel animation, in which a still camera shoots each frame. In each case, we take what we see to be an instance of camera movement. What matters, Bordwell argues, are the "perceptual cues which determine a 'camera-movement effect' onscreen *regardless of whether the camera moved in production or not*."[5]

Importantly, flexibility about the physical camera is part of live-action cinema. Julie Turnock, for example, details the ways in which the blockbuster films of the 1970s relied on animation to create the spectacles driving their popularity. Simulated camera movement is central to the Stargate sequence in *2001: A Space Odyssey*, which overtly draws on a tradition of experimental animation to create new perceptual effects. But it is equally important in *Star Wars* (George Lucas, 1977), especially with its imagery of hyperspace travel. Turnock writes:

> *Star Wars* is also using animation—the moving shapes in graphic relation to other shapes and colors—to generate the illusionistic sense of kinetic forward momentum. Most strikingly, the opening of *Star Wars* and the jump to hyperspace, as well as many of the space battles, use the perspectival illusion of movement into deep space in a similar way to [Jordan Belson's] *Allures* [1961] to dynamize the space on the screen and make the viewer feel he or she is moving through and into space.[6]

As Turnock argues, the creation of the impression of a forward camera movement makes us feel as though we are moving through space with the camera. The impression is not filtered through a character, but directly presented to us: we feel that we are there, moving through space ourselves—an impossible, fantastic experience.

This long history matters. If digital camera movements purport to give us new ways of moving through the world they reveal, using new technologies to give new visual experiences to viewers, such claims to originality resonate across the history of cinema. Here is William Paul: "Cinerama's greatest sign of power was the rapid forward tracking shot which became the key signature of practically every Cinemara film, from the travelogues of the early fifties to the fiction films of the sixties. . . . [T]he rapid track forward is terrifying because it underscores our passivity and threatens to deny our individuation from the image."[7] Alexander Bakshy wrote in 1927: "Thanks to the moving camera [the spectator] is able to view the scene from all kinds of angles, leaping from a long-distance view to a close-range inspection of every detail."[8] And a 1903 advertisement for a phantom ride stated that "the view taken from the front of the train running at high speed is one even the tourists riding over the line are not privileged to enjoy."[9]

New technologies of the moving camera do not necessarily produce new conceptual problems. Drone-mounted cameras, for example, are now found in feature films as well as in nature documentaries. Yet although *Winged Migration* (Jacques Perrin, 2001) was filmed without drones, the camera still moved in and through flocks of birds. Forms of remote video display were also present earlier in a predigital era, which Katherine Chandler discusses in regard to television-guided planes during World War II. A pilot, steering from a remote location, would see "through 'its' perspective. . . . [T]he point of view from the camera onboard becomes his hypothetical position."[10]

New technologies, new movements, new perspectives: this is the story that runs through the history of camera movement, reinventing itself at each new technological episode, yet with the same parameters. A nonhuman perspective is of course nothing new; in *Apotheosis* (1970), for example, John Lennon and Yoko Ono mount the camera on an unseen balloon as it rises up from the city and above the clouds, a kind of transcendent phantom ride.[11] Indeed, Patrick Keating argues that the history of camera movement in Hollywood cinema revolves around a tension between a constitutive anthropomorphism and a belief that the camera can exceed the terms of human vision. If the former is often rhetorically dominant, the idea that the camera creates forms of perception that have no correlate in our everyday experience is deeply powerful: "Hollywood filmmakers delighted in the idea that the camera could go anywhere and find anything."[12] Yet each model, anthropomorphic and nonanthropomorphic alike, draws on the logic of the epistemic fantasy. Chandler, for example, notes of the pilot of a World War II drone that his language vacillates between the first person—"Yeah, *I* got shot down once or twice"—and a more objective remove—"Anti-aircraft fire brought *it* down."[13] We know that we are not with the camera as it moves through the world, but yet we *want* to be there, even when it is explicitly positioned as nonhuman.

My point is not about the fantasy of immersive identification, nor about the prehistory to the digital—that point, in particular, has been made by others—but rather that the focus on the novelty of digital camera movements is the wrong topic. To be clear, new cameras certainly do move in hitherto unprecedented ways.[14] But when Brown and Jones (and others) describe digital cameras as qualitatively unlike anything that has come before, they overlook the long history of conceptual tensions around the idea of the camera—part of which I have tried to articulate in this book. In a similar vein, Ryan Pierson has argued that what the new camera movements make explicit is our longstanding inability to describe what the camera is, and how it can function.[15] Pierson uses animation to develop his argument, since it's there that many of the stable categories that undergird film style, ontology, and technology are subverted. He looks to an experimental tradition of Norman McLaren and Caroline Leaf (among others) to see an instability not just in "camera" but in the "world of the film," but it's present as well in more popular forms. In Ub Iwerks's *Funny Face* (1932), for example, two characters bounce on a bed and go up through the roof of the house; the camera, looking horizontally at a cross-section of the house, follows them up and into the sky. Yet when it follows them down, an apparently straightforward movement, the house has apparently swiveled 45 degrees, so that we can watch them roll down the roof and fall into a barrel of water below. The twist of the film world is what, to Pierson, marks the irrelevance of the category of the camera and the need to shift our account to a description of the world on-screen, at least when it comes to animation and, he argues, spectacular digital camera movements.

To conclude this book, I want to argue that a key problem to address is what happens when we move beyond the idea of a *single* camera that is taken to create a perspectival organization of the world for the spectator. Multiple-camera compositions are everywhere in contemporary cinema. Sometimes the multiple cameras are hidden, as in the bank of still cameras that generate the "bullet-time" effect in *The Matrix* (Lana Wachowski and Lily Wachowski, 1999); the two cameras that are needed to produce 3D stereoscopic effects; or the camera arrays that create virtual reality environments. Yet multiple cameras can also be part of the explicit construction of the image, as with split-screen compositions. Thinking about digital camera movements—and understanding their challenges to existing interpretive frameworks—means addressing what it means when there is no longer (only) one camera that's moving. Part of the aim of this chapter is thus to survey several iterations of this dynamic. But I also mean to show how the presence of multiple cameras being used to generate the image(s) in the frame, especially in the context of camera movements, generates new ways of thinking about key questions of film theory: perception and experience, models of montage, and the very status of the camera itself.[16]

2.

A common move in new media debates has been to replace the photograph with the computer as the ground for the image. This is what D. N. Rodowick has in mind when he writes, discussing the computer as a medium, "No longer a passive surface for receiving projections, the screen now becomes a manipulable surface for executing algorithms."[17] The image is no longer fixed, and the capacity for visual transformation is taken to be part of the nature of digital media. This position can be pushed further. A screen for moving image media is not a computer, but it can be made to resemble the desktop. Celebrating the centennial of cinema's birth, Lev Manovich saw the emergence of a new kind of screen: "No single window completely dominates the viewer's attention. In this sense the possibility of simultaneously observing a few images which coexist within one screen can be compared with the phenomenon of zapping—the quick switching of television channels that allows the viewer to follow more than program. In both instances, the viewer no longer concentrates on a single image."[18] Manovich emphasizes the site of display, the displacement of the image away from a single organizing perspective—what he, along with other theorists like Anne Friedberg and Hito Steyerl, associates with a tradition that dates back to Alberti—and the creation of multiple frames of organization at the same moment. Manovich even tries to realize this vision in *Soft Cinema* (2006), an installation work in which a search function selects clips from an archive that then form a somewhat randomly generated narrative presented on multiple frames within the screen.[19]

The multiframe screen is taken to emblematize the new era of computer-based image production and manipulation. Friedberg argues that "as the 'personal computer' began to invade daily life, a new 'interface' to the screen began to produce new modes of cinematic, television, and video display."[20] A common mode has been the use of inserted frames. Ang Lee's *Hulk* (2003), for example, occasionally employs a smaller image within the overall composition. Usually it creates a counterpoint to what we're seeing: an event taking place elsewhere, or more commonly someone approaching the character in the larger image. Of course this visual feel is part of an adaptation of a comic book, so that the multiple screens reflect the look of a page. But it is also a formal strategy internal to the grammar of narrative cinema. Lee effectively makes sequential montage into spatial montage, a reorientation of the principles of shot/reverse-shot so that the shots happen simultaneously. He sees, in other words, a way to use multiple frames within the image to produce a more effective form of storytelling, one that gives a sense of immediacy to the effect of the montage. In Friedberg's terms, "the sequential spatiality and cross-cut temporality of single-screen film-making has been replaced by simultaneous non-sequential display."[21]

Lee's use of multiple frames as a form of montage has a long gene-alogy within the history of cinema. *The Thomas Crown Affair* (Nor-man Jewison, 1968) uses the technique both to model conversations and to put multiple parts of a scene into relation with each other. The end of *Charade* (Stanley Donen, 1963) uses the technique to display all the guises that Cary Grant's character has taken through the film. And perhaps most wonderfully, in *Suspense* (1913) Lois Weber transforms the logic of crosscutting into a triple image: the tramp breaking into the home on the left, the wife on the phone on the right, and in between them the husband receiving the call and rushing home. Other versions of the practice include superimposition as well as rear-screen projec-tions and matte processes.

These are all questions of montage, ways to creatively adapt standard practices. Yet as with most models of montage, the underlying discourse around them assumes the shot is static, or that camera movement is inessential, part of the way, as in *Hulk*, that a familiar shot/reverse-shot pattern is revised. In some cases, camera movement is taken to be a type of attraction, used to present something directly to the viewer, as in the opening racing sequence in John Frankenheimer's *Grand Prix* (1966), which creates a tripartite split of the frame to better present the differ-ing speeds and styles of the racers.

As with the other problems of film and media theory I've discussed throughout this book, the terms of debate shift when camera move-ment is taken into consideration, especially when the camera moves in different ways in different frames within the same image. In Mike Figgis's *Timecode* (2000), for example, the frame is divided into four quadrants throughout the film. Each quadrant contains a single take of roughly ninety minutes that follows a character (or cluster of characters) through this time. It's a gimmick film, and enough of a gimmick that a fake movie pitch within the film, one that is rightly mocked, essentially describes *Timecode* itself: dressed up with a pseudo-intellectual argu-ment for the small digital camera's ability to record extended scenes, and pitted against the Soviet school of montage theory. The splitting of the frame into quadrants, each with an extended shot, in a sense epitomizes a Bazinian fantasy in which we can choose what actions and events we focus on, much as we do, visually, in our everyday lives. This is the translation of time into space, sequentiality into simultaneity: montage between shots to montage within the image. Much of the critical literature on *Timecode* has thus followed the challenge imposed by its layout: Do we look at individual screens or at all four at once? Is this a model for multiscreen construction or simply a version of a familiar way of creating narrative organization?[22] Sound obviously helps guide us, but Figgis often blurs multiple sound sources together, so it's not always a reliable guide to where we should—or do—look. Figgis even performed the film "live" on several occasions, mixing the sound to create different paths of experience through the same narrative events.

While its use of long takes places *TimeCode* within a tradition of single-shot films, a curious consequence of Figgis's stylistic decision emerges with the use of the moving camera. Take a moment a little over twenty minutes into the film, during one of its narrative pauses. In the top left quadrant, Rose and Lauren are in their limousine; we see the city streets receding behind them as the limousine drives forward, and the camera is also moving slightly away from them (see figure 20). In the top right, Emma is talking to her therapist; the camera swivels around them and pulls back slightly to frame her. In the bottom right, studio executives discuss scripts—and receive massages—while the camera tracks and pans swiftly between them; the sound at this moment is coming from their dialogue about inane (and insane) plots. And in the bottom left, Lester discusses the audition of a young actress, Victoria, the camera following their interactions (and also the interventions of Lester's assistant); they then walk towards the camera, which retreats in front of them to keep both in the frame.

These camera movements each use a handheld digital camera, but they go in different directions and have different orientations toward the events they show. Taken together, they pose a set of interpretive questions: What should we make of these simultaneous movements? How do we respond to them? Can we feel ourselves moving with each camera? With one at a time? Or do we see this entire screen as an image in which movement is taking place—in which, following Pierson, the world is unstable—yet the multiplication of views precludes our ability to inhabit any one?

FIGURE 20. *Timecode* (Mike Figgis, 2000). Simultaneous camera movements.

To appreciate how the moving camera is working here, consider as a comparison a sequence from *Speedy* (Ted Wilde, 1928), one of Harold Lloyd's last silent films, which depicts his adventures as a taxicab driver. After failing to pick up passengers, he winds up giving a ride to Babe Ruth. Enamored of his celebrity passenger, Lloyd pays little attention to the busy streets he's driving down, repeatedly missing cars apparently only by fractions of inches. Much of this is shot from the rear seat, as we see Lloyd driving—or neglecting to do so—while in front of the car are scenes of chaotic city traffic. But fascinatingly, there are three other types of camera movement in the sequence. One is from Lloyd's perspective, looking back at Ruth; behind him is a small rear window through which we can see, overexposed, scenes from the outside. A second is an occasional shot from alongside the car, with both car and camera moving to the right; what stands out here is the horizontal movement of the camera, unique among the shots in the sequence. And last is a kind of subjective shot, framed over the hood ornament of the car and moving through the busy streets. Clearly sped up, this latter category conveys a sense of immersion and exhilaration.[23]

The sequence from *Speedy* is part of the normal Hollywood style, interspersing moments of visual excitement with spectatorial identification—and suspense. The different kinds of camera movement complicate this; there is no single thing that movement is, nor is there any single kind of thing that the camera does in order to generate that movement.[24]

The shift to simultaneity, spatializing what was sequential, changes our perception by allowing the different forms of movement to inflect each other. As *Timecode* begins, for example, each quadrant is gradually activated, starting with the therapist section in the top right. In the others, Figgis places a set of abstract patterns moving past the camera. They seem almost like the animated movement effects by Belson that Turnock describes in relation to *Star Wars*, as their movement generates an impression of moving into depth. But Figgis seems to want to use them only as a contrast to what follows, as if to suggest that the fantasy of movement into depth misses the way different motion forms contain different perceptual requirements and effects. Gradually this image is joined by the top left quadrant, showing an outdoor staircase leading up and to the left, with the driveway at the right part of the frame. A wide-angle lens distorts the space. Across the bottom two quadrants a sine wave runs to the right. In the top left quadrant, Lauren begins to descend the staircase, moving forward from depth and walking around the curve; the sine wave underneath is replaced by a series of dots moving in the opposite direction, to the left. As Lauren descends, that camera pivots with her to the left and then follows her as she walks toward two cars in the background—movements that are magnified by the visual distortion effected by the lens. The effect, however, goes beyond the single quadrant. The camera in the top right remains stationary, but its proximity to the movement in the adjacent quadrant means that the space there begins to subtly warp and shift; it is impossible not to see the stationary shot as if it, too, were in motion. It's an unsettling effect, one that creates perceptual instability.

Figgis uses this kind of effect at several points in the film. The final earthquake, for example, is represented with the camera shaking in three of the four quadrants, but the absence of shaking in the fourth means that we in fact perceive it as in motion *with respect to* the other quadrants. It's not that, as Friedberg suggests, we see the image as a whole, or that our attention is necessarily split between the quadrants; the movement in each quadrant comes to shape or inflect any way we look at the frame. Later in the film, as characters in each quadrant rest from various activities, the cameras assigned to each quadrant are moving at the same time. What results is a series of shifting affinities. At one point, Lester is in the bottom left with the camera moving backward—a movement that rhymes with the action in the top right, as Emma goes to the bathroom in a bookstore. Then a moment later the camera with Lester stops its movement, and the camera in the top left starts moving backward, creating a new link between the top two quadrants. Then the cameras in the bottom two quadrants begin to move, but they do so horizontally and create a connection between Lester's movements and Rose going into a bathroom. Then Lester's assistant starts to walk toward the camera, which retreats backward and suddenly creates a match with Lauren in the quadrant above. And on and on it goes.

What's happening in these sequences is not a matching of forms so much as a way to create links between otherwise unrelated actions. It's a perceptual game, a complex negotiation between the fantasy of immersive identification that camera movements can produce and the way that the multiplication of cameras forces an orientation that is geared more toward the surface of the image, and the way it transforms as different areas move. This technique is not unique to Figgis. Jordan Schonig has drawn attention to the way Ken Jacobs's *Georgetown Loop* (1996) displaces the dynamics of immersion onto the perception of the surface. In that work, a phantom ride is shown on half the screen and then, after finishing, is repeated—but with its mirror image next to it:

> What results is a mesmerizing kaleidoscopic effect: our attention is immediately drawn to the central axis between the images, from which two-dimensional abstract swirls of space contract and expand in various degrees of speed and intensity. . . . Instead of seeing a framed mobile perspective that reveals and conceals the world with its movement through space, we are compelled to see formless matter spontaneously emerge from the central axis and glide laterally across the screen's surface.[25]

The very terms of how we organize our thinking about the moving camera no longer hold once the number of cameras begins to proliferate.

3.

The most ubiquitous use of multiple cameras in contemporary media remains 3D cinema. Usually, 3D cameras are built in such a way that they mimic the distance between our eyes—the interocular distance—in order to produce an image of the world that feels roughly like the way we experience the world. An online manual spells this out:

> In order for your footage to best simulate what viewers would see with their own eyes, it's important to match the human interocular distance as closely as possible. This means that the distance between the centers of your camera lenses should be approximately 2.5". Ignoring the interocular distance can result in some surprising and even unpleasant effects. Move the cameras too far apart, and the world will look like it's been miniaturized. Move them too close together, and suddenly the smallest object appears gigantic. 2.5". Learn it. Live it. Love it.[26]

If you miss the mark, the manual notes, smooth mode of access to the film world will be prevented and will result instead in "surprising and even unpleasant effects."

The shift from one to two cameras has significant conceptual consequences. Brooke Belisle, for example, has recently used the rise of 3D cinema to revise the standard history of the transition from photography to cinema. I noted in chapter 6 that the standard history generally carries with it an assumption about single-point perspective, the organization of Renaissance perspective that is taken to be built into the lens of the camera. Belisle argues for an alternate genealogy based on stereoscopy, whose dual images operate along a different—if related—assumption about a connection between human vision and mechanical vision. She writes,

"The difference between images is what enables stereoscopic depth, and it also anchors the analogy between eyes and cameras that was used to explain this depth to nineteenth-century spectators." The perception of depth in the image suggests "that the dimensionality we perceive in the world could be reiterated by the dimensions of photographic representation. The perception of depth that a stereograph could prompt both drew upon and helped authorize an analogy between human vision and photographic imaging."[27] This analogy is central to the basic operation of 3D models, but it's especially prominent in the camera movement that is the hallmark of 3D cinema, namely movement along the z-axis into the depths of the image.[28]

Yet such revisionist history risks remaining stuck in a formula based on perceptual verisimilitude. While rejecting single-point perspective and the assumption of a monocular viewpoint in favor of a stereoscopic model, Belisle retains everyday vision as a guiding norm. It is not just that stereoscopy provides a better genealogy for an emergent 3D cinema; the binocular perception of stereoscopy is based on the claim that it is *better* at reproducing our everyday perception of the world. Belisle is careful herself to avoid that claim, but I want to emphasize how the combination of multiple cameras, augmented by camera movement, can force a reconsideration of an underlying verisimilar model.

Several avant-garde experiments have troubled the relationship between vision and technology, creating an alternate aesthetic strategy that unsettles an affinity between image and world. A recent work by OpenEndedGroup (Marc Downie and Paul Kaiser), *Ulysses in the Subway* (2016), is organized around an audio recording made by Ken Jacobs of a journey through the subway and home to his apartment. Downie and Kaiser took the audio material, up to two thousand samples each frame, and built algorithmically generated 3D animated imagery from that material.[29] Sometimes the nonrepresentational imagery seems to respond directly to the sound we hear, following familiar patterns of sound waves: increasing and decreasing in height depending on the volume, and with peaks and troughs that roughly match what we're hearing. At other points, however, the relation is less clear, as when two bands of modulated light run across the top and bottom of the frame. Still other passages create patterns, as if dancing figures, rippling out across the frame.

Watching *Ulysses in the Subway*, we often feel that we are at the position of a static camera—or a camera effect—in front of which various patterns are passing. Yet at key moments it seems as though our position is actually in motion. Sometimes that occurs when the visual patterns suddenly open up the z-axis, and it seems as though we are moving into rather than across space. But it also happens when Downie and Kaiser decide to insert footage from G. W. Blitzer's phantom ride, *Interior New York Subway* (1905), in which the camera, attached to the front of one train, follows another through the subway. "An unseen energy swallows space," Gunning quotes from an early review of phantom rides.[30] Here the film appears as if an apparition, at first emerging from behind the virtuosic patterns generated by the sound recording, before becoming the sole focus on the screen. The effect is unsettling. Because the abstract image generally emerges from the screen, as if in rounded space, the phantom ride doesn't shift to the z-axis so much as begin to stretch space backward. This ensures that the clip is not marked as a kind of cinematic realism to be contrasted with the visual abstraction of the rest of the film; it functions instead as part of the overall visual effect. And because Blitzer's film foregrounds the place of camera movement, we may begin to wonder whether what we're seeing during much of the work is best understood as a visualization moving in front of a camera or a camera moving past a sort of sound sculpture. As the camera moves, space begins to stretch and come apart.

Downie and Kaiser's use of camera movements in 3D works against the technological simulation of everyday perception. We become attuned to the dimensionality of the image as something other than we can ordinarily experience, as calling into question the relation between figure and ground—and sound and image. In this it is fitting that Jacobs is the subject of the film, since 3D experiments have been central to his work. During the 1990s and 2000s, for example, he began to develop versions of 3D imagery, especially what he called "eternalisms." Belisle describes this technique:

> arranging images, interspersed with black frames, in carefully prescribed patterns along the horizontal timeline of film-editing software. With jump cuts operating at microintervals, and simulating a shutter by interleaving black frames, this process creates flicker effects that cross spatial and temporal depth to produce wavering illusions of three-dimensionality and movement.[31]

These movements render our point of view dramatically uncertain. We don't know where to locate ourselves, or whether the image is moving or we are. In some of Jacobs's most recent work, the deployment of eternalisms with abstract expressionist painting—such as *Joan Mitchell: Departures* (2018) or his multiple studies of Jackson Pollock's *White*

Light (1954)—makes the introduction of depth and movement into still images breathtaking and unsettling. Even as they animate the still images, the looping structures, repeating multiple times before turning to a new, brief movement, push the film into the realm of the mechanical—or perhaps the hypnotic. By explicitly evoking Jacobs, Downie and Kaiser align their own work with a 3D practice that uses the relation between the cameras to realign the way we see the world.

This perceptual unsettling is a key point for experiments with 3D cameras. Because the image is based on the use of two disparate images, captured by different cameras, the relation between them can be reconfigured. Although he has an ambivalent relation with the American avant-garde, Jean-Luc Godard's recent 3D films explore similar territory. Indeed, one of the overlooked aspects of Godard's late films and videos is their interest in technology. Think of his early embrace of video in works like *Ici et ailleurs* (1976) and *Numéro deux* (1975). Or his famous pronouncement in *Sauve qui peut (la vie)* (1980) that the relation between cinema and video is like that between Cain and Abel, but it is *cinema* that is the murderous brother, jealous of the other's success. And for all of Godard's love of images of film editing, like the blind editor featured in *JLG/JLG: Autoportrait de décembre* (1995), his virtuosic displays of editing prowess in *Histoire(s) du cinema* are all done through video.

Godard's technophilia culminates in his recent 3D work, in which, along with the familiar lists of composers and authors whose works comprise the soundscape of the film, he also provides a list of the different cameras he uses. The first of these new works, *Les trois désastres* (*The Three Disasters*, 2013), is a short film—part of the omnibus *3X3D* (2013)—that is, in many respects, exactly the kind of 3D film that we would expect Godard to make. Drawing on the themes, preoccupations, and style of *Histoire(s) du cinema*, it renders that work's multiplane superimpositions into three dimensions. Flat planes of images move back and forth; a screen appears over an otherwise normally rendered scene, and as it moves from in front to in back of that scene, the effect is stunning. Two focal lengths are presented, one in each eye, and it's difficult to figure out how to look at what's on the screen. We struggle to see what we're being shown, much less make sense of the connections being drawn. It's as if Godard decided to amplify the difficulty not only of thinking about but even of processing his already difficult videographic montage.

Given the power of *Les trois désastres*, it is noteworthy that Godard embarks on a very different project in *Adieu au langage* (*Goodbye to*

Language, 2014). Many of the hallmarks of his late style are still there, from the density of references and quotations to the insertion of clips from the history of cinema. But his use of 3D changes. Both Godard and his cinematographer, Fabrice Aragno, have spoken extensively about the way they created their own 3D rigs, positioning two cameras—of different sorts—side by side to allow for their experiments. This approach allowed them to dispense with one of the fundamental axioms of 3D cinema: the attempt to replicate interocular distance, the gap between our eyes that allows us to see in three dimensions. Aragno notes, "Hollywood says you shouldn't have more than six centimeters between cameras, so I began at 12 to see what happened."[32] (When the online manual I quoted earlier suggests that we unlearn everything in order to make better 3D movies, it does not include proper interocular distance as one of the things we should forget.) Farther apart, closer together: once Godard and Aragno dispensed with the need to reproduce interocular distance, they could experiment with the production of new kinds of images and new kinds of spatial organizations. Aragno asserts: "All today's digital technology wants to do is reconstitute reality, to duplicate it perfectly. It's the opposite of cinema or art in general."[33]

Of the three major 3D techniques in *Adieu au langage*, two clearly have this perceptual unsettling as their aim. The first involves the distortion of space. This usually happens when the cameras are brought too close together, which has the effect of stretching out space in curious ways; Godard is creating and manipulating an asymmetry in the interocular distance of the cameras and that of the projector. A second effect involves ghosting, the creation of phantom images within the field of vision (your nose is the most obvious example). Godard creates cinematic ghosts by pushing the cameras close enough to an object so that part of it cannot be brought into focus with our eyes. The ghost emerges, that is, because the angles of each camera are sufficiently distinct—they are sufficiently far apart—that they produce incompatible perspectival organizations; no amount of looking can make them match up. Godard is particularly fond of using this effect with trees, not only because they provide multiple planes for convergence—or lack thereof—but also because doing do refuses the idea of a vision of nature without technological mediation.

In each of these two effects, an attempt is made to transform our perception of the world, to make us newly aware of it. Perhaps this is the lesson of the film's star, Godard's dog, Roxy Miéville. Godard's resolute focus on Roxy seems to ask us to imagine what it's like to experience the world as she does, to have a perception stripped of conceptual content, of linguistic meaning. This fits a long-standing cinematic (and indeed aesthetic) trope. Think here of Stan Brakhage's evocation of "an eye which does not respond to the name of everything but which must know each object encountered in life through an adventure of perception. How many colors are there in a field of grass to the crawling baby unaware of 'Green'?"[34] Or recall André Bazin's words: "Only the impassive lens, stripping its object of all those ways of seeing it, those piled-up preconceptions, that spiritual dust and grime with which my eyes have covered it, is able to present it in all its virginal purity to my attention and consequently to my love."[35] This is the fantasy of cinema's ability to create a fresh, or maybe—as Victor Shklovsky might put it—refreshed perception, one that is figured as a return to an original state: the baby, virginal purity, and so on.

But that form of innocence doesn't really fit Godard's project. He's not interested in something new in that sense, the creation of an entirely new language of cinema. Rather, as he does throughout his career, Godard starts with the basic building blocks of cinema—for him, narrative cinema—and then works to undo and revise them by fundamentally rethinking their structures and functions.

This is where we get the most spectacular of all of the 3D techniques in *Adieu au langage*: the radical separation of the two cameras, hence of our two eyes. Early on, a woman—Ivitch—comes to talk to a man reading a book, and in the midst of their conversation she is grabbed from offscreen off to the right while the man stays still. As she is pulled away, the "right eye camera" separates from the "left eye camera" to follow her (see figure 21). Since the left eye remains static, our vision literally comes apart for a period of time—only to return when she breaks free and returns to the initial framing, at which point the two images coalesce again into a single one. Nico Baumabach describes the moment of rupture as creating a superimposition, but that is more what 2D video does to simulate the 3D effect.[36] What happens in 3D is genuinely painful, yet exhilarating. If we keep both eyes open, we watch our brain attempt to process two incompatible spaces, fail to do so—and then, almost miraculously, succeed in creating a new, semicoherent space that combines the visual fields of both eyes. Or we can shut one eye, then the other, alternating between eyes to create a montage of our own choosing between the two images. This is what many reviewers, and even Godard himself at times, recommended for the audience.

FIGURE 21. *Adieu au langage* (*Goodbye to Language*; Jean-Luc Godard, 2014). The separation of cameras.

What I want to suggest is that these moments function as camera movement. It is not the case that the entire camera array is moving, but *a* camera is—and it moves with a character to open up new aspects of space. *Adieu au langage* is filled with different kinds of camera movements. There is a gorgeous crane shot over an outdoor parking lot, in which the shadow of the operator on the crane becomes visible part of the way into the shot, but space has been oddly miniaturized. There are a number of horizontal tracking shots across living rooms of houses, often showing the TV on and characters sitting in chairs. In each of these cases, the manipulation of the technology of 3D pushes on the idea that the moving camera represents space in a faithful manner; we get, instead, distortions, compressions, and expansions. So when one of the cameras turns to follow a character offscreen, the movement draws us—or at least one of our eyes—in a new direction, in which the continuity of the camera runs into the perceptual dislocation of the 3D technology.

It's central to Godard's project that he is using the most basic of all techniques in classical Hollywood cinema: shot/reverse-shot, in which we look at a character looking offscreen, and the next shot shows us what he or see sees. This interest runs throughout Godard's career, as he expressed in an interview on *Pierrot le fou* (1965): "A director like Delbert Mann . . . follows a pattern. Shot—the character speaks; reverse angle, someone answers."[37] And it recurs in his twenty-first-century films, mostly explicitly in *Notre musique* (2004), in which he shows stills from *His Girl Friday* (1940); a similar gesture is present in *Éloge de l'amour* (2001).[38] Godard's proposal is that shot/reverse-shot is essentially two images being held up and judged against each other.

We see this clearly in the second instance in *Adieu au langage* when the two cameras come apart. Again, it involves a man and a woman, naked in their country house, and so to the formal technique is added an explicit logic of comparison or juxtaposition. Not just of one shot against one another, but of genders as well: man and woman, the logic of the couple that is also a fundamental montage component in Godard's work. (Sergei Eisenstein would agree with this, as well as the way the combination of the two bodies suggests the act of sex itself.) What's going on here is not the sequential logic of montage, the link of one shot to another; rather, it's *montage between the eyes*, a way of revising forms of cinematic montage on an almost biological foundation. (Perhaps this is why there are so many allusions to biological processes in the film, such as the moments of literal toilet humor.)

I take the idea of montage between the eyes to be Godard's fundamental realization about 3D cinema: that because the image in each eye is different, they are always being placed in relation to one another. It's important to see how far reaching this model is. On it, *every image* in *Adieu au langage* is an act of montage. Indeed, what are the techniques of ghosting and spatial distortion but instances of montage between the eyes? It is just made explicit when Godard piggybacks on the familiar shot/reverse-shot construction.

What 3D does for Godard is make it clear that the image we get in each eye is slightly different, grounding this recognition in the technical fact of the apparatus. The difference, again, is not the precondition for but the very fact of montage, a lesson that emerges through the use of the moving camera. Yet—and this is what *Adieu au langage* suggests—all this is true regardless of the presence of the 3D apparatus: each eye always takes in a different view, however slight, of the world. 3D illustrates what is true of all cinema, and perhaps true of our embeddedness within a world in the first place. Put slightly differently, in *Adieu au langage* Godard uses the technics and technology of 3D image recording and projection to suggest that perception is nothing more or less than montage: that we see the world as a montage structure, one that our brains (or minds) expertly combine into a seamless flow. The separation of our eyes in the redefined shot/reverse-shot sequences allows us to see how this works; it holds out to us the way we process the elements of a montage structure. And if this is who we are, if we really are creatures who perceive and inhabit the world through a foundation of montage, then maybe we can say that *Adieu au langage*—even at its most virtuosic—is faithfully recording and representing to us our own experience. Even when it comes apart.

4.

One of the press photos for *Adieu au langage* shows Godard and Aragno with some of their homemade 3D rigs, three of which are placed on toy train tracks that run across the carpet. Aragno is bent over the cameras, working on something, and Godard is reclining in an easy chair behind him, smoking a cigar and clearly enjoying the toys. The photo is a lovely emblem of his technophilia, the effect enhanced by its clever evocation of Orson Welles's description of the RKO studio as "the biggest electric train set any boy ever had."

In many ways, Welles has been one of the presiding spirits for this book, especially the way his use of camera movements does not—despite what Bazin said about them—respect the integrity of time and space but rather plays with cinematic norms and audience fantasies. From early on in *Citizen Kane*, Welles employs forward tracking shots to move through impossible spaces in order to get closer to, see, or discover something thought to be of importance. Take Thompson's appearance at Thatcher's Library, where the camera follows him as he walks into the reading room; the door closes, and the camera tracks toward it before executing a quick dissolve that positions it inside the room—still moving forward at the same pace. At the same time that Welles establishes the camera as having something like an investigative gaze, moving independently to find out information on its own, he is also playing with *our* desire to see, and in particular our desire to see something we'd normally be prevented from seeing; starting with the "No Trespassing" sign in the first moments of the film, the camera moves past barriers that ought to prohibit our passage. These are the epistemological fantasies that Welles is so adept at evoking.[39]

The game Welles plays—and which Godard plainly loves—is one in which he subverts, takes apart, and exposes the conventions of cinema without pushing us out of the film. Two famous tracking shots, both organized around Susan Alexander's nightclub, show how this works. The first occurs immediately after Thompson has been given his assignment. Welles cuts directly from the screening room to a billboard of Susan, with lightning flashing and rain falling. Thunder rolls, and the camera lifts up, moving above a rooftop, then tracking forward toward the neon sign advertising "El Rancho/Floor Show/Twice Nightly"—somehow passing between the first two lines—and continues onward toward a skylight. As the camera approaches it, we can see the nightclub beneath. The shot starts to go out of focus, there are several flashes of lightning, and then the camera is suddenly inside the nightclub, still tracking toward Susan, seated alone at a table. The lightning flashes, which cover up the dissolve and so make an impossible movement seem normal, are the magician's wave of the hand, a brief distraction of our attention that allows the trick to happen unnoticed.

But that's not enough for Welles. He has to make it clear to us *how* we're being tricked, while at the same time still have us believe what we see. Later in the film, we return to the nightclub, and Welles repeats the virtuosic shot through the skylight. This time, the lightning flash is gone and the second shot—from inside the club—is stationary; the bare bones of the trick are exposed to our view. And yet we still "fall" for it, still allow ourselves to be led through the skylight. This is the art of the magician: Welles knows how to manipulate our familiarity with conventions, knows how to show us that we're being manipulated and yet still have us absorbed in the game being played in front of our eyes.

It is no small part of Welles's entire cinematic project to take aim at such epistemic fantasies. While this tendency is found at the very beginning of his career, it becomes prominent in what James Naremore describes as his late trilogy: *The Immortal Story* (1968), *F for Fake* (1973), and the posthumously released *The Other Side of the Wind* (2018).[40] What unites these films is not just their interest in aging (and also sex), but their preoccupation with the deep fantasies we have about core components of cinema. *The Immortal Story* takes up narrative and our desire to have stories correspond to something in the world; if the events don't already exist, the conceit of the film is that they will have to be brought about so that the story—any story—will be true for at least one person. *F for Fake* merges a preoccupation with forgery and deceit with the operation of montage itself, working through the question of whether—and how—we come to connect two things placed next to each other. *The Other Side of the Wind* addresses perhaps the central ontological fiction of cinema: that we can be hidden from the camera, that there are zones of privacy and intimacy in our lives—not least our fantasy of lives on-screen. This is a question that always fascinated Welles, even if at times only implicitly so, but with *The Other Side of the Wind* it becomes the central topic of the film itself.

The film tells the story of Jake Hannaford, an aging director from the classical Hollywood days—played by John Huston—now returned from Europe and trying to make a movie to compete with newer kinds of filmmaking, both European art cinema and the sexploitation films associated with Russ Meyer. The narrative chronicles a party for his seventieth birthday, after which—as we learn at the outset of the film—he will die in a car crash, likely of suicide. Interspersed among the party sequences and the increasing drunkenness, depression, and despair, is footage from the movie Hannaford is making. The party resembles what Joseph McBride describes as "a parody of *cinema verité*," as the opening narrator declares that the film is put together from footage shot that night.[41]

Throughout this book, my account of epistemic fantasies of the moving camera has relied on a tension surrounding the fantasy of being in the world of the film and the fiction that no camera is present. That tension has even seemed at times to be a requirement of such fantasies. In setting this out, however, I've largely bypassed nonfiction film, as if the recognition that a camera really did exist in the world—and that some specifiable person was holding it—precluded the dynamics of identification, imagination, and expression that I've been trying to isolate.

Yet there is of course a range of anxieties about our relation to the camera in nonfiction film. What I want to pull out here, then, are some problems of camera movement that have been important to nonfiction cinema.[42] Much as Welles responds to the epistemic fantasies implicit in Hollywood cinema in his early films, he takes up core features of nonfiction filmmaking practices that attempt to resolve or negotiate the presence of the camera in the world itself.

The most famous of these negotiations is direct cinema, with its fantasy of filming people without them being aware of or modifying their behavior in relation to the presence of the camera. Often this was achieved by focusing on situations in which people were intensely absorbed in their actions or their own thoughts—for example, the shots of John F. Kennedy as he waits for the news about election night in *Primary* (Drew Associates, 1960) while the camera watches, seemingly unnoticed, nearby. Yet there are also moments in which the camera undertakes such virtuosic movement that it serves to make *viewers* forgot that they are watching through a technological guise. This paradoxical effect is found in the signature shot of *Primary*, when the camera follows Kennedy through a crowded rally and up onto the stage. The virtuosity of its movement and the spectator's interest in Kennedy's own performance cause the camera—despite its explicit presence—to submerge beneath our awareness.

Another kind of epistemic fantasy is found in one of the contemporary responses to direct cinema, namely Jean Rouch's model of cinema verité. This is most famously present in *Chronique d'un été* (*Chronicle of a Summer*, 1961), in which Rouch and Edgar Morin use the camera to provoke or stimulate discussion and so enable deeper truths to emerge. But Rouch developed other strategies for negotiating the camera, especially in his ethnographic work. In *Tourou et Bitti: Les tambours d'avant* (1971), Rouch sets out to film a possession ritual, aiming to show how spirits "mount" the dancers. The film begins as Rouch enters the village of Simiri, where a ceremony is underway to summon spirits to end a drought; while nothing has happened for the first three days of the ceremony, his entry into the village square with his camera causes that possession to occur. In a single, ten-minute shot, Rouch records the interaction between the dancer and the drummers, circling the clearing in the middle of the village as more people (and more spirits) join the dance. (He also shows the children of the village watching their parents, learning how the ritual takes shape and what its purpose might be.) As the shot nears its end, Rouch notes that the sacrifices are about to begin and then remarks, "I should have gone on filming, but I wanted to make a movie, return to the start of my story, and I pulled back slowly to see what the schoolchildren saw: A small village square in the setting sun where, in a secret ceremony, men and gods spoke of coming harvests." As these words are spoken in voice-over, Rouch draws back from the village square, back in the direction from which he originally entered, and tilts the camera up to reveal the sun.

The common way of understanding *Tourou et Bitti* comes from Rouch himself. In "On the Vicissitudes of the Self," Rouch claimed that the effect of the virtuosic sequence shot placed him in a kind of *ciné-trance*, and that the state of mind he was in as he wandered through the village was sufficient to induce the spirits to arrive.[43] They recognized in him a familiar being, a self who was already possessed, which meant that it was safe for them to finally emerge into the village. Rather than an observer looking at and examining the ceremony, Rouch becomes a central participant in the ritual itself. The virtuosity of his work with the camera, his ability to move in and with the dancers, transforms not only the dance but his status in the world of the dancers. Paul Stoller describes the effect as the newly created being of "Rouch-the-camera," a self who is able to act within the terms of the possession rituals.[44]

The solution that Rouch devises thus rests on a fantasy of immersion, the idea that it is possible to engage in the world directly, despite—even because of—the intermediary technology. It's a fantasy found repeatedly in documentary cinema. Errol Morris's use of his "Interrotron," in which interviews are mediated through a television screen—each person's face appears on a screen in front of the other, with a camera filming from behind the screen—is done so as to minimize the disruption caused by the movie camera. Because we're used to talking to screens, Morris suggests, they can be made into something natural, almost unnoticed.

Welles takes a different tack. Like much of his work of the 1970s, the style of *The Other Side of the Wind* is a far cry from the extended camera movements and long takes that defined his Hollywood career. The virtuosity of those films feels so easy, almost brashly so—as if Welles could produce any effect he wanted. But by this point, working independently and no longer commanding the resources of a studio, the labor of style is now evident. The shots are rarely extended in duration; one shot quickly leads into another, which then almost overlaps with the following shot in staccato bursts of editing. The camera is perpetually roving, moving its focus between people and events. And because the camera is handheld, this movement provides a palpable sense of its presence in the world of the film.

"What's the fundamental aesthetic difference between a zoom and a dolly?" asks a character in the film. A young director, played by Peter Bogdanovich, answers glibly: "What possible difference can that make . . . except to another dolly." Obviously Welles knows the answer, and has known for a long time. The opening shot of *Touch of Evil* is rightly regarded as one of his technical masterpieces, a stunning feat of virtuosity that is nonetheless intimately connected to the story it tells. Yet immediately after that shot, when the sound of the explosion is heard, Welles adds two additional shots: the first is a shot of the explosion itself, which contains a fast zoom into the burning car; the second is of Miguel Vargas running toward the explosion, a handheld shot that retreats swiftly to keep him focused in the frame. In three shots, Welles summarizes different kinds of movement: tracking shot (on a crane), zoom, and handheld.

But if Welles knows the difference, it doesn't mean the question is irrelevant. Both kinds of movements are declarations of the presence of the filmmaker, a moment whereby we are made to realize—precisely because of the roughness of the movement—that a camera is present. This recognition is amplified in *The Other Side of the Wind* by the way that, each time a character turns around, it seems there is a camera, or set of cameras, waiting to film them. Welles is not interested in catching life unawares or in provoking a higher truth. Instead, he emphasizes the sense of a world seen, of being seen, the consequences of the fact that, as Walter Benjamin put it in the 1930s, "any person today can lay claim to being filmed."[45] Welles never lets us forget this. Even in the parody film that Hannaford is projecting, the camera is made explicit. When the main actor refuses to continue, he walks off the set while the camera, commanded by Hannaford to keep filming, turns to follow.

To what end? Welles is never interested in dissipating illusions, pure and simple. His is not a Brechtian cinema—but nor is it, as so many critics argued in the heyday of political modernism, a principally illusionistic one.[46] Everywhere in *The Other Side of the Wind* we find cameras. When Hannaford tries to seduce the young girl, a quick cut shows multiple cameras poking through the trees, filming them. We see the cameras and recognize that we are seeing through them—that we are complicit in the invasion of privacy, but also in the refusal of anyone to halt actions—but as they move to show us something new, we continue to go along with them. Welles even works through the way that different cameras—35mm vs. 16mm, color vs. black and white—and different techniques—dolly vs. zoom vs. handheld—provide different forms of access to the world of the film, different ways of knowing something about it, and different forms of visual pleasure. At once inside and outside the film, Welles sidesteps the problem of the camera in documentary by burying the viewer under a barrage of cameras; it no longer matters whether a camera is present for the simple reason that cameras are always present.

Welles holds open a set of questions. Do we care about the cameras or the image? How do we look at a film? How do we track our own fantasies and desires about movies? These are the kinds of questions I've been trying to address in this book, to get a sense of how to think about them. The moving camera is central to this, both as the repository of many of our fantasies about moving images and as a site of uncertainty within familiar forms of thinking. To take camera movements seriously is to open up a new zone, at once theoretical, historical, and critical, for exploration. It is to give up on certain fantasies of schematic understandings and replace them with self-aware forms of viewing. It is to pay attention to how our fantasies and desires structure our relation to films, while recognizing how those films seek to elicit and play with those very fantasies and desires. It is to be immersed in the film and critically distant at one and the same time, feeling the forms of motion while thinking about the interpretive arcs on which they carry us.

Notes

Roland Barthes, "Leaving the Movie Theater" [1975], in *The Rustle of Language*, trans. Richard Howard (New York: Hill and Wang, 1986), 345–49; 347.

CHAPTER 1. TALKING ABOUT THE MOVING CAMERA

1. Eric Grode, "'1917' Isn't the First (Supposedly) One-Shot Film: Here's a Timeline," *New York Times*, December 25, 2019.

2. "Suddenly we're right in the midst of it all": quoted in Tom Gunning, "Landscape and the Fantasy of Moving Pictures: Early Cinema's Phantom Rides," in *Cinema and Landscape*, ed. Graeme Harper and Jonathan Ryder (Chicago: University of Chicago Press, 2010), 31–70; 51; "swept along in the rush": quoted in Tom Gunning, "An Unseen Energy Swallows Space: The Space in Early Film and Its Relation to American Avant-Garde Film," in *Film Before Griffith*, ed. John Fell (Berkeley: University of California Press, 1984), 355–66; 363.

3. Blain Brown, *Cinematography Theory and Practice: Imagemaking for Cinematographers, Directors, and Videographers* (Amsterdam: Focal Press, 2002), 76.

4. Patrick Keating, *The Dynamic Frame: Camera Movement in Classical Hollywood* (New York: Columbia University Press, 2019), 2.

5. This dual fact is described in an article about the television coverage of the protests following the killing of George Floyd in May 2020: "The illusion is as old as Thomas Edison and the Lumière brothers: The camera is your eye, it roams the world, seeing and recording it transparently, as if its aperture is consciousness itself. Of course that's not true, but the illusion is part of the camera's

power to amuse us, inform us and mislead us, and it is essential to both the camera's democratic and totalitarian power." Philip Kennicott, "Through the Lens of a CNN Camera on the Ground, a View of American Disintegration," *Washington Post*, May 29, 2020. I am grateful to David Levin for this reference.

6. For early examples, see Irving Pichel, "Seeing with the Camera," *Hollywood Quarterly* 1, no. 2 (1946): 138–45; Jean Mitry, *The Aesthetics and Psychology of the Cinema*, trans. Christopher King (Bloomington: University of Indiana Press, 2000), 183ff.; and David Bordwell, "Camera Movement and Cinematic Space," *Cine-Tracts* 1, no. 2 (1977): 19–25.

7. André Bazin, *Jean Renoir*, ed. François Truffaut, trans. W. W. Halsey II and William H. Simon (New York: Da Capo Press, 1992), 46.

8. Annette Michelson, "Toward Snow" [1971], in *The Avant-Garde Film: A Reader of Theory and Criticism*, ed. P. Adams Sitney (New York: Anthology Film Archives, 1987), 172–83; 175. Snow himself would lament "that the movement of the camera as a separate expressive entity in film is completely unexplored." "Application to the Canadian Film Development Corporation" [1969], in *The Collected Writings of Michael Snow*, ed. Michael Snow and Louise Dompierre (Waterloo, ON: Wilfrid Laurier University Press, 1994), 59.

9. Brian Henderson, *A Critique of Film Theory* (New York: E. P. Dutton, 1980), 74.

10. Alfred Hitchcock, "Hitchcock Talks about Lights, Camera, Action (1967)," in *Hitchcock on Hitchcock: Selected Writings and Interviews*, ed. Sidney Gottlieb (Berkeley: University of California Press, 1997), 310.

11. Mitry, *The Aesthetics and Psychology of Cinema*, 185. See also Jakob Nielsen, "Camera Movement Revisited," 16, no. 9 (February 2009), www.16-9.dk/2009-02/side11_inenglish.htm.

12. Nick Hall, *The Zoom: Drama at the Touch of a Lever* (New Brunswick, NJ: Rutgers University Press, 2018), 6–15. See also Keating, *The Dynamic Frame*, 68–79.

13. Éric Rohmer and Claude Chabrol, *Hitchcock: The First Forty-Four Films*, trans. Stanley Hochman (New York: Frederick Ungar, 1979), 84.

14. Gilberto Perez, *The Material Ghost: Films and Their Medium* (Baltimore, MD: Johns Hopkins University Press, 1998), 91. See also Victor Perkins, "The Cinema of Nicholas Ray," in *Movies and Methods*, ed. Bill Nichols (Berkeley: University of California Press, 1976): 1:251–62.

15. Bordwell, "Camera Movement and Cinematic Space," 19.

16. On the zoom, see Adam O'Brien, "When a Film Remembers Its Filming: The New Hollywood Zoom," *Journal of Media Practice* 13, no. 3 (2012): 227–37; Paul Willemen, "The Zoom in Popular Cinema: A Question of Performance," *Inter-Asia Cultural Studies* 14, no. 1 (2013): 104–9; Chris Fujiwara, "Zooming through Space" [1998], HILOBROW, January 5, 2012, www.hilobrow.com/2012/01/05/zooming-through-space/; and Hall, *The Zoom*. On Steadicam, see Jean-Pierre Geuens, "Visuality and Power: The Work of the Steadicam," *Film Quarterly* 47, no. 2 (Winter 1993–94): 8–17; and Katie Bird, "'Dancing, Flying Camera Jockeys': Invisible Labor, Craft Discourse, and Embodied Steadicam and Panaglide Technique from 1972 to 1985," *Velvet Light Trap* 80 (Fall 2017): 48–65.

17. On the cosmic zoom, see Jennifer Barker, "Neither Here nor There: Synaesthesia and the Cosmic Zoom," *New Review of Film and Television Studies* 7, no. 3 (September 2009): 311–24. Jordan Schonig has written about a technique he describes as the "chained camera" in "The Chained Camera: On the Ethics and Politics of the Follow-Shot Aesthetic," *New Review of Film and Television Studies* 16, no. 3 (2018): 164–94. On camera movement and animation, see Russell George, "Some Spatial Characteristics of the Hollywood Cartoon," *Screen* 31, no. 3 (1990): 296–321; and Ryan Pierson, "Whole-Screen Metamorphosis and the Imagined Camera (Notes on Perspectival Movement in Animation)," *Animation: An Interdisciplinary Journal* 10, no. 1 (2015): 6–21. On handheld cinematography, see Adam Hart, "Extensions of Our Body Moving, Dancing: The American Avant-Garde's Theories of Handheld Subjectivity," *Discourse* 41, no. 1 (Winter 2019): 37–67; see also Keating, *The Dynamic Frame*, 234–35.

18. J. L. Austin, "A Plea for Excuses," in *Philosophical Papers*, 3rd ed., ed. J. O Urmson and G. J. Warnock (Oxford: Oxford University Press, 1979), 175–204; 183.

19. Keating, *The Dynamic Frame*, 79.

20. Keating, *The Dynamic Frame*, 56.

21. Quoted in Edward Branigan, *Projecting a Camera: Language-Games in Film Theory* (New York: Routledge, 2006), 40.

22. Pichel, "Seeing with the Camera," 140.

23. Quoted in Keating, *The Dynamic Frame*, 186.

24. Bordwell, "Camera Movement and Cinematic Space," 21, 23.

25. Quoted in Annette Michelson, "About Snow," *October* 8 (Spring 1973): 111–25; 123.

26. Bruce Bennett, "The Normativity of 3D: Cinematic Journeys, 'Imperial Visuality' and Unchained Cameras," *Jump Cut: A Review of Contemporary Media* 55 (Fall 2013), www.ejumpcut.org/archive/jc55.2013/Bennett-3D/index.html.

27. Slavoj Zizek, "The Camera's Posthuman Eye," in Henry Bond, *Lacan at the Scene* (Cambridge, MA: MIT Press, 2009), xi–xv; xiii.

28. Alexander Galloway, *Gaming: Essays on Algorithmic Culture* (Minneapolis: University of Minnesota Press, 2006), 29–69; and Will Brooker, "Camera-Eye, CG-Eye: Videogames and the 'Cinematic,'" *Cinema Journal* 48, no. 3 (Spring 2008): 122–28.

29. Tom Gunning, "Rounding Out the Moving Image: Camera Movement and Volumetric Space" (paper delivered at the Society for Cinema and Media Studies, Montreal, March 26, 2015) (emphasis added).

30. Tom Gunning, "Nothing Will Have Taken Place—Except Place: The Unsettling Nature of Camera Movement," in *Screen Space Reconfigured*, ed. Susanne Saether and Synne Tollerud Bull (Amsterdam: Amsterdam University Press, 2020), 263–81; 267.

31. Thomas Elsaesser and Malte Hagener, "Cinema as Eye," in *Film Theory: An Introduction through the Senses*, 2nd ed. (New York: Routledge, 2015), 94–123.

32. Vivian Sobchack, "Toward Inhabited Space: The Semiotic Structure of Camera Movement in the Cinema," *Semiotica* 41, no. 1/4 (1982): 317–55; 320.

33. See, among many instances, André Bazin, "The Evolution of the Language of Cinema," in *What Is Cinema?*, trans. Hugh Gray (Berkeley: University of California Press, 1967), 1:37.

34. Sobchack, "Toward Inhabited Space," 327.

35. See especially Vivian Sobchack, "The Active Eye: A Phenomenology of Cinematic Vision," *Quarterly Review of Film and Video* 12, no. 3 (1990): 21-36.

36. Quoted in Serena Ferrara, *Steadicam: Techniques and Aesthetics* (Oxford: Focal Press, 2001), 123-24.

37. Jennifer Barker, *The Tactile Eye: Touch and the Cinematic Experience* (Berkeley: University of California Press, 2009), 75. On anthropomorphic accounts of the camera, see Branigan, *Projecting a Camera*, 36-39.

38. Scott C. Richmond, *Cinema's Bodily Illusions: Flying, Floating, and Hallucinating* (Minneapolis: University of Minnesota Press, 2016), 8.

39. Richmond, *Cinema's Bodily Illusions*, 74 (emphasis added); see also 16, 84, 105, 109-10, 140.

40. Elizabeth Reich and Scott C. Richmond, "Introduction: Cinematic Identifications," *Film Criticism* 39, no. 2 (Winter 2014-15): 3-24; 12.

41. Jordan Schonig, *The Shape of Motion: Cinema and the Aesthetics of Movement* (New York: Oxford University Press, forthcoming). See also Keating, *The Dynamic Frame*, 186, 241. As illustrated by Schonig's work and much of the best recent work on camera movement, experimental and animated films are sites where key assumptions about camera movement can be tested, explored, and even exploded. See, for example, John Powers, "Moving through Stasis in Stan Brakhage's *Passage Through: A Ritual*," *Screen* 60, no. 3 (Autumn 2019): 410-27. Part of the project of my book is to see some of the same questions emerge in startling forms against the background of narrative fiction film, where the model of the camera as spectator's surrogate dominates thinking about camera movement.

42. Joe McElhaney, *The Death of Classical Cinema: Hitchcock, Lang, Minnelli* (Albany: State University of New York Press, 2006), 162-63.

43. Stanley Cavell speaks to such fantasies when he writes that "Capra and Hitchcock's films make nakedly clear the power of film to materialize and to satisfy (hence to dematerialize and to thwart) human wishes that escape the satisfaction of the world as it stands." "What Becomes of Things on Film?," in *Themes Out of School* (Chicago: University of Chicago Press, 1984), 173-83; 180.

44. Damon R. Young observes that "this inherent transgressiveness of the act of looking in on private space through a window" is "redoubled," perhaps even "retroactively justified," by the illicit scene it reveals. *Making Sex Public and Other Cinematic Fantasies* (Durham, NC: Duke University Press, 2018), 195. Young also helpfully catalogs the camera movements in Hitchcock's films that go through windows (270n23).

45. On *The Big Clock*, see Keating, *The Dynamic Frame*, 248-49.

46. See, for example, Mark Hansen, *New Philosophy for New Media* (Cambridge, MA: MIT Press, 2006).

47. Hito Steyerl, "In Free Fall: A Thought Experiment on Vertical Perspective," *e-flux* 24 (April 2011), www.e-flux.com/journal/24/67860/in-free-fall-a-thought-experiment-on-vertical-perspective/.

48. Lev Manovich, "An Archeology of a Computer Screen," *Kunstforum International* 132 (Fall 1995): 124–35.

49. Shane Denson, "Crazy Cameras, Discorrelated Images, and the Post-Perceptual Mediation of Post-Cinematic Affect," in *Post-Cinema: Theorizing 21st Century Film*, ed. Shane Denson and Julia Leyda (Falmer, UK: REFRAME Books, 2016), 193–233; 216.

50. Shane Denson, Therese Grishamn, and Julia Leyda, "Post-Continuity, the Irrational Camera, Thoughts on 3D," in Denson and Leyda, *Post-Cinema*, 933–75; 939.

51. Shane Denson, *Discorrelated Images* (Durham, NC: Duke University Press, 2020), 26.

52. Pierson, "Whole-Screen Metamorphosis and the Imagined Camera," 7.

53. Richmond, *Cinema's Bodily Illusions*, 136.

54. Kristen Whissel, "Parallax Effects: Epistemology, Affect and Digital 3D Cinema," *Journal of Visual Culture* 15, no. 2 (2016): 233–49; 238. Holly Willis also reads the shot this way; see *Fast Forward: The Future(s) of the Cinematic Arts* (New York: Wallflower Press, 2016), 142–43.

55. Denson, *Discorrelated Images*, 9.

56. Denson, *Discorrelated Images*, 8.

57. Denson does acknowledge that such perspectival games took place in the predigital era, but associates them with an avant-garde seeking to undo mainstream cinema.

58. John Gibbs and Douglas Pye, "Introduction 1" to *The Long Take: Critical Approaches*, ed. John Gibbs and Douglas Pye (London: Palgrave Macmillan, 2017), 1–26; 6–7.

59. Jonathan Rosenbaum, "Portabella and Continuity," in *Goodbye Cinema, Hello Cinephilia: Film Culture in Transition* (Chicago: University of Chicago Press, 2010), 131–35; 134.

60. Jonathan Rosenbaum articulates this position when he wonders why "we're all still using the same terms for practices and objects that are radically different from one another." ("End of Beginning: The New Cinephilia," in *Screen Dynamics: Mapping the Borders of Cinema*, ed. Gertrud Koch and Volker Pantenburg (Vienna: Synema, 2012), 30–41; 31. See also Holly Willis's claim that "shifts in digital tools remain so far removed from the working methods of many filmmakers that we lack the language to even describe or define new practices." *Fast Forward*, 143.

61. D. N. Rodowick observes that "dominant cultural contexts for imagining what cameras *are* limit our sense of what cameras *do*" in *What Philosophy Wants from Images* (Chicago: University of Chicago Press, 2017), 105–6.

CHAPTER 2. THE LURE OF THE IMAGE

1. Jean-Louis Baudry, "The Apparatus: Metapsychological Approaches to the Impression of Reality in the Cinema," in *Narrative, Apparatus, Ideology: A Film Theory Reader*, ed. Phil Rosen (Columbia University Press: New York, 1986), 299–318: 302.

2. Plato, *Republic*, trans. G. M. A. Grube (Indianapolis, IN: Hackett, 1992), 518c.

3. Serge Daney, "The Therrorized (Godardian Pedagogy)" [1976], trans. Bill Krohn and Charles Cameron Ball, www.diagonalthoughts.com/?p=1620. See also Michael Cramer, *Utopian Television: Rossellini, Watkins, and Godard beyond Cinema* (Minneapolis: University of Minnesota Press, 2017).

4. Ovid, *Metamorphoses*, trans. Allen Mandelbaum (New York: Harcourt Brace, 1993), III.405–11.

5. Marshall McLuhan draws from the myth a conclusion about people "being fascinated by any extension of themselves in any material other than themselves"; Narcissus, he says, "had adapted to his extension of himself and had become a closed system." *Understanding Media: The Extensions of Man* (Cambridge, MA: MIT Press, 1994), 41.

6. For a reworking of these ideas more in line with the thinking developed in this chapter, see Hans Loewald, "Instinct Theory, Object Relations, and Psychic Structure Formation" [1978]," in *The Essential Loewald: Collected Papers and Monographs* (Hagerstown, MD: University Publishing Group, 2000), 207–18.

7. That is, with this myth, and in contrast to what many theorists and filmmakers hoped for, sound is not a pedagogic corrective to the image. I am grateful to Nicole Morse for discussions on this point.

8. Leon Battista Alberti, *On Painting*, trans. Cecil Grayton (New York: Penguin Books, 1991), 61. See also Richard Neer, "Poussin, Titian and Tradition: *The Birth of Bacchus* and the Genealogy of Images," *Word & Image* 18, no. 3 (2002): 267–81; 275.

9. Roland Barthes, "Leaving the Movie Theater" [1975], in *The Rustle of Language*, trans. Richard Howard (New York: Hill and Wang, 1986), 345–49; 345.

10. Barthes, "Leaving the Movie Theater," 347.

11. Barthes, "Leaving the Movie Theater," 348.

12. Writing at roughly the same moment, Jean-Louis Comolli also uses the idea of the "lure" to talk about the film image. But where Barthes is interested in our fascination with the image itself, with the image as such, Comolli argues that the film image manifests a constructed vision of reality that serves as a way to naturalize more ideological meanings. The reality effect thus becomes the hook for politics. See Jean-Louis Comolli, *Cinema against Spectacle: Technique and Ideology Revisited*, ed. and trans. Daniel Fairfax (Amsterdam: Amsterdam University Press, 2015), 224, 230.

13. Barthes, "Leaving the Movie Theater," 349. Barthes's formulation bears striking parallels to the remedy Kracauer proposed for the seductions of new movie palaces in the 1920s: to look at the architectural details, the surrounding décor—all the things that would distract a viewer from the image. See Siegfried Kracauer, "Cult of Distraction," in *The Mass Ornament: Weimar Essays*, ed. and trans. Thomas Levin (Cambridge, MA: Harvard University Press, 1995), 323–28.

14. For an alternate telling of Plato's Allegory of the Cave that focuses on the images shown, see Denis Diderot, "Fragonard—Salon of 1765," in *Selected Writings on Art and Literature*, trans. Geoffrey Bremner (London: Penguin Books, 1994), 219–29.

15. La Rochefoucauld, *Maxims*, trans. Leonard Tancock (London: Penguin Books, 1959), 49.

16. La Rochefoucauld, *Maxims*, 102.

17. Jean-Paul Sartre, *What Is Literature? And Other Essays* (Cambridge, MA: Harvard University Press, 1988), 224; and Roland Barthes, *Writing Degree Zero*, trans. Annette Lavers and Colin Smith (New York: Hill and Wang, 1967), 15.

18. On the history of *Cahiers du cinéma*, see Emilie Bickerton, *A Short History of Cahiers du cinéma* (London, Verso, 2009); and Antoine de Baecque, *Les Cahiers du cinéma: Histoire d'une revue* (Paris: Cahiers du cinéma, 1991).

19. Serge Daney, "The Tracking Shot in *Kapo*," in *Postcards from the Cinema*, trans. Paul Douglas Grant (New York: Berg, 2007), 17–35. Daney makes a similar claim elsewhere; see, for example, Bill Krohn, "On Daney (1977)," in *Letters from Hollywood, 1977–2017* (Albany: State University of New York Press, 2000), 9–33.

20. Jacques Rivette, "On Abjection" [1961], trans. David Phelps with the assistance of Jeremi Szaniawski. www.dvdbeaver.com/rivette/OK/abjection.html.

21. Laurent Jullier and Jean-Marc Leveratto, "The Story of a Myth: "The 'Tracking Shot in *Kapò*' or the Making of French Film Ideology," *Mise au point* 8 (April 2016), https://map.revues.org/2069.

22. See Lisa Downing and Libby Saxton, *Film and Ethics: Foreclosed Encounters* (New York: Routledge, 2010), 22–35; and Pavle Levi, *Jolted Images: Unbound Analytic* (Amsterdam: Amsterdam University Press, 2017), 111–16.

23. Daney's "The Forbidden Zoom," trans. Ginette Vincendeau, *Framework* 32/33 (1986): 176–77, is more concerned with a form/content problem.

24. Daney, "The Tracking Shot in *Kapo*," 20.

25. On bad taste, see C. F. Cornford, "The Question of Bad Taste," *British Journal of Aesthetics* 8, no. 3 (1968), 215–26; Theodore Gracyk, "Having Bad Taste," *British Journal of Aesthetics* 30, no. 2 (1990), 117–31; and Pierre Bourdieu, *Distinction: A Social Critique of the Judgment of Taste*, trans. Richard Nice (Cambridge, MA: Harvard University Press, 1987). See also Carl Wilson, *Let's Talk about Love: A Journey to the End of Taste* (New York: Continuum, 2007).

26. This reading of Franju's film forms the conclusion of Siegfried Kracauer's *Theory of Film: The Redemption of Physical Reality* (Princeton, NJ: Princeton University Press, 1997), 305–6. On these broader debates, see Miriam Hansen, "'Schindler's List Is Not Shoah': The Second Commandment, Popular Modernism, and Public Memory," *Critical Inquiry* 22, no. 2 (Winter 1996): 292–312; and Georges Didi-Huberman, *Images in Spite of All: Four Photographs from Auschwitz*, trans. Shane Lillis (Chicago: University of Chicago Press, 2008). Gertrud Koch has extended this line of thought to excavate an anti-imagist strain in political film more broadly; see "Mimesis and *Bilderverbot*," *Screen* 34, no. 3 (October 1993): 211–22.

27. André Bazin, "Le Ghetto concentrationnaire," *Cahiers du cinéma* 9 (1952): 58–60.

28. Daney is alive to this last example: "With even more substantial directors than Pontecorvo, I often stumbled upon this smuggler's way of adding extra parasitic beauty or complicit information to scenes that didn't need it. . . .

[Nothing troubled me so much as] Anna Magnani's revealing skirt after she is shot dead in *Rome, Open City*. Rossellini was also hitting 'below the belt,' but in such a new way that it would take years to know towards which abyss it was taking us. Where does the event end? Where is the cruelty? Where does obscenity begin and where does pornography end? I knew these were questions constitutive of the 'post-camp' cinema. A cinema that I began to call, because we are the same age, 'modern.'" Daney, "The Tracking Shot in *Kapo*," 27.

29. Daney, "The Tracking Shot in *Kapo*," 17.

30. Sergei Eisenstein, "The Materialist Approach to Form," in *Selected Work*, vol. 1, *Writings, 1922–34* (London: BFI Publishing, 1988), 59–64; 62.

31. Brian Henderson, *A Critique of Film Theory* (New York: E.P. Dutton, 1980): 62–81.

32. Luc Moullet, "Sam Fuller: In Marlowe's Footsteps" (1959) and Jean Domarchi et al., "Hiroshima, notre amour" (1959), in *Cahiers du cinéma, the 1950s: Neo-Realism, Hollywood, New Wave*, ed. Jim Hillier (Cambridge, MA: Harvard University Press, 1985). On Moullet, see Jonathan Rosenbaum, "À la recherche de Luc Moullet: 25 Propositions" and "Moullet retrouvé (2006/2009)," in *Goodbye Cinema, Hello Cinephilia: Film Culture in Transition* (Chicago: University of Chicago Press, 2010), 31–43, 320–24. See also Sam Di Iorio, "The Woodcutter's Gaze: Luc Moullet and Cahiers du Cinéma 1956–1969," *SubStance* 34, no. 3 (2005): 79–95.

33. Quoted in Jullier and Leveratto, "The Story of a Myth."

34. It no doubt matters for Rivette that Emmanuelle Riva was both the object of the "tracking shot in *Kapo*" and the star of *Hiroshima mon amour*.

35. Daney, "The Tracking Shot in *Kapo*," 34.

36. Sam Di Iorio, "Three Tracking Shots: Jacques Rivette towards a Masterless Cinema," *Contemporary French Civilization* 32, no. 2 (Summer 2008): 85–112; 86.

37. Di Iorio, "Three Tracking Shots," 96–98.

38. Jean Paulhan, *The Flowers of Tarbes, or Terror in Literature*, trans. Michael Syrotinski (Urbana: University of Illinois Press, 2006), 23–24.

39. It's not exclusively Brechtian. See, for example, John David Rhodes, "Belabored: Style as Work," *Framework* 53, no. 1 (2012): 47–64, or Thorstein Veblen's praise of "the honorific marks of hand labor" in *The Theory of the Leisure Class* (New York: A. M. Kelly, 1965), 159–60.

40. Daney, "The Tracking Shot in *Kapo*," 17.

41. Nico Baumbach, *Cinema/Politics/Philosophy* (New York Columbia University Press, 2018): 16.

42. See David Bordwell, *On the History of Film Style* (Cambridge, MA: Harvard University Press, 1998), 4.

43. This is obviously a sketch of a larger account. For some of that work, see Richard Neer, "Connoisseurship and the Stakes of Style," *Critical Inquiry* 32, no. 1 (2005): 1–26; and Constantine Nakassis, *Doing Style: Youth and Mass Mediation in South India* (Chicago: University of Chicago Press, 2016).

44. As Richard Moran observes, a person "might well be disturbed by what he finds himself feeling at the movies. Such reactions would be hard to understand if what he felt was as remote from his real temperament as the events on

the screen are remote from his real beliefs about the world. The person who finds himself chortling with appreciation at a racist joke cannot excuse himself by insisting that he no more really shares in the attitude his laughter expresses than he really believes the fictional truths that make up the details of the story." "The Expression of Feeling in Imagination," *Philosophical Review* 103, no. 1 (1994): 74–106; 93–94.

45. Details of description matter. Michael Wood describes these shots as zooms and thus fails to see how they entrap the spectator as well as Scottie; see *Alfred Hitchcock: The Man Who Knew Too Much* (Boston: New Harvest, 2015), 90–91.

46. See Patrick Keating, *The Dynamic Frame: Camera Movement in Classical Hollywood* (New York: Columbia University Press, 2019), 277.

47. Walter Benjamin, "The Work of Art in the Age of Its Technological Reproducibility: Third Version," in *Selected Writings*, vol. 4, *1938–1940*, ed. Howard Eiland and Michael Jennings (Cambridge, MA: Harvard University Press, 2003), 251–83; 268; and Béla Bálazs, *Early Film Theory*, ed. Erica Carter, trans. Rodney Livingstone (New York: Berghahn Books, 2010), 173. On the vicissitudes of this myth, see Sven Lindqvist, *The Myth of Wu Tao-Tzu*, trans. Joan Tate (London: Granta, 2012).

48. This does not mean that we want to live in the world shown by a film—that's not the point in the discussion of *Kapo*—but that we imagine moving through it as the camera does, being in the world in *that* way.

49. Daney, "The Tracking Shot in *Kapo*," 20, 34. It is worth noting that Daney displaces this anxiety onto the younger generation of filmgoers: they won't get what's wrong with *Kapo*, won't understand its formal challenge.

50. Quoted in *Les inrockuptibles* (March 1992).

51. Daney, "The Tracking Shot in *Kapo*," 26.

52. Daney, "The Tracking Shot in *Kapo*," 34.

53. Daney, "The Therrorized (Godardian Pedagogy)."

54. Krohn, "On Daney (1977)," 31.

55. See Sergei Eisenstein, "Dickens, Griffith, and Ourselves," in *Selected Works*, vol. 3, *Writings 1934–1947*, ed. Richard Taylor (London: British Film Institute, 1996), 193–238.

56. Krohn, "On Daney (1977)," 31.

57. Daney, "The Tracking Shot in *Kapo*," 34.

58. Daney, "The Tracking Shot in *Kapo*," 33.

59. Daney, "The Tracking Shot in *Kapo*," 34.

60. Daney, "The Tracking Shot in *Kapo*," 34.

61. On these topics, see my *Late Godard and the Possibilities of Cinema* (Berkeley: University of California Press, 2012), 221–37.

62. Daney, "The Tracking Shot in *Kapo*," 35.

63. Serge Daney, "Montage Obligatory: The War, the Gulf, and the Small Screen," trans. Laurent Kretzschmar, *Rouge* 8 (2006), www.rouge.com.au/8 /montage.html.

64. Paulhan, *The Flowers of Tarbes*, 2.

65. Gilles Deleuze, "What Is a *Dispositif?*," in *Michel Foucault, Philosopher*, ed. and trans Timothy Armstrong (New York: Routledge, 1991), 159–68; 160.

66. See Michel Foucault, "The Confession of the Flesh," in *Power/Knowledge: Selected Interviews and Other Writings, 1972–1977*, ed. and trans. Colin Gordon (New York: Pantheon Books, 1980), 194–228. See also Davide Panagia, "On the Political Ontology of the *Dispositif*," *Critical Inquiry* 45, no. 3 (Spring 2019): 714–46.

67. Baudry, "The Apparatus," 312.

68. Will Straw, "Pulling Apart the Apparatus," *Recherches sémiotiques/ Semiotic Inquiry* 31 (2011): 59–73; 62.

69. Jean-Louis Baudry, "Ideological Effects of the Basic Cinematographic Apparatus," in Rosen, *Narrative, Apparatus, Ideology*, 286–98; 288–89.

70. See, for example, Daniel Dayan, "The Tutor-Code of Classical Cinema," *Film Quarterly* 28, no. 1 (Fall 1974): 22–31.

71. Baudry, "Ideological Effects of the Basic Cinematographic Apparatus," 292.

72. David Bordwell, "Camera Movement and Cinematic Space," *Cine-Tracts* 1, no. 2 (1977): 19.

73. Anne Friedberg, *Window Shopping: Cinema and the Postmodern* (Berkeley: University of California Press, 1994), 147. See also Anne Friedberg, *The Virtual Window: From Alberti to Microsoft* (Cambridge, MA: MIT Press, 2006), 74–78.

74. Sarah Keller has noted the importance of identification to models of cinephilia; see *Anxious Cinephilia: Pleasure and Peril at the Movies* (New York: Columbia University Press, 2020), 90–97.

CHAPTER 3. WHERE ARE WE?

1. See Kenneth Johnson, "The Point of View of the Wandering Camera," *Cinema Journal* 32, no. 2 (Winter 1993): 49–56; and Jennifer Barker, *The Tactile Eye: Touch and the Cinematic Experience* (Berkeley: University of California Press, 2009), 80–81.

2. Quoted in George Wilson, *Narration in Light: Studies in Cinematic Point of View* (Baltimore, MD: Johns Hopkins University Press, 1986), 55.

3. See Noël Burch, "Nana, or the Two Kinds of Space," in *Theory of Film Practice*, trans. Helen Lane (Princeton, NJ: Princeton University Press, 1981), 17–31.

4. Dziga Vertov, "The Council of Three," in *Kino-Eye: The Writings of Dziga Vertov*, ed. Annette Michelson, trans. Kevin O'Brien (Berkeley: University of California Press 1984), 14–21; 16–7.

5. James Naremore, *The Magic World of Orson Welles*, rev. ed. (Dallas, TX: Southern Methodist University Press, 1989), 22–23. Welles of course claimed that he was the first to grasp this affinity.

6. Walter Benjamin, "The Work of Art in the Age of Its Technological Reproducibility: Third Version," in *Selected Writings*, vol. 4, *1938–1940*, ed. Howard Eiland and Michael Jennings (Cambridge, MA: Harvard University Press, 2003), 251–83; 265.

7. To take just one example: Annette Michelson worries that Stan Brakhage's analogy between camera and body "calls into question the instrument's

fundamental power as expressed in the metaphor of the camera as eye." "Film and the Radical Aspiration," in *The Film Culture Reader*, ed. P. Adams Sitney (New York: Cooper Square Press, 2000), 404–21; 419.

8. Christian Quendler, *The Camera-Eye Metaphor in Cinema* (New York: Routledge, 2017), 1.

9. Christian Metz, *The Imaginary Signifier: Psychoanalysis and the Cinema*, trans. Celia Britton, Annwyl Williams, Ben Brewster, and Alfred Guzzetti (Bloomington: University of Indiana Press, 1986), 46, 49.

10. Metz, *The Imaginary Signifier*, 51.

11. Kaja Silverman, "What Is a Camera?, or: History in the Field of Vision," *Discourse* 15, no. 3 (1993): 3–56; 52–53.

12. Kristen Whissel, *Picturing American Modernity: Traffic, Technology, and the Silent Cinema* (Durham, NC: Duke University Press, 2008), 96.

13. Gregory Currie, *Image and Mind: Film, Philosophy, and Cognitive Science* (Cambridge, UK: Cambridge University Press, 1995), 171.

14. George Wilson, *Seeing Fictions in Film: The Epistemology of Movies* (New York: Oxford University Press, 2011), 37. Wilson is in fact arguing against Currie, who is himself arguing against earlier work by Wilson. I bring them together here because the terms of their disagreement mark them as distinct from the intuitive view.

15. Wilson, *Seeing Fictions in Film*, 79n3. While Branigan does discuss camera movements, he generally does so in terms of narrative motivation. See Edward Branigan, *Point of View in the Cinema: A Theory of Narration and Subjectivity in Classical Film* (Berlin: Mouton Publishers, 1984), 42–56.

16. A similar anxiety is also present in Arthur Danto's "Moving Pictures," in which the topic of camera movement suddenly leads to the introduction of equivocations like "phenomenologically speaking" and "I tend to feel" into an argument otherwise devoid of them. See Arthur Danto, "Moving Pictures" [1979], in *Philosophy of Film and Motion Pictures: An Anthology*, ed. Noël Carroll and Jinhee Choi (Malden: Blackwell Publishing, 2006), 100–12; 110. Katherine Thomson-Jones provides the one account I have come across that takes the moving camera seriously as a significant problem for these debates, though her focus is more on how the forward-moving camera obviates the need for the assumption of a narrating agency within the world of the film. See Katherine Thomson-Jones, "Narration in Motion," *British Journal of Aesthetics* 52, no. 1 (2012): 33–43.

17. Jean Mitry, *The Aesthetics and Psychology of the Cinema*, trans. Christopher King (Bloomington: University of Indiana Press, 2000), 214, 218.

18. Adam Hart, "Killer POV: First-Person Camera and Sympathetic Identification in Modern Horror," *Imaginations* 9, no. 1 (2018): 69–86.

19. Thomson-Jones, "Narration in Motion," 40.

20. David Bordwell, "Camera Movement and Cinematic Space," *Cine-Tracts* 1, no. 2 (1977): 19–25; 23. His larger argument in the essay is of course more complex.

21. See, for example, Maurice Merleau-Ponty, *Phenomenology of Perception*, trans. Colin Smith (New York: Routledge, 1962), 203.

22. See Vivian Sobchack, *The Address of the Eye: A Phenomenology of Visual Experience* (Princeton, NJ: Princeton University Press, 1992), 59. Sobchack

stands in here for a broader and more diverse phenomenological film theory. I don't think the simplification that results is egregious, though problems of alternative models do arise.

23. Noël Carroll, *The Philosophy of Motion Pictures* (Malden, MA: Blackwell Publishing, 2008), 126.

24. Danto, "Moving Pictures," 110.

25. Edward Branigan, *Projecting a Camera: Language-Games in Film Theory* (New York: Routledge, 2006), 36.

26. Vittorio Gallese and Michele Guerra, "The Feeling of Motion: Camera Movements and Motor Cognition," *Cinéma & Cie* 14, nos. 22/23 (2014): 103–12; 106.

27. Vittorio Gallese and Michele Guerra, *The Empathic Screen: Cinema and Neuroscience*, trans. Frances Anderson (Oxford: Oxford University Press, 2020), 91–92. Malcolm Turvery has criticized their approach in terms similar to the discussion here; see "Mirror Neurons and Film Studies: A Cautionary Tale from a Serious Pessimist," *Projections* 14, no. 3 (2020): 21–46.

28. Patrick Keating, *The Dynamic Frame: Camera Movement in Classical Hollywood* (New York: Columbia University Press, 2019), 45. He continues: "*The Cat and the Canary* comments on the uncanny nature of camerawork itself, ridiculing the oft-posed analogy between the camera and the human by representing the camera's eerie point of view as simultaneously human and inhuman."

29. On these qualities, see Carol Clover, "The Eye of Horror," in *Viewing Positions: Ways of Seeing Film*, ed. Linda Williams (New Brunswick, NJ: Rutgers University Press, 1995), 184–230; and Steve Neale, "*Halloween*: Suspense, Aggression and the Look," in *Planks of Reason: Essays on the Horror Film*, ed. Barry Grant (Metuchen, NJ: Scarecrow, 1984), 331–45.

30. Sobchack, *The Address of the Eye*, 62, 179.

31. Branigan, *Projecting a Camera*, 42.

32. The case is slightly more complicated because Mrs. Johnson does not *quite* look at the camera when she opens the door. But if the direction of her look means we are not exactly at George's position—a fact we are aware of—as soon as the camera begins to move, we feel that we are moving with him, that we have taken up his position. I am grateful to Jordan Schonig for this observation.

33. As with *The Magnificent Ambersons*, he doesn't quite look directly at it, but the affinity between Faust and the camera is sufficiently strong that we read it as a direct look—plus, since Faust is invisible, we accept that the major can only look in a general direction.

34. Joris Ivens, *The Camera and I* (New York: International Publishers, 1949), 42.

35. Sobchack, *The Address of the Eye*, 240.

36. Not surprisingly, many extended subjective shots are motivated by extreme psychological states. In addition to drugs, there are dreams (*Killer's Kiss* [Stanley Kubrick, 1955]), fantasies (*The Sea Inside* [Alejandro Amenábar, 2004]), and science fiction devices (*Being John Malkovich* [Spike Jonze, 1999]). On the vogue for point of view shots in classical Hollywood, see Keating, *The Dynamic Frame*, 195–208, 276, 279.

37. James Conant, "The World of a Movie," in *Making a Difference: Rethinking Humanism and the Humanities*, ed. Niklas Forsberg and Susanne Jansson (Stockholm: Thales, 2009), 293–324; 302–3.

38. Conant, "The World of a Movie," 314–5.

39. How we identify with characters, and the relation of that identification to point-of-view shots, is a larger topic; see Murray Smith, "Altered States: Character and Emotional Response in Cinema," *Cinema Journal* 33, no. 4 (1994): 34–56, and Murray Smith,, "Imagining from the Inside," in *Film Theory and Philosophy*, ed. Richard Allen and Murray Smith (New York: Oxford University Press, 1997), 412–30; and Jinhee Choi, "Leaving It Up to the Imagination: POV Shots and Imagining from the Inside," *Journal of Aesthetics and Art Criticism* 63, no. 1 (Winter 2005): 17–25. These debates have a history in literary theory, especially around the idea of "free indirect discourse"; on its application to cinema, see Pier Paolo Pasolini, "Comments on Free Indirect Discourse" and "The Cinema of Poetry," in *Heretical Empiricism*, trans. Ben Lawton and Louise K. Barnett (Bloomington: University of Indiana Press, 1988), 79–101, 167–86; Gilles Deleuze, *Cinema 1: The Movement-Image*, trans. Hugh Tomlinson and Barbara Habberjam (Minneapolis: University of Minnesota Press, 1986), 71–76; and Louis-Georges Schwartz, "Typewriter: Free Indirect Discourse in Deleuze's 'Cinema,'" *SubStance* 34, no. 3 (2005): 107–35.

40. Kendall Walton, "Fearing Fictions," *Journal of Philosophy* 75, no. 1 (January 1978): 5–27; 5. Walton's answer will be that Charles makes believe that he is in the world of the fiction with the slime approaching him; Charles feels, fictionally, the emotions he would have felt if he were actually there. The conclusion is that "make-believedly [Charles] is afraid," that he feels a kind of "quasi-fear" (13).

41. See Kendall Walton, "How Remote Are Fictional Worlds from the Real World?," *Journal of Aesthetics and Art Criticism* 37, no. 1 (1979): 11–23. My reading of Walton is shaped by Richard Moran's "The Expression of Feeling in Imagination," *Philosophical Review* 103, no. 1 (1994): 74–106.

42. Kendall Walton, *Mimesis as Make-Believe* (Cambridge, MA: Harvard University Press, 1990), 277.

43. Scott C. Richmond, *Cinema's Bodily Illusions: Flying, Floating, and Hallucinating* (Minneapolis: University of Minnesota Press, 2016), 8.

44. Richmond, *Cinema's Bodily Illusions*, 54–55.

45. See Ariel Rogers, *Cinematic Appeals: The Experience of New Movie Technologies* (New York: Columbia University Press, 2013), 210ff.

46. Sara Ross, "Invitation to the Voyage: The Flight Sequence in Contemporary 3D Cinema," *Film History* 24 (2012): 210–20; 219.

47. Scott C. Richmond, "The Exorbitant Lightness of Bodies, or How to Look at Superheroes: Ilinx, Identification, and *Spider-Man*," *Discourse* 34, no. 1 (2012): 113–44; 129–30. See also Scott C. Richmond, "On Learning to Fly at the Movies: *Avatar* and *How to Train Your Dragon*," *Journal of Narrative Theory* 46, no. 2 (Summer 2016): 254–83.

48. Richard Wollheim, *Painting as an Art* (Princeton, NJ: Princeton University Press, 1987), 102. There is an unsurprising contrast here with Michael

258 | Notes to Pages 76–80

Fried's interest in seeing people absorbed in activities as surrogates for the relation of the beholder to the image (364–65n34).

49. See Richard Wollheim, "Imagination and Identification," in *On Art and the Mind: Essays and Lectures* (Cambridge, MA: Harvard University Press, 1974), 54–83; 73–74. See also Joel Snyder, "Picturing Vision," *Critical Inquiry* 6, no. 3 (Spring 1980): 499–526; 510.

50. Wollheim, *Painting as an Art*, 139. See also Michael Baxandall, *Painting and Experience in Fifteenth Century Italy* (New York: Oxford University Press, 1972), 76.

51. Wollheim, *Painting as an Art*, 164.

52. There is a larger question of why we are prone to posit internal spectators. One way of answering it would be to follow through on John Bowlby's claim that ethological findings "encourage speculation that for humans, as well perhaps as for other primates, it is as natural to attribute states of mind to self and to others as it is to attribute spatial qualities to the world around us." *Attachment and Loss*, vol. 1, *Attachment*, 2nd ed. (New York: Basic Books, 1982), 370. Another would involve Merleau-Ponty's discussion of the way we perceive objects in the world as existing within a wider horizon; "to look at an object is to inhabit it," he writes, suggesting that we see the world both from its position and from the perspective of everything that surrounds it in three-dimensional space. *Phenomenology of Perception*, 68.

53. These debates begin with Michel Foucault, *The Order of Things: An Archeology of the Human Sciences*, trans. Alan Sheridan (New York: Vintage, 1973), 3–16. For a summary of these debates and a revised account of the painting, see Joel Snyder, "'Las Meninas' and the Mirror of the Prince," *Critical Inquiry* 11, no. 4 (1985): 539–72.

54. This repetition is noted in David Bordwell, Janet Staiger, and Kristin Thompson, *The Classical Hollywood Cinema* (New York: Routledge, 1985), 346.

55. John MacKay has pointed out a similar dynamic in Vertov's *Lullaby* (1937), where the moving camera is used to articulate various ways of inhabiting the world.

56. Wollheim, *Painting as an Art*, 102–3.

57. Wollheim, *Painting as an Art*, 162.

58. Wollheim, *Painting as an Art*, 183.

59. It begins, more or less, with an essay by Bernard Williams, in which he emphasizes that "I as perceiver do not necessarily belong inside the world that I visualize, any more than I necessarily do so in the world that I imagine." "Imagination and the Self," in *Problems of the Self: Philosophical Papers 1956–1972* (Cambridge, UK: Cambridge University Press, 1973), 26–45; 34–35.

60. Richard Wollheim, *The Thread of Life* (Cambridge, UK: Cambridge University Press, 1984), 104.

61. Moran, "The Expression of Feeling in Imagination," 91. See also J. David Velleman, "Self to Self," *Philosophical Review* 105, no. 1 (1996): 39–76.

62. Moran, "The Expression of Feeling in Imagination," 91, 93.

63. Christopher Jude McCarroll, *Remembering from the Outside: Personal Memory and the Perspectival Mind* (New York: Oxford University Press, 2019), 36.

64. McCarroll, *Remembering from the Outside*, 143. On related aspects of Sartre's account of self-understanding, see Matthew Boyle, "Sartre on Bodily Transparency," *Manuscrito* 41, no. 4 (2018): 33–70.

65. McCarroll, *Remembering from the Outside*, 88–89. On the way one can generate "internal kinesthetic imagery from an external visual perspective," see page 136.

66. McCarroll, *Remembering from the Outside*, 133.

67. McCarroll, *Remembering from the Outside*, 196.

68. Warren Buckland, "Narration and Focalisation in *Wings of Desire*," *CineAction* 56 (2001): 26–33; 31.

69. Ofer Eliaz, *Cinematic Cryptonymies: The Absent Body in Postwar Film* (Detroit: Wayne State University Press, 2018), 71.

70. Keating, *The Dynamic Frame*, 121. See also his discussion of a shot from *The Man Who Laughs* (Paul Leni, 1928), in which Gwynplaine is holding onto a ledge: "The camera suddenly cranes down to the ground . . . [It] represents Gwynplaine's fear of falling rather than the fall itself" (52).

71. Branigan, *Point of View in the Cinema*, 109.

72. Bordwell, "Camera Movement and Cinematic Space," 25.

73. Adam Hart, "Extensions of Our Body Moving, Dancing: The American Avant-Garde's Theories of Handheld Subjectivity," *Discourse* 41, no. 1 (Winter 2019): 37–67; 48–52.

74. For an analysis of these formal strategies, see David Bordwell, *The Films of Carl-Theodor Dreyer* (Berkeley: University of California Press, 1981), 93–115.

75. This topic bears on the role of "folk psychology" in thinking about the philosophy of mind; for a summary of these debates, see Stephen Stich and Shaun Nichols, "Folk Psychology," in *The Blackwell Guide to Philosophy of Mind* (Oxford: Basil Blackwell, 2003), 235–55; and David Bordwell, "Common Sense + Film Theory = Common-Sense Film Theory?," May 2011, www .davidbordwell.net/essays/commonsense.php. Also relevant is Christian Metz's discussion of the importance of fantasy and cognitive desire in our basic comprehension of film. See "*Trucage* and the Film," trans. Françoise Meltzer, *Critical Inquiry* 3, no. 4 (Summer 1977): 657–75, esp. 669–70.

CHAPTER 4. VARIABLE DYNAMICS OF POINT OF VIEW

1. Laura Mulvey, "Visual Pleasure and Narrative Cinema," in *Visual and Other Pleasures*, 2nd ed. (New York: Palgrave MacMillan, 2009), 14–27; 26, 20.

2. The phrase is from Theodor W. Adorno, quoted in Michael Cahn, "Subversive Mimesis: Theodor W. Adorno and the Modern Impasse of Critique," in *The Literary and Philosophical Debate*, vol. 1 of *Mimesis in Contemporary Theory*, ed. Mihai Spariosu (Philadelphia: Benjamins, 1984), 34.

3. I discuss this sequence in greater detail in "Rethinking Bazin: Ontology and Realist Aesthetics," *Critical Inquiry* 32 (Spring 2006): 443–81; 464–69.

4. Patrick Keating, *The Dynamic Frame: Camera Movement in Classical Hollywood* (New York: Columbia University Press, 2019), 199–200.

5. The ethical claims of *Waltz with Bashir* are pegged to the way this shot, and its heightened sense of interiority, is followed by a reverse-shot that shows, for the first time in the film, video footage from the massacre's aftermath. The effect is to move outside of Folman's own experience, suggesting that the events do not, in the end, primarily belong to or matter in relation to his memory—that they are part of a world beyond his point of view.

6. Lotte Eisner, *Fritz Lang* (New York: Da Capo Press, 1976), 160, 166–67.

7. In this Lang resembles Eisenstein, who also largely eschews the moving camera.

8. See Thomas Elsaesser, *Metropolis* (London: BFI Publishing, 2000), 9–12.

9. For a broader account of German cinema in the 1920s, with particular attention to the valences of point of view, see Katharina Loew, *Special Effects and German Silent Film: Techno-Romantic Cinema* (Amsterdam: Amsterdam University Press, 2021), 227–72.

10. See Eisner, *Fritz Lang*, 91.

11. Eisner, *Fritz Lang*, 91.

12. There is a similar shot later in the film, when the elevators crash down into the workers' city and the camera rushes forward to push up against Maria's face—again simultaneously responding to the force of the explosion, giving it physical weight for the viewer, and expressing her sense of terror at the destruction she sees.

13. *Die Spinnen* and *Der müde Tod* both have moments when the camera is mounted on a moving vehicle—a train in the former and a flying carpet in the latter—but these are not marked significantly as *camera* movements. A more ambiguous example is a late scene in *Dr. Mabuse*, in which the camera is mounted on Von Wenck's car as he drives after the magic word "Melior."

14. Tom Gunning isolates these techniques as indicators of "visionary scenes"; see *The Films of Fritz Lang: Allegories of Vision and Modernity* (London: BFI Publishing, 2000).

15. Keating notes a similar type of shot that revolves around hypnosis in Paul Fejos's *The Last Performance* (1923) (see Keating, *The Dynamic Frame*, 42). Interestingly, Fejos had worked with Lang in 1923, during the making of *Dr. Mabuse*.

16. George Wilson, *Seeing Fictions in Film: The Epistemology of Movies* (New York: Oxford University Press, 2011), 149.

17. Wilson notes that questions about point of view are not sufficient on their own to account for what's going on in a given shot, but he glosses this gap in terms of our larger knowledge of a scene's "epistemic structure." *Seeing Fictions in Film*, 163–64.

18. Rudolf Arnheim, *Film as Art* (Berkeley: University of California Press, 1957), 102–3; and Siegfried Kracauer, *From Caligari to Hitler: A Psychological History of German Film*, ed. Leonardo Quaresima (Princeton, NJ: Princeton University Press, 2004), 83.

19. Gunning, *The Films of Fritz Lang*, 109.

20. Kracauer, *From Caligari to Hitler*, 83. This address to the spectator is analogous to what Paul Willemen, adapting Mulvey, describes as the "fourth

look" of the cinema in *Looks and Frictions* (Bloomington: Indiana University Press, 1994).

21. Noël Burch, *In and Out of Synch: The Awakening of a Cine-Dreamer*, trans. Ben Brewster (Aldershot, UK: Scolar Press, 1991), 215; and Gunning, *The Films of Fritz Lang*, 110.

22. Kracauer, *From Caligari to Hitler*, 94 ("complete triumph"). On this topic, Theodor W. Adorno remarks: "The subject too is not static like a camera on a tripod; rather, the subject also moves, by virtue of its relationship to the object that is inherently in motion." *Hegel: Three Studies*, trans. Shierry Weber Nicholsen (Cambridge, MA: MIT Press, 1993), 99.

23. Bernhard Diebold, "Expressionism and the Cinema," in *The Promise of Cinema: German Film Theory 1907–1933*, ed. Anton Kaes, Nicholas Baer, and Michael Cowan (Berkeley: University of California Press, 2016), 415–20; 419.

24. Adam Hart, "Killer POV: First-Person Camera and Sympathetic Identification in Modern Horror," *Imaginations* 9, no. 1 (2018): 69–86; 74.

25. Hart, "Killer POV," 77.

26. A later shot in *Metropolis*, in which Maria squirms in fear as Rotwang approaches her within his house, follows a similar logic. Although there is no camera movement, the same dynamic—that we look from Rotwang's optical point of view but experience the shot as an expression of Maria's state of mind—guides its structure.

27. The sequence is also filmed in a very different manner, eschewing not only camera movements but point-of-view shots more generally.

28. William Rothman, *Hitchcock—The Murderous Gaze* (Cambridge, MA: Harvard University Press, 1982), 282. In a sense, Hitchcock is providing a version of the "cuckoo clock" speech by Orson Welles in *The Third Man* (Carol Reed, 1949), in which Reed's focus on the rhythms of Welles's words helps draw us into inhabiting a moral position we would otherwise think to be vile.

29. As Gunning notes in *The Films of Fritz Lang*, xi–xii, Lang's films are humanly moving despite the reductive psychology of his characters.

30. Gunning, *The Films of Fritz Lang*, 185.

31. I mean here to evoke the notion of the "unchained camera" (*Entfesselte Kamera*) that Karl Freund used to characterize his technical achievements. See Lotte Eisner, *The Haunted Screen: Expressionism in German Cinema and the Influence of Max Reinhardt*, trans. Roger Greaves (London: Thames and Hudson, 1969), 212–21. See also Lotar Holland, "Subjective Movement," in Kaes, Baer, and Cowan, *The Promise of Cinema*, 512–15. On the moving camera and the transition to sound, see Keating, *The Dynamic Frame*, 56ff.

32. Although *Testament* does have several spectacular camera movements—as in the sharp pans and tilts that coincide with Dr. Baum's glimpse of Mabuse's apparition—its use of camera movement is more in line with familiar stylistic templates.

33. Leo Braudy, *The World in a Frame: What We See in Films* (Chicago: University of Chicago Press, 2002), 48.

34. On camera movement in Murnau's film, see, for example, Marc Silberman, *German Cinema: Texts in Context* (Detroit: Wayne State University Press,

1995), 19–33; and Sabine Müller, "Embodied Cognition and Camera Mobility in F. W. Murnau's *The Last Laugh* and Fritz Lang's *M*," *Paragraph* 37, no. 1 (2014): 32–46.

35. See Kracauer, *From Caligari to Hitler*, 221.

36. Müller incorrectly describes the camera as stationary, only using a pan ("Embodied Cognition and Camera Mobility," 38); it is vital to the effect of the shot that the camera physically moves through space.

37. See Anton Kaes, *M* (London: BFI Publishing, 1999), 9–13; Gunning, *The Films of Fritz Lang*, 165–68.

38. Lang's other depiction of domestic pleasure, in *The Big Heat* (1953), is likewise shattered early in the film.

39. Lang on the lynching scene in *Fury* (1936): "I roll the camera forward as a man would walk and thus approach the jail. The audience becomes the mob" (quoted in Keating, *The Dynamic Frame*, 95).

40. Gunning offers a more generous reading: "While in debt to a long tradition of European Orientalist fantasies (with all the richness of imagery and dubious ideology) Lang's Indian films . . . attempt to establish an alternative film-making style to the classical Hollywood narrative forms" (Gunning, *The Films of Fritz Lang*, 458).

41. On this tension, see, for example, Dipesh Chakrabarty, "Romantic Archives: Literature and the Politics of Identity in Bengal," *Critical Inquiry* 30, no. 3 (Spring 2004): 654–82.

42. Darius Cooper, *In Black and White: Hollywood and the Melodrama of Guru Dutt* (Calcutta: Seagull Press, 2005), 7. See also Ira Bhaskar, "Emotion, Subjectivity, and the Limits of Desire: Melodrama and Modernity in Bombay Cinema, 1940s–'50s," in *Gender Meets Genre in Postwar Cinemas*, ed. Christine Gledhill (Champaign: University of Illinois Press, 2012): 161–76. On the politics of melodrama, see, for example, Salomé Skvirsky, "The Price of Heaven: Remaking Politics in *All that Heaven Allows*, *Ali: Fear Eats the Soul*, and *Far from Heaven*," *Cinema Journal* 47, no. 3 (Spring 2008): 90–121.

43. For a general discussion of the song sequences, see Daisy Rockwell, "Visionary Choreographies: Guru Dutt's Experiments in Film Song Picturisation," *South Asian Popular Culture* 1, no. 2 (2003): 109–24.

44. Richard Dyer, *Only Entertainment* (London: Routledge, 2002), 20. Dyer is clear that the presentation of utopian potential is much less frequently in the world of narrative—as opposed to the "world of the numbers" (30).

45. For a discussion of economic and technological reasons for the persistence of this autonomy, see Sangita Gopal and Sujata Moorti, Introduction to *Global Bollywood: Travels of Hindi Song and Dance* (Minneapolis: University of Minnesota Press, 2008), 1–60. See also Usha Iyer, *Dancing Women: Choreographic Corporeal Histories of Hindi Cinema* (New York: Oxford University Press, 2020).

46. Rochona Majumdar, "Song-Time, the Time of Narratives, and the Changing Idea of Nation in Post-Independence Cinema," *boundary* 2 (forthcoming).

47. For some of the background to this political and cinematic project, see Ashish Rajadhyaksha, *Indian Cinema: A Very Short Introduction* (Oxford: Oxford University Press, 2016), 49–72.

48. For versions of such readings, see Allison Griffiths, "Discourses of Nationalism in Guru Dutt's *Pyaasa*," *Deep Focus* 6 (1996): 24–31; Sudhir Mahadevan, *A Very Old Machine: The Many Origins of the Cinema in India* (Albany: State University of New York Press, 2015), 83–104; Cooper, *In Black and White*, 7, 87; and Rashmi Doraiswamy, *Guru Dutt through Light and Shade* (New Delhi: Wisdom Tree, 2008), 32.

49. Lucy Fischer, *Cinematernity: Film, Motherhood, Genre* (Princeton, NJ: Princeton University Press, 1996), 224.

50. Nasreen Munni Kabir, *Guru Dutt: A Life in Cinema*, new ed. (New Delhi: Oxford University Press, 2005), 127.

51. Ravi Vasudevan notes the presence of point-of-view shots in the film but doesn't discuss them further; see *The Melodramatic Public: Film Form and Spectatorship in Indian Cinema* (New York: Palgrave MacMillan, 2011), 118ff.

52. The subtitles on different prints of *Pyaasa* vary tremendously; I have consulted Nasreen Munni Kabir, *The Dialogue of Pyaasa: Guru Dutt's Immortal Classic* (New Delhi: Om Books International, 2001).

53. See Pooja Rangan's astute comment that voice is "a sonic metaphor for point of view." "Auditing the Call Centre Voice: Accented Speech and Listening in Sonali Gulati's *Nalini by Day, Nancy by Night* (2005)," in *Vocal Projections: Voices in Documentary*, ed. Annabella Honess Roe and Maria Pramaggiore (New York: Bloomsbury Academic, 2019), 29–44; 31. This is complicated in *Pyaasa* not only by the use of playback singers but also because Vijay's songs in the film are sung by two different singers, Hemant Kumar and Mohammad Rafi.

54. Siegfried Kracauer, "Boredom," in *The Mass Ornament: Weimar Essays*, ed. and trans. Thomas Levin (Cambridge, MA: Harvard University Press, 1995), 331–34; 332. On this model of flexible identifications, see Miriam Bratu Hansen, *Cinema and Experience* (Berkeley: University of California Press, 2012), 18–19.

55. See also Ashish Rajadhyaksha, "Why Film Narratives Exist," *Inter-Asia Cultural Studies* 14, no. 1 (2013): 62–75.

56. Kabir says that it's Vijay's memory (*Guru Dutt*, 125), but what's evoked, even if it is sometimes filtered through Vijay's recollections, is something more like a shared experience.

57. The association is intentional on Dutt's part (see Kabir, *Guru Dutt*, 131).

58. The emphasis on the reciprocal arrangement of gazes is central. In *Chori Chori* (Anant Thakur, 1956), for example, a late song sequence uses camera movements in toward Nargis's face that are then followed by movements away as she sings, but the camera's movement is not straight, and it is not aligned with the sight of others. If the ostensible effect is there—words strike her, and she sings out to the world—the dynamic of gazes is missing.

59. This is also pointed out in Griffiths, "Discourses of Nationalism in Guru Dutt's *Pyaasa*," 29.

60. On the differing political ambitions of Ghatak and Dutt, see Nandini Bhattercharya, "Nation (De)composed: Ritwik Ghatak, Guru Dutt, Saadat Hasan Manto, and the Shifting Shapes of National Memory," in *The Indian*

Partition in Literature and Films, ed. Rini Bhattarcharya Mehta and Debali Mookerjea-Leonard (New York: Routledge, 2015), 107–18.

61. I take the term from Adebayo Williams, "Intellectuals and the Crisis of Democratization in Nigeria: Towards a Theory of Postcolonial Anomie," *Theory and Society* 27, no. 2 (1998), 287–307.

62. The song reflects not only the political preoccupations of the lyricist, Sahir Ludhianvi, but also a mode of address to the audience found in progressive street theater of the time. I am grateful to Usha Iyer for this observation.

63. Sergei Eisenstein, "Dickens, Griffith, and Ourselves," *Writings, 1934–1947*, vol. 3 of *Selected Works*, trans. Michael Glenny, ed. Richard Taylor (London: BFI, 1996), 193–238.

64. Robert Warshow, "Re-Viewing the Russian Movies" [1955], in *The Immediate Experience* (New York: Anchor Books, 1964), 201–12.

65. Or this is a depiction of the uprising—any uprising—from the point of view of the French, to whom it all appears spontaneous because they cannot imagine its planning.

66. Keating, *The Dynamic Frame*, 131. Curiously, one of the places a version of a collective point of view is achieved is in disaster movies.

67. Dutt will also associate the audience with a mob in *Kaagaz Ke Phool* (Paper Flowers, 1959), though with less of a political orientation.

68. Quoted in Kabir, *Guru Dutt*, 136. Kabir also notes that the scene with Gulab was added on at the end to decrease the sense of Vijay's isolation; initially, the film ended with his departure from Meena—totally alone (122).

69. Cooper, by contrast, argues that the failure of love for Meena is the cause of his existential despair; see *In Black and White*, 87.

70. This is what Mahadevan argues in *A Very Old Machine*, 84–89.

CHAPTER 5. MAX OPHULS AND THE LIMITS OF VIRTUOSITY

1. In Jean Domarchi et al., "Hiroshima, notre amour," in *Cahiers du cinéma, the 1950s: Neo-Realism, Hollywood, New Wave*, ed. Jim Hillier (Cambridge, MA: Harvard University Press, 1985), 59. Translation modified.

2. Mary Ann Doane notes that "accusations against the emptiness of technique abound in Ophuls criticism. . . . [They are] attacks concerning an overemphasis upon technological or formal feats at the expense of 'substance' or 'ethics.'" *Femmes Fatales: Feminism, Film Theory, Psychoanalysis* (New York: Routledge, 1991), 120. Andrew Sarris remarks that Ophuls "seemed inordinately devoted to baroque opulence." *The American Cinema: Directors and Directions, 1929–1968* (New York: E. P. Dutton, 1968), 71.

3. Stephen Heath, "The Question Oshima," in *Questions of Cinema* (Bloomington: University of Indiana Press, 1981), 145–64; 163.

4. See, in particular, Susan White, *The Cinema of Max Ophuls: Magisterial Vision and the Figure of Woman* (New York: Columbia University Press, 1995).

5. A partial exception to this trend is V. F. Perkins, who describes how the big ideas of the films resonate downward through a "mixture of tones." "Scarlet, No Empress," *Film Quarterly* 65, no. 2 (2011): 28–31; 31. See also

see V. F. Perkins, "*Letter from an Unknown Woman*," *Movie* 29/30 (1982): 61–72; V. F. Perkins, "'Same Tune Again!': Repetition and Framing in *Letter from an Unknown Woman*," *CineAction* 52 (2000): 40–48; and V. F. Perkins, "La Maison Tellier," *Film Quarterly* 63, no. 2 (2009): 66–71.

6. Among various topics, discussions have been about the ethics of form in lyric poetry, the relation of author to narrator in first-person fiction, and the modes of sympathetic identification made possible by free-indirect discourse in the novel. For examples, see, respectively, Robert Kaufmann, "Aura, Still," *October* 99 (Winter 2002): 45–80; Joshua Landy, *Philosophy as Fiction: Self, Deception, and Knowledge in Proust* (Oxford: Oxford University Press, 2004); and Andrew Miller, *The Burdens of Perfection: On Ethics and Reading in Nineteenth Century British Literature* (Ithaca, NY: Cornell University Press, 2008).

7. See Candace Vogler, "The Moral of the Story," *Critical Inquiry* 34, no. 1 (Fall 2007): 5–35.

8. Sergei Eisenstein, "Dickens, Griffith, and Ourselves," in *Selected Works*, vol. 3, *Writings 1934–1947*, ed. Richard Taylor (London: British Film Institute, 1996); André Bazin, "The Virtues and Limitations of Montage," in *What Is Cinema?*, trans. Hugh Gray (Berkeley: University of California Press, 1967), 1:41–52; and Jean-Louis Baudry, "Ideological Effects of the Basic Cinematographic Apparatus," in *Narrative, Apparatus, Ideology: A Film Theory Reader*, ed. Phil Rosen (Columbia University Press: New York, 1986), 286–98.

9. In an article written several years after this chapter was originally published as an essay, Sabine Müller argued that F. W. Murnau's moving camera provides a "double perspective" on the film's story; see "Embodied Cognition and Camera Mobility in F. W. Murnau's *The Last Laugh* and Fritz Lang's *M*," *Paragraph* 37, no. 1 (2014): 32–46; 41.

10. Quoted in Lutz Bacher, *Max Ophuls in the Hollywood Studios* (New Brunswick, NJ: Rutgers University Press, 1996).

11. Their action is apparently without purpose: they descend one staircase only to climb the other. I think the two women exist mainly to solve a formal problem. Ophuls has to have someone walk back across the foyer so that he can get to the place where Lisa and her husband will appear, but he doesn't want any figure to block our vision of them. The only place the women can go, then, is up the staircase. It's a solution that has the added advantage of prefiguring the movement of Lisa and her husband up the same staircase a moment later.

12. Gilberto Perez wonderfully compares this kind of sequence to Antonioni: "Characters entering and leaving frame, disappearing and reappearing, the camera moving with one character, then with another, in one direction, then in another, exploring, inspecting the scene, finding the lost sight of, encountering the unanticipated." *The Eloquent Screen: A Rhetoric of Film* (Minneapolis: University of Minnesota Press, 2019), 260.

13. Perkins emphasizes this tendency as well in "*Letter from an Unknown Woman*," 72.

14. This is roughly George Wilson's reading, part of his larger argument that the film systematically undermines Lisa's perspective as narrator; see *Narration in Light: Studies in Cinematic Point of View* (Baltimore, MD: Johns Hopkins University Press, 1986), 103–25.

15. Wilson discerns a similar structure from the perspective of narrative authority. Though my interpretation of the film differs from his, I see it as complementary rather than contradictory. Robin Wood argues for the presence of a similar perspective in this shot, albeit on different terms; see "Ewig hin der Liebe Glück," in *Letter from an Unknown Woman*, ed. Virginia Wright Wexman and Karen Hollinger (New Brunswick, NJ: Rutgers University Press, 1986), 220.

16. A more appropriate thing to say is that the form of the camera movement helps us understand the psychological state of the characters in the first place.

17. In a similar vein, Karl Schoonover has emphasized the importance of "capitalist modernity's accumulative materiality" to the world of Ophuls's American films; see "The Cinema of Disposal: Max Ophuls and Accumulation in America," *differences* 29, no. 1 (2018): 33–65; 49.

18. I take this observation from Laura Mulvey, "Max Ophuls's Auteurist Adaptations" in *True to the Spirit: Film Adaptation and the Question of Fidelity*, ed. Colin MacCabe, Kathleen Murray, and Rick Warner (New York: Oxford University Press, 2011), 75–90.

19. According to George Annenkov, Ophuls made the change to evoke an earlier film starring his two central actors, Charles Boyer and Danielle Darrieux (*Mayerling* [Anatole Litvak, 1936]), in which Boyer had played a lieutenant: "This time, we'll make him a General." *Max Ophuls* (Paris: Le Terrain Vague, 1962), 67–68.

20. Her cry, "Where's the second shot?," echoes the duel at the end of *Liebelei*.

21. The first title card reads, "*Madame de . . . était une femme très élégante, très brillante, très fêtée. Elle semblait promise à une joile vie sans histoire.*" The second reads, "*Rien ne serait probablement arrive sans ce bijou.*"

22. A similarly deictic title is Budd Boetticher's *Seven Men from Now* (1956), whose "now" points to the moment in which the narrative begins.

23. Although no reason for the debt is given in the film, Louise de Vilmorin's novella says that she has habitually understated her expenses to her husband and now can't bring herself to confess the truth (his ability to pay it off is taken for granted). As a result, she finds herself in the position of having to sell something of her own.

24. On the relation between the openings of these two films, see John Gibbs, "Opening Movements in Ophuls: Long Takes, Leading Characters and Luxuries," in *The Long Take: Critical Approaches*, ed. John Gibbs and Douglas Pye (London: Palgrave Macmillan, 2017), 89–102.

25. See also Adrian Danks, "'Only Superficially Superficial': The Tragedy of Sophistication in *Madame de . . .*," *Senses of Cinema* 25 (March–April 2003), http://sensesofcinema.com/2003/cteq/madame_de-2/; and Katerina Virvidaki, *Testing Coherence in Narrative Film* (London: Palgrave Macmillan, 2017): 45–67.

26. Perez, *The Eloquent Screen*, 254.

27. Compare to Stanley Cavell, *Pursuits of Happiness* (Cambridge, MA: Harvard University Press, 1981), 1–8.

28. These three kinds of value are found in both Karl Marx, *Grundrisse*, trans. Martin Nicolaus (London: Penguin Books, 1973), and Georg Simmel,

The Philosophy of Money, trans. Tom Bottomore and David Frisby, 2nd ed. (London: Routledge, 1990). See also Joseph Bitney, "Passionate Exchanges: Melodrama and the Commodity Form" (PhD diss., University of Chicago, 2020).

29. The terms of this discussion are drawn from Barbara Herman, *Moral Literacy* (Cambridge, MA: Harvard University Press, 2007).

30. For this interpretation, see Alan Williams, *Max Ophuls and the Cinema of Desire: Style and Spectacle in Four Films, 1948–1955* (New York: Arno Press, 1980); Andrew Britton, "Metaphor and Mimesis: *Madame de . . . ,*" *Movie* 29/30 (Summer 1982): 91–107; and White, *The Cinema of Max Ophuls.*

31. White, *The Cinema of Max Ophuls,* 57–58, 62. This is the most common reading of the film.

32. Williams, for example, argues that the earrings "belong to both her and her husband, and represent the contract between them. In selling the earrings, Louise rejects her marriage." *Max Ophuls and the Cinema of Desire,* 131–32.

33. G. W. F. Hegel, *Philosophy of Right,* trans. T. M. Knox (London: Oxford University Press, 1967), § 117.

34. Unlike the Marquis in Renoir's *La règle du jeu,* André does not say that he has decided to become "worthy of my wife"; he has simply tired of his lover and uses the earrings to smooth over an awkward scene.

35. André certainly feels pain at Louise's actions, especially when he first discovers the deception; my point is that he does not take her to have rejected their marriage.

36. We later learn that André in fact finds this situation to be quite painful; he plays a role he does not enjoy.

37. Ophuls's dismissal of the category of fate is systematic. In the scene when André comes home from the opera to search for the earrings Louise claims to have lost, he is followed up the stairs by Louise's maid, who says, "I don't believe it. What a catastrophe. I predicted it—four diamonds and two black sevens means great loss. . . . At first, I thought the loss would come later. But with diamonds before sevens." We know she is lying here, attempting to distract André from thinking too much about what might have actually happened; she is aware that Louise sold the jewels, even wishing her well as she left on her errand. Fate, in the form of some supernatural agency, is invoked to serve as a deception or distraction. Two other examples in the film follow this pattern. The first is when the maid announces to Louise that she sees in the cards "a great love . . . reciprocated," at which Louise becomes interested in fortune-telling for the first time. (She had previously scoffed, as the cards only say that she is about to go away on a voyage, and that there will trouble for her husband because of the king or a foreigner: self-evident facts.) The second is when André remarks to Lola that the number 13—the number of the berth she occupies on the train to Constantinople—is good luck. While Lola may take this statement seriously, it seems clear that André means to smooth over the difficult fact that he is effectively sending her away and so ending their relationship. In these cases, the categories of fate, luck, and destiny are not things that actually obtain in the world of the film but are speech acts used (somewhat cynically) by various characters to achieve their ends.

38. There is a nice expression of the relation between dance and society in a letter written by Schiller, although the terms are different: "I know of no better image for the ideal of a beautiful society than a well executed English dance, composed of many complicated figures and turns.... Everything fits so skillfully, yet so spontaneously, that everyone seems to be following his own lead, without every getting in anyone's way. Such a dance is the perfect symbol of one's own individually asserted freedom as well as of one's respect for the freedom of the other." Quoted in Paul de Man, "Aesthetic Formalization: Kleist's *Über das Marionettentheater*," in *The Rhetoric of Romanticism* (New York: Columbia University Press, 1984), 263–90; 263.

39. It's for this reason that I am hesitant to say, as others have, that Ophuls values movement above all else.

40. We might also see *Madame de . . .* as part of a long line of novels and films in which adultery does not in itself constitute a damaging moral act or a reason for the lessening of the claims to happiness of the central characters. In different ways, both *Casablanca* (Michael Curtiz, 1942) and *Hiroshima mon amour* provide examples of this.

41. See, for example, Herman, *Moral Literacy*, 135–43, 176–202.

42. In a sequence filled with mirrors and doublings, we can think of the musician as the mirror image of the journalist whose movement across a room allowed the dancing to begin: here, he brings it to a close.

43. The social world returns in a brutal way: after a moment's silence, the sound of a trumpet blares out, announcing the beginning of a hunt—an activity in which, as Renoir's *La Règle du jeu* would have shown Ophuls, society becomes deadly.

44. The idea that love—as opposed to passion or desire?—can only flourish outside the gaze of society receives two other expressions later in the film. One is Louise's declaration to Donati, "I only want to be looked at by you." The other is André's curious action as he declares his own love for Louise: he shuts all the windows to her room.

45. Love, Goethe notes, desires eternity: "an ecstasy that must endure forever! / Forever!—For its end would be despair, / No, without end! No end!" Johann Wolfgang von Goethe, *Faust*, trans. Walter Arndt (New York: W. W. Norton, 1976), lines 3192–94.

46. At the end of the film, when both Fritz and Christine are dead, Ophuls will reprise the ride: we hear the words they spoke to each other while the camera retraces their earlier route, again coming to rest on the graveyard.

47. Ludwig Wittgenstein, *Tractatus Logico-Philosophicus*, trans. C. K. Ogden (London: Routledge, 1981), 6.4311. Or Goethe: "Alone the present moment—is our bliss." Goethe, *Faust*, line 9382.

48. This dynamic is of long-standing interest for Ophuls. He talks about "misreading" the sign over the Frankfurt opera house so that, instead of *Dem Wahren, Schönen, Guten* (To Truth, Beauty, Goodness), it becomes *Den schönen, guten Waren* (To beautiful, good wares). See Max Ophuls, "Thoughts on Film," in *Ophuls*, ed. Paul Willemen (London: BFI, 1972), 33–50; 35–36.

49. It's a posture similar to how Gilberto Perez describes the use of beauty in Godard's *Nouvelle vague* (1990), which "disallows the complacency both

of those who would simply enjoy beauty without looking into the conditions that make for it, and of those who would simply dismiss it as the plaything of a privileged few without recognizing its capacity to transcend and even subvert their claim to ownership." "Self-Illuminated," *London Review of Books*, April 1, 2004, 6.

50. "We are all literalists most or all of our lives. Presentness is grace." Michael Fried, "Art and Objecthood," in *Art and Objecthood* (Chicago: University of Chicago Press, 1998), 148–72; 168.

51. Ophuls, "Thoughts on Film," 42; and Immanuel Kant, *Critique of the Power of Judgment*, trans. Paul Guyer and Eric Matthews (Cambridge, UK: Cambridge University Press, 2000), Ak. 317–19.

52. *Liebelei, Letter from an Unknown Woman*, and *Madame de . . .* are all set in this world, and each ends with a duel.

53. Stanley Cavell, *The World Viewed*, enl. ed. (New York: Viking Press, 1979), 23.

54. See Mulvey, "Max Ophuls's Auteurist Adaptations."

55. Some of the American films are partial exceptions.

56. See Bertolt Brecht, *The Threepenny Opera*, trans. Hugh McDiarmid (London: Methuen, 1973).

57. See White, *The Cinema of Max Ophuls*, 209.

58. In addition to the camera movements and wipes, other devices such as intrascenic dissolves carry the rhetorical weight of the aesthetic and ethical project in *La Signora di Tutti*.

59. This combination of a downward movement with an upward tilt is also found in the first shot of *Lola Montès*, when the camera descends to the floor of the circus.

60. Joe McElhaney describes these shots as operating around a double void: both the absent Leonora and "the world being unfolded, the spectacle that is unfolding." "Bits of Business: The American Films of Max Ophüls," *Lola* 6 (December 2015), www.lolajournal.com/6/ophuls.html.

61. One assistant said while working on *Caught*: "He makes the camera disappear. It just happened to be there catching the action—like a silent witness." Quoted in Bacher, *Max Ophuls in the Hollywood Studios*, 223.

62. Godard remarks, "With each shot, each transition, each composition, Hitchcock does the only thing possible for the rather paradoxical but compelling reason that he could do anything he liked." "*The Wrong Man*," in *Godard on Godard*, ed. Tom Milne (New York: Da Capo Press, 1972).

CHAPTER 6. TERRENCE MALICK AND PERSPECTIVE

1. Robert Koehler, "What the Hell Happened with Terrence Malick," *Cineaste* 38, no. 4 (Fall 2013): 4–9; 6.

2. See, for example, David Bordwell, "Intensified Continuity: Visual Style in Contemporary American Film," *Film Quarterly* 55, no. 3 (2002): 16–28; and Steven Shaviro, "Post-Continuity: An Introduction," in *Post-Cinema: Theorizing 21st-Century Film*, ed. Shane Denson and Julia Leyda (Falmer: REFRAME Books, 2016), 51–64.

3. See John Landreville, "Alternative Ethics for Ecocinema: *The Tree of Life* and Post-Continuity Aesthetics," *New Review of Film and Television Studies* 17, no. 1 (2019): 99–119.

4. Tom Gunning, "*The New World*: Dwelling in Malick's New World," The Criterion Collection, July 25, 2016, www.criterion.com/current/posts/4161-the-new-world-dwelling-in-malick-s-new-world.

5. Thomas Deane Tucker, "Worlding the West: An Ontopology of *Badlands*," in *Terrence Malick: Film and Philosophy*, ed. Thomas Deane Tucker and Stuart Kendall (New York: Bloomsbury, 2011), 80–100; 101. For a survey of this literature, see Robert Sinnerbrink, *Terrence Malick: Filmmaker and Philosopher* (London: Bloomsbury Academic, 2019). For a discussion of the major themes in these readings, see Martin Rossouw, "There's Something about Malick: Film-Philosophy, Contemplative Style, and Ethics of Transformation," *New Review of Film and Television Studies* 15, no. 3 (2017): 279–98. On the emergence of philosophical debates in critical work on Malick, see John Rhym, "The Paradigmatic Shift in the Critical Reception of Terrence Malick's *Badlands* and the Emergence of a Heideggerian Cinema," *Quarterly Review of Film and Video* 27, no. 4 (June 2010): 255–66.

6. This happens, for example, when Marc Furstenau and Leslie MacAvoy write: "Malick's films, especially *The Thin Red Line*, are instances of what may be called a Heideggerian cinema. Malick's approach to filmmaking is strongly influenced by the philosophy of Martin Heidegger, of which he has a thorough and intimate understanding." "Terrence Malick's Heideggerian Cinema: War and the Question of Being in *The Thin Red Line*," in *The Cinema of Terrence Malick: Poetic Visions of America*, 2nd ed., ed. Hannah Patterson (New York: Wallflower Press, 2007), 179–91; 180. See also Simon Critchley, "Calm—On Terrence Malick's *The Thin Red Line*," *Film-Philosophy* 6 (2002), www.film-philosophy.com/vol6-2002/n48critchley.

7. Matthew Evertson, "Fields of Vision: Human Presence in the Plain Landscapes of Terrence Malick and Wright Morris," in Tucker and Kendall, *Terrence Malick: Film and Philosophy*, 101–25, esp. 111.

8. John Steinbeck, *Grapes of Wrath* (New York: Penguin Books, [1939] 1992), 79.

9. Robert Pippin, for example, notes the widely shared view that art's philosophical ambitions should be understood "not as making any tacitly assertoric or even discursive claim but rather as disclosive and disclosive generally of a kind of truth unavailable discursively." "Vernacular Metaphysics: On Terrence Malick's *The Thin Red Line*," *Critical Inquiry* 39, no. 2 (Winter 2013): 247–75; 271.

10. Lloyd Michaels, *Terrence Malick* (Urbana: University of Illinois Press, 2009), 4, 63.

11. Jaimey Fisher, "Nature Scaled to Body: Literary Adaptation, Space, and Genre in Terrence Malick's *The Thin Red Line* (1998) and G.W. Pabst's *Westfront 1918* (1930)," *New Review of Film and Television Studies* 17, no. 1 (2019): 57–80; 58. On "contemplative style," see, for example, Rossouw, "There's Something about Malick."

12. The exception might be Welsh's voice-over comment as he walks by a captain talking to troops about the military as family: "They want you dead, or in their lie." I am grateful to Rick Warner for reminding me of this sequence.

13. Maurice Merleau-Ponty, "Indirect Language and the Voices of Silence," in *The Merleau-Ponty Aesthetics Reader: Philosophy and Painting*, ed. and trans. Michael Smith (Evanston, IL: Northwestern University Press, 1993), 76–120; 87.

14. André Bazin, "The Ontology of the Photographic Image," in *What Is Cinema?*, trans. Hugh Gray (Berkeley: University of California Press, 1967), 1:9–16; 12. Translation modified.

15. Hubert Damisch, "Five Notes for a Phenomenology of the Photographic Image," in *Classic Essays on Photography*, ed. Alan Trachtenberg (New Haven, CT: Leete's Island Books, 1980), 287–90; Jacques Aumont, "The Point of View," trans. Arthur Denner, *Quarterly Review of Film and Video* 11 (1989): 1–22; and Anne Friedberg, *The Virtual Window: From Alberti to Microsoft* (Cambridge, MA: MIT Press, 2006), 74.

16. Richard de Cordova, "From Lumière to Pathé: The Break-Up of Perspectival Space," *Ciné-Tracts* 4, nos. 2–3 (1981): 55–63; 57.

17. On the temptation for such metaphorical extensions, see James Conant, "The Dialectic of Perspectivism 1," *Sats—Nordic Journal of Philosophy* 6, no. 2 (2005): 5–50.

18. Erwin Panofsky, *Perspective as Symbolic Form*, trans. Christopher Wood (New York: Zone Books, 1997), 31, 42.

19. Panofsky, *Perspective as Symbolic Form*, 34. Heidegger, writing several decades later, would use this argument to articulate what he describes as "The Age of the World Picture."

20. Hubert Damisch, *The Origin of Perspective*, trans. John Goodman (Cambridge, MA: MIT Press, 1994), 13–14.

21. For some antiperspectival strategies, see Nicholas Baer, "Post-Perspectivalist Perspectives in 'The Cabinet of Dr. Caligari,'" in *The New Berlin, 1912–1932*, ed. Inga Rossi-Schrimpf (Brussels: Racine, 2018), 93–99; Kaja Silverman, "What Is a Camera?, or: History in the Field of Vision," *Discourse* 15, no. 3 (1993): 3–56.

22. Jacques Rivette, "Mizoguchi Viewed from Here," in *Cahiers du cinéma, the 1950s: Neo-Realism, Hollywood, New Wave*, ed. Jim Hillier (Cambridge, MA: Harvard University Press, 1985), 265.

23. See, for example, Thomas Lamarre, "The Multiplanar Image," *Mechademia: Emerging Worlds of Anime and Manga* 1 (2006): 120–43; and Ryan Pierson, "Whole-Screen Metamorphosis and the Imagined Camera (Notes on Perspectival Movement in Animation)," *Animation: An Interdisciplinary Journal* 10, no. 1 (2015): 6–21.

24. Stan Brakhage, "Metaphors on Vision," in *Essential Brakhage: Selected Writings on Filmmaking by Stan Brakhage*, ed. Bruce R. McPherson (Kingston, NY: McPherson, 2001), 12.

25. Jedediah Purdy, *For Common Things: Irony, Trust, and Commitment in America Today* (New York: Vintage Books, 2000), 9–10.

26. A key background is the treatment of irony in German Romanticism; see, for example, Friedrich Schlegel, *Lucinde and the Fragments*, trans. Peter Firchow (Minneapolis: University of Minnesota Press, 1971).

27. On Malick and irony, see also Rick Warner, "Malick's Emergent Lyricism in *Badlands* and *Days of Heaven*," in *The Other Hollywood Renaissance*, ed. R. Barton Palmer, Murray Pomerance, and Dominic Lennard (Edinburgh: Edinburgh University Press, 2020), 177–88.

28. Søren Kierkegaard, *Concluding Unscientific Postscript to "Philosophical Fragments"*, ed. and trans. Howard Hong and Edna Hong (Princeton, NJ: Princeton University Press, 1992), 1:277n. This phrase is also cited by Jonathan Lear in an account of irony that has shaped my view of the topic; see Jonathan Lear, *A Case for Irony* (Cambridge, MA: Harvard University Press, 2011), 19.

29. Richard Neer remarks: "What matters, therefore, must be the general fact of allusiveness, more than any particular instance of it; the general fact that these characters speak words that are not their own and yet are all the more meaningful for that." "Terrence Malick's *The New World*," https://nonsite.org/feature/terrence-malicks-new-world.

30. Pippin, "Vernacular Metaphysics."

31. That does not mean they are easy to make sense of even on their own terms: "There can be no answers to these questions. . . . These questions are asked not in order to be answered, but in order to help us to understand the extensibility of being that can be voiced only as that which it is not, as that which always fails to be adequate to the film's vision." Leo Bersani and Ulysse Dutoit, *Forms of Being: Cinema, Subjectivity, Aesthetics* (London: BFI. 2004), 170–71.

32. Pippin, "Vernacular Metaphysics," 255. The best account of Malick's use of voice-overs is Jeremy Millington, "Critical Voices: Points of View in and on *The Thin Red Line*," *CineAction* 81 (2010): 28–38.

33. Pippin, "Vernacular Metaphysics," 251, 257. Michel Chion, for example, makes this error in *The Thin Red Line*, trans. Trista Selous (London: BFI, 2004), 72.

34. See James Conant, "Putting Two and Two Together: Kierkegaard, Wittgenstein and the Point of View for Their Work as Authors," in *The Grammar of Religious Belief*, ed. D. Z. Phillips (New York: St. Martin's Press, 1996), 248–331; and Joshua Landy, *How to Do Things with Fictions* (Oxford: Oxford University Press, 2012).

35. Gunning, "*The New World*: Dwelling in Malick's New World."

36. Lee Carruthers, *Doing Time: Temporality, Hermeneutics, and Contemporary Cinema* (Albany: State University of New York Press, 2016), 129–30.

37. Bersani and Dutoit, for example, write: "All the shots of sunlight streaming down through the branches of trees, of mountains in the distance just as the sun begins to penetrate the morning mist, of birds poised on a branch, of circling eddies of water: all these images, on the whole images of calm beauty (not of the unceasing strife the Colonel claims to see in nature), represent the vast, non-human setting of *The Thin Red Line* as a mostly immobile, indifferent witness to the human agitations within it." *Forms of Being*, 159.

38. Neer, "Terrence Malick's *The New World*."

39. Steven Rybin, *Terrence Malick and the Thought of Film* (Plymouth, MA: Lexington Books, 2012), 18.

40. Landreville, "Alternative Ethics for Ecocinema," 114.

41. Katie Bird, "'Dancing, Flying Camera Jockeys': Invisible Labor, Craft Discourse, and Embodied Steadicam and Panaglide Technique from 1972 to 1985," *Velvet Light Trap* 80 (Fall 2017): 48–65; 51.

42. Millington, "Critical Voices," 34.

43. Sinnerbrink, *Terrence Malick: Filmmaker and Philosopher*, 161–206.

44. Stanley Cavell, *The World Viewed*, enl. ed. (New York: Viking Press, 1979), 129. Cavell continues with an important parenthetical: "It may be worth calling this view objective, if you know that you have in mind not some unassessed contrast with subjectivity, but a mood in which reality becomes reified for you, a mood of nothing but eyes, dissociated from feeling."

45. Terrence Malick, Translator's introduction to Martin Heidegger, *The Essence of Reasons*, trans. Terrence Malick (Evanston, IL: Northwestern University Press, 1969), xi–xviii; xiv–xv.

46. Malick, Translator's introduction, xv.

47. Gunning, "*The New World*: Dwelling in Malick's New World."

48. Neer, "Terrence Malick's *The New World*."

49. Neer, "Terrence Malick's *The New World*."

50. Henry David Thoreau, *Walden* (New York: Library of America, 1985), 321–587; 429.

51. Neer, "Terrence Malick's *The New World*."

52. Jean-Jacques Rousseau, "On the Social Contract," in *Rousseau's Political Writings*, ed. Alan Ritter and Julia Conaway Bondanella, trans. Julia Conaway Bondanella (New York: W. W. Norton, 1988), 84–173; 85.

53. Neer, "Terrence Malick's *The New World*." Sinnerbrink describes this as Malick's "knowing kind of romanticism." *Terrence Malick: Filmmaker and Philosopher*, 101.

54. Britt Harrison notes the formal parallels between these scenes in "*The New World*: Heideggerian or Humanist Cinema?," *Aesthetic Investigations* 3, no. 2 (2020): 200–27; 214–18.

55. Rousseau, "On the Social Contract," 92. On the role of freedom in Rousseau, see (among others) Joshua Cohen, *Rousseau: A Free Community of Equals* (New York: Oxford University Pres, 2010); and Frederick Neuhouser, *Rousseau's Theodicy of Self-Love: Evil, Rationality, and the Drive for Recognition* (New York: Oxford University Press, 2008), esp. 50–51.

56. Sinnerbrink, *Terrence Malick: Filmmaker and Philosopher*, 108, 106.

57. Stanley Cavell, *Pursuits of Happiness* (Cambridge, MA: Harvard University Press, 1981), 159.

58. Cavell, *Pursuits of Happiness*, 60.

59. Cavell, *Pursuits of Happiness*, 49.

60. Cavell, *Pursuits of Happiness*, 109.

61. Lear, *A Case for Irony*, 13.

62. Lear, *A Case for Irony*, 20.

63. Even the ending of *Song to Song*, when Faye and BV reunite away from Austin in order to live at one with the earth, is more fully fleshed out.

64. For example, in the first few shots after Rolfe enters the film, Malick moves the camera in two distinct ways. Shots of Rolfe are shown with the camera moving in straight lines, usually horizontally, and show him walking through the settlement looking at Rebecca. ("When first I saw her," he says in voice-over, "she was regarded as someone finished, broken.") The shots of her, by contrast, have a tighter framing, and the camera moves with and around her activities. When the pair first walk together, the camera is directly behind them, following their movement along the inside of the settlement's wooden walls. The sense of Rolfe's separation from her, and her unreachability in her own world—a world of memory and loss—is conveyed in the camera's differing forms of movement. The same separation occurs when Rolfe and Rebecca walk through the forest before he proposes to her: their movements are isolated from one another, and their gazes do not cross; even after his declaration of love, they look away from rather than at each other.

65. Lear, *A Case for Irony*, 30.

66. Cavell, *Pursuits of Happiness*, 103.

67. Neer, "Terrence Malick's *The New World*."

68. This is the connection Conant emphasizes in "The Dialectic of Perspectivism."

69. See Søren Kierkegaard, *Fear and Trembling/Repetition*, ed. and trans. Howard Hong and Edna Hong (Princeton, NJ: Princeton University Press, 1983), 204.

70. G. W. F. Hegel, *Phenomenology of Spirit,* trans. A. V. Miller (Oxford: Oxford University Press, 1977), § 808.

71. Ralph Waldo Emerson, "Nature," in *The Essential Writings of Ralph Waldo Emerson*, ed. Brooks Atkinson (New York: Modern Library, 2000), 3–42; 6.

72. It is of course true that the film's flashbacks, if that is what they are, include many aspects that Jack could not himself have witnessed. Here Malick draws on a Hollywood convention that uses flashbacks as a way to go into a past time, within which standard narrative devices can then operate. As David Bordwell puts it, "The *range of knowledge* in the flashback portion is often not identical with that of the character doing the remembering. It is common for the flashback to show us more than the character can know (e.g., scenes in which she or he is not present)." *Narration in the Fiction Film* (Madison: University of Wisconsin Press, 1985), 162. On this reading, Malick is dramatically expanding this convention, pushing it to extremes in order to explode the conventions of human scale on which it is based. Steven Rybin suggests this point in *Terrence Malick and the Thought of Film*, 175–76).

73. I am grateful to Robert Pippin for clarifying this point.

74. Carruthers writes: "Here is the human form in its pliancy and vulnerability, overcome by such things as old age, laughter, sleep, wonder, 'the glory,' in Malick's language—each swiftly enumerated." *Doing Time*, 137.

75. The one scene in the past that mimics the feel of the present occurs at the father's work at an oil refinery. Amid all the metal sheen and structure, the camera can only move forward, backward, or horizontally.

76. Søren Kierkegaard, *Eighteen Upbuilding Discourses*, ed. and trans. Howard Hong and Edna Hong (Princeton, NJ: Princeton University Press, 1990), 110–11.

77. Kierkegaard, *Fear and Trembling/Repetition*, 210.

78. Joanna Picciotto, *Labors of Innocence in Early Modern England* (Cambridge, MA: Harvard University Press, 2010), 403. I am grateful to Jen Waldron for conversations on this topic.

79. See, for example, John Milton, *Paradise Lost* (London: Penguin Books, 2003), I.284–94.

80. See Jody Duncan Jesser, "Creationisms," *Cinefex* 128 (January 2012): 66–85; 74–75.

81. See Berthold Hoeckner, *Film, Music, Memory* (Chicago: University of Chicago Press, 2019), 48.

CHAPTER 7. BEYOND THE (SINGLE) CAMERA

1. William Brown, "Man without a Movie Camera—Movies without Men: Towards a Posthumanist Cinema," in *Film Theory and Contemporary Hollywood Movies*, ed. Warren Buckland (New York: Routledge, 2009), 66–85; 75.

2. Mike Jones, "Vanishing Point: Spatial Composition and the Virtual Camera," *Animation: An Interdisciplinary Journal* 2, no. 3 (2007): 225–43; 235. Ariel Rogers offers a more nuanced version of such claims in a discussion of *Avatar*: "The appeal of this novel experience of gravity-defying mobility [involves] harnessing 3D to promise viewers a feeling of physically impossible kinesis within a physically impossible milieu." *Cinematic Appeals: The Experience of New Movie Technologies* (New York: Columbia University Press, 2013), 216.

3. Jones, "Vanishing Point," 241.

4. David Bordwell, "Camera Movement and Cinematic Space," *Cine-Tracts* 1, no. 2 (1977): 19–25; 20.

5. Bordwell, "Camera Movement and Cinematic Space," 21 (emphasis in original).

6. Julie Turnock, *Plastic Reality: Special Effects, Technology, and the Emergence of 1970s Bluckbuster Aesthetics* (New York: Columbia University Press, 2015), 167. For a more general discussion of the use of animation practices and practitioners for special effects, see pages 43–55.

7. William Paul, "The Aesthetics of Emergence," *Film History* 5 (1993): 321–55; 339.

8. Quoted in Patrick Keating, *The Dynamic Frame: Camera Movement in Classical Hollywood* (New York: Columbia University Press, 2019), 39.

9. Quoted in Tom Gunning, "Landscape and the Fantasy of Moving Pictures: Early Cinema's Phantom Rides," in *Cinema and Landscape*, ed. Graeme Harper and Jonathan Ryder (Chicago: University of Chicago Press, 2010), 31–70; 55.

10. Katherine Chandler, "American Kamikaze: Television-Guided Assault Drones in World War II," in *Life in the Age of Drone Warfare*, ed. Lisa Parks

and Caren Kaplan (Durham, NC: Duke University Press, 2017), 89–111; 105. For more on the relation between photography and flight as projects for "extending the capacity of the human eye," see Denis Cosgrove and William L. Fox, *Photography and Flight* (London: Reaktion Books, 2010).

11. I am grateful to J. Carlos Kase for this example.

12. Keating, *The Dynamic Frame*, 241. He notes: "When it suits the needs of the film, the camera imitates a person. When it doesn't, the anthropomorphic fiction is dropped" (86).

13. Chandler, "American Kamikaze," 105.

14. As I finish this manuscript, a popular video of a drone flying through a bowling alley eloquently demonstrates this fact (www.youtube.com/watch?v=VgS54fqKxfo).

15. Ryan Pierson, "Whole-Screen Metamorphosis and the Imagined Camera (Notes on Perspectival Movement in Animation)," *Animation: An Interdisciplinary Journal* 10, no. 1 (2015): 6–21; 7–8.

16. I do not discuss virtual reality here, although its technology allows many of the perceptual shifts I describe. For one such example, see *Loops VR* (OpenEndedGroup, 2018). See also Ariel Rogers, *On the Screen: Displaying the Moving Image, 1926–1942* (New York: Columbia University Press, 2019): 199–209; and Brooke Belisle, "Whole World Within Reach: Google Earth VR," *Journal of Visual Culture* 19, no. 1 (2020): 112–36, esp. 122–25.

17. D. N. Rodowick, *The Virtual Life of Film* (Cambridge, MA: Harvard University Press, 2007), 129.

18. Lev Manovich, "An Archeology of a Computer Screen," *Kunstforum International* 132 (Fall 1995): 124–35.

19. For a more successful use of multiframe construction, see the projects of Forensic Architecture (https://forensic-architecture.org/).

20. Anne Friedberg, *The Virtual Window: From Alberti to Microsoft* (Cambridge, MA: MIT Press, 2006), 220.

21. Friedberg, *The Virtual Window*, 218.

22. For examples of this argument, see Friedberg, *The Virtual Window*, 218; and Holly Willis, *New Digital Cinema: Reinventing the Moving Image* (New York: Wallflower Press, 2005), 40.

23. Lauren Rabinovitz connects these shots to the tradition of the phantom ride in *Electric Dreamland: Amusement Parks, Movies, and American Modernity* (New York: Columbia University Press, 2012), 159–60.

24. Jordan Schonig would classify such shots within "cinema's motion forms," the various patterns and groupings of movement that guide the way we see and respond to the moving image. See *The Shape of Motion: Cinema and the Aesthetics of Movement* (New York: Oxford University Press, forthcoming).

25. Jordan Schonig, "Seeing Aspects of the Moving Camera: On the Twofoldness of the Mobile Frame," *Synoptique* 5, no. 2 (2017): 57–78; 65–66.

26. Tony Bruno, "Shooting for 3D," *Videomaker*, n.d., https://www.videomaker.com/article/14912-shooting-for-3d

27. Brooke Belisle, "From Stereoscopic Depth to Deep Learning," in *Deep Mediations*, ed. Karen Redrobe (Durham, NC: Duke University Press, 2021), 329–50; 333, 334. See also Brooke Belisle, "The Dimensional Image: Overlaps

in Stereoscopic, Cinematic, and Digital Depth," *Film Criticism* 37–38 (2013): 117–37.

28. See, for example, Kristen Whissel, "Parallax Effects: Epistemology, Affect and Digital 3D Cinema," *Journal of Visual Culture* 15, no. 2 (2016): 233–49.

29. See Downie and Kaiser's description of *Ulysses in the Subway*, http://openendedgroup.com/artworks/ulysses.html.

30. See Tom Gunning, "An Unseen Energy Swallows Space: The Space in Early Film and Its Relation to American Avant-Garde Film," in *Film Before Griffith*, ed. John Fell (Berkeley: University of California Press, 1984), 355–66.

31. Brooke Belisle, "Depth Readings: Ken Jacobs's Digital, Stereographic Films," *Cinema Journal* 53, no. 2 (2014): 1–26; 11.

32. Vadim Rizov, "Goodbye to 3D Rules," *Filmmaker Magazine*, October 24, 2014, https://filmmakermagazine.com/87878-goodbye-to-3-d-rules/#.XIvyqoRKjzL.

33. Quoted in Andrew Utterson, "Practice Makes Imperfect: Technology and the Creative Imperfections of Jean-Luc Godard's Three-Dimensional (3D) Cinema," *Quarterly Review of Film and Television* 34, no. 3 (2017): 295–308; 306.

34. Stan Brakhage, "Metaphors on Vision," in *Essential Brakhage: Selected Writings on Filmmaking by Stan Brakhage*, ed. Bruce R. McPherson (Kingston, NY: McPherson, 2001), 12.

35. André Bazin, "The Ontology of the Photographic Image," in *What Is Cinema?*, trans. Hugh Gray (Berkeley: University of California Press, 1967), 1:9–16; 15.

36. Nico Baumbach, "Starting Over," *Film Comment* 50, no. 6 (2014): 34–41; 37. For a general discussion of Godard's use of 3D, see David Bordwell, "*Adieu au langage*: 2 + 2 x 3D," *Observations on Film Art* (blog), September 7, 2014, http://www.davidbordwell.net/blog/2014/09/07/adieu-au-langage-2-2-x-3d/.

37. Jean-Luc Godard, "Let's Talk about *Pierrot*," in *Godard on Godard*, trans. and ed. Tom Milne (New York: Da Capo Press, 1972), 215–34; 223.

38. See Rick Warner, "Essaying the Forms of Popular Cinema: Godard, Farocki and the Principle of Shot/Countershot" in *The Essay Film: Dialogue, Politics, Utopia*, ed. Elizabeth Papazian and Caroline Eades (New York: Columbia University Press, 2016), 28–67; and Rick Warner, "Godard's Stereoscopic Essay: Thinking in and with *Adieu au langage*," in *The Global Auteur: Politics and Philosophy in 21st Century Cinema*, ed. Seung-hoon Jeong and Jeremi Szaniawski (New York: Bloomsbury, 2016), 61–78.

39. This paragraph and the next two are drawn from my "Bazin's Modernism," *Paragraph* 36, no. 1 (2010): 10–30; 23–24.

40. James Naremore, "The Death of the Auteur: Orson Welles's *The Other Side of the Wind*," *Cineaste* 44, no. 1 (2018): 8–12; 8.

41. Joseph McBride, "'Twilight in the Smog': Notes on *The Other Side of the Wind*," *Sight&Sound* 28, no. 11 (November 2018): 32–37; 34.

42. See also David MacDougall, "When Less Is Less: The Long Take in Documentary," *Film Quarterly* 46, no. 2 (1992): 36–46.

43. Jean Rouch, "On the Vicissitudes of the Self," in *Cine-Ethnography*, ed. Steven Feld (Minneapolis: University of Minnesota Press, 2003), 87–101; 101.

44. Paul Stoller, *The Cinematic Griot: The Ethnography of Jean Rouch* (Chicago: University of Chicago, 1992), 170.

45. Walter Benjamin, "The Work of Art in the Age of Its Technological Reproducibility, Second Version," in *Walter Benjamin, Selected Writings*, vol. 3, *1935–1938*, eds. Howard Eiland and Michael W. Jennings (Cambridge, MA: Harvard University Press, 2002), 99–133; 114.

46. See, for example, Noël Burch and Jorge Dana, "Propositions," trans. Diana Matais and Christopher King, *Afterimage* 5 (1974): 40–66; 55.

Index

2012 (Emmerich, 2009), 74

Adieu au langage [*Goodbye to Language*] (Godard, 2014), 233–38, 236*fig.*
Adorno, Theodor W., 261n22
agency, 57, 76, 141, 147; of the camera, 165; moral, 136; narrating, 255n16; of spectators/viewers, 53; supernatural, 67, 267n37
Alberti, Leon Battista, 27, 175, 224
Allures (Belson, 1961), 221
Amator [*Camera Buff*] (Kieślowski, 1979), 58–59, 61, 63, 67; perceptual game in, 59; point of view in, 58*fig.*, 59, 60, 68, 70
Amazing Transparent Man, The (Ulmer, 1960), 68–69, 256n33
Angels in America (Nichols, 2004), 220
animation, 8, 66, 83, 94, 177, 219, 221, 223, 247n17
anime, 177
anthropomorphism, of camera, 9, 11–13, 222, 276n12
antiperspectivalism, 19, 21, 173, 203, 208, 217; animation of the eye and, 174; in history of cinema, 176–77; human versus divine temporal orders, 205–6, 207; rejection of linear time and, 205. *See also* perspective
Antonioni, Michelangelo, 2, 8, 19, 265n12

Apotheosis (Lennon and Ono, 1970), 222
apparatus theory, 25, 40, 45, 54, 55, 136–37
Arabesque for Kenneth Anger (Menken, 1955), 72
Aragno, Fabrice, 234, 238
Arendt, Hannah, 128
Arnheim, Rudolf, 102
art cinema, 35, 84 240
audiences, 5, 10, 26, 61, 118, 120, 123; camera's agency and, 11–12; conventions of narrative film and, 91; direct encounter with screen, 102; fantasies of, 238; feeling of utopia and, 119; formal devices of Hollywood cinema and, 136; Malick's voice-overs and, 179; montage and, 36; moralism in art and, 30; narrative revelations of camera and, 167; of "phantom rides," 4; political cinema and, 26; self-sufficient world of the film and, 163; subjective shots and, 101; 3D effect and, 235; tracking shots and, 21. *See also* spectators/viewers
Aumont, Jacques, 175
Austin, J. L., 8
Avatar (Cameron, 2009), 74, 275n2

Bach, Johann Sebastian, 218
Bacher, Lutz, 138
Badlands (Malick, 1973), 172, 182

Founded in 1893,
UNIVERSITY OF CALIFORNIA PRESS
publishes bold, progressive books and journals
on topics in the arts, humanities, social sciences,
and natural sciences—with a focus on social
justice issues—that inspire thought and action
among readers worldwide.

The UC PRESS FOUNDATION
raises funds to uphold the press's vital role
as an independent, nonprofit publisher, and
receives philanthropic support from a wide
range of individuals and institutions—and from
committed readers like you. To learn more, visit
ucpress.edu/supportus.